# STOP THE EVIL

# CASUALTY SHEET.

Name: _William H. Howe_

Rank: _Private_       Company: _A_   Regiment: _116_

Arm: _Inf_       State: _Pa._

Nature of Casualty: _Hanged, for the offense of Desertion and Murder, Aug. 26, 1864. — G. O., No. 26, Dept. of the Susquehanna, Apr. 9, 1864. — See List of U. S. soldiers executed by U. S. military authorities Pages 8 & 9 See also, 5981, A, – A. G. O._

_(E. B.) Aug. 7 - 85_

_W. S. Burton_
Clerk.

_Oct. 12 - 85_

_Exd B & N_

# STOP THE EVIL

## A Civil War History of Desertion and Murder

Robert I. Alotta

Presidio Press
San Rafael, California
London, England

973. 74
ALo

Library of Congress Cataloging in Publication Data

Alotta, Robert I
    Stop the evil.

    Bibliography: p.
    Includes index.
    1. Howe, William H., d. 1864.  2. United States –
History – Civil War, 1861–1865 – Desertions.
3. Desertion, Military – United States.  4. Trials
(Military offenses) – United States.  5. Soldiers –
United States – Biography.  I. Title.
E527.5 116th.H68A44        973.7'4        78-10425
ISBN 0-89141-018-X

Book design by Hal Lockwood

Jacket design by Leslie Fuller

Printed in the United States of America

To the lucky few
who learn
from the errors of others.

# Contents

# Illustrations

# Preface

Shocked with disbelief and filled with horror over the revelations of the Pentagon papers and the Watergate disclosures, the American people forced themselves to look to their leaders for guidance and for a denouncement of the charges.

In an effort to protect and preserve their power, the nation's leaders sought to make the accusers the scapegoats. These accusers were not elected officials. They were just ordinary men who didn't totally comprehend what government was all about: this seemed to be the public official's position. And so, Daniel Ellsberg and John Dean were set up as examples before the American people of fellow-citizens who had gone wrong.

This setting of an example to safeguard a system—at the expense of a man's reputation or even his life—is nothing new. It is not the sole creation of the twentieth-century political mind. Nor is it original for a government "of the people, by the people, and for the people" to subvert or suspend the time-honored systems of checks and balances to preserve and protect the incumbent elected officials and to exclude those who are not compatible with current thinking.

The American people had been taken advantage of during the Nixon years and the Ellsbergs and Deans made sure the people knew it. Realizing, at long last, that they had been "had," the American people focused their pent-up frustrations on the central figure in the entire federal mess. They crucified Richard M. Nixon and forced him to resign the presidency – the first American president ever to leave under such circumstances.

How was it possible, Americans thought, that such a horror could befall this land – this land of Washington, Jefferson and Lincoln? How could elected and appointed officials use their positions in such a despicable manner, merely to advance their own personal power, prestige and wealth?

The electorate forgot that the president was no more, and no less, than any other citizen in this country. He was not a king who ruled by some divine right; he was not a god. He was a man who made promises to the people and was elected by them to carry out those promises. He was a man who swore to defend the Constitution. But, like everyone else, the president was a man – a man who, like all of us, could fall under the spell of temptation.

The wrongs of the Nixon administration were not the worst that this nation has ever encountered, but simply the worst that twentieth-century Americans had witnessed. Other men and other administrations in this nation's history did the same things as Nixon. They, however, were fortunate and were not found out while they lived. Some did things that were infinitely more disastrous to the American way of life than Richard Nixon. No one died as a result of the Watergate disclosures. But men did die as a result of actions carried out during the administration of Abraham Lincoln.

Revered by millions as the "Great Emancipator," Lincoln surrounded himself with men who made Haldeman and Ehrlichman look like choirboys. Lincoln's henchmen were no better – and, in some sense, much worse – than the crowd that recently populated and prostituted the Oval Office.

Through the use of military force, the Lincoln administration "maintained the peace" at polling places during Civil War elections. In some cases, men who had been elected by the people were arrested if their philosophy did not reflect the thinking of the incumbent administration. Citizens of a free nation – a democracy – were restricted from exercising the right of free speech. It was a dark day in the life of America. But the darkness was overshadowed by the spectre of the Civil War.

Because of the war, government officials could suspend the rights of the individual in the interest of national security. They could encourage informers to make anonymous reports on other citizens. By suspending the writ of habeas corpus, they could force men to prove their innocence, rather than be proven guilty by an approved court of law.

The military assumed a dominant role in the judicial life of the Union states. This assumption of power was feared by the founding fathers during the early days of America's emergence from a colony to a nation. Politically inspired men used every occasion—every opportunity—to improve their position and increase their power.

The tale of "brother against brother; father against son," which children have been taught to associate with the Civil War, was not limited to the confrontation between North and South. It existed in the North to a much greater degree than historians have previously indicated. Lincoln's policies during those turbulent years, whether conceived by him or others, destroyed the democratic system for which "four score and twenty years" before, the patriots of the Revolution had died.

It cannot be the role of the historian to state that the leaders in those days abused their power for strict personal gain or advancement. Unlike investigative reporters today, we cannot confront the accused with the charges and evaluate the nuances of his response—the lifting of an eyebrow, the stammer and stutter of confusion. We cannot listen to tape recordings of supposed secret conversations. The historian must rely on documents and public statements issued by these officials who, of course, would not state publicly that they had abused their offices. We also have official documents to peruse. In these we can find slight variations from the public position. Through the miracles of technology, we have access to newspapers of the period, complete with editorials and letters to the editors. Even with this reservoir of information, the historian can only relate the events and activities, interpret them in their context, and suggest that all was not as it seemed. It is then up to the individual reader to perceive the facts, compare them and make a judgment.

*Stop the Evil* is the story of the persecution of one unwitting man—a poor, ignorant boy from the rural community of Frederick Township, Montgomery County, Pennsylvania—William H. Howe.

We traced the life, times and death of William Howe, through newspapers, books, manuscripts, official documents and letters. We could not help but see similarities between the events in Howe's life and those of Eddie Slovik in World War II and William Calley in the Vietnam War. All of these men were used by their government to deter others from following the same course of action. At the same time, they served as examples of the power of government over the people.

By reading the story of William H. Howe, as it is projected across the background of the times in which he lived and died, perhaps we shall realize that "what is past is prologue."

# Acknowledgments

It goes without saying that the research of a book of this nature could not have been completed without the assistance of others. I have been quite fortunate in having a number of men and women who have assisted me in uncovering the story of William H. Howe. Because each in his or her own way was important, the listing of names is not in any specific order—except the disorder of my mind at this particular time.

The people at the Free Library of Philadelphia have, as always, been most cooperative and have extended themselves "above and beyond the call of duty." In particular, those in the newspaper department were extremely tolerant of my requests for roll after roll of microfilm for the newspapers published in Philadelphia during the Civil War years. Especially helpful were Willie (Frank) Green and Samuel Holt.

In the map collection, Jerry Post was superb. His knowledge of maps, and where to find them, helped me immensely. The inter-library loan department expedited a great deal of material which, unless I traveled there to get them, I could never have obtained from the U.S. Army Military Institute at Carlisle Barracks, Pa., and elsewhere. Even the staff at the library was astonished at the amount of material we were able to receive on loan. And, the staff of government publications department lugged volume after volume of the *Official Records* without a murmur, even though I called for the same volume time after time.

Michael P. Musick and Dale E. Floyd at the Navy and Old Army Branch, Military Archives Division, in the National Archives were most helpful and knowledgeable. My telephone bills attest to the depth to which we pursued the subject, with me in Philadelphia and them in Washington. Dale Floyd requires special mention. After the manuscript was completed, he located the missing court-martial proceedings, which supplied answers to several questions and took me from the realm of conjecture to that of fact.

In the "up country" where Howe once lived and where he is buried, I received a helping hand, several gallons of water for a steaming radiator, and an objective perspective from the Rev. Albert I. Douglass, pastor of St. Luke's, Keelor's Church, in Obelisk, Pa., where Howe had once worshipped. With Pastor Douglass, I found William Howe's grave . . . and the homestead. William F. Speier, Jr., present owner of the Howe place in Perkiomenville, was cooperative as was his father-in-law David Torrance who knows where the body's buried. Pastor Douglass went with me to visit The Schwenkfelder Library in Pennsburg, Pa., where I met Claire Conway and Edgar Grubb. Mr. Grubb, who has been researching the Howe family for years, made material available to me which might have taken months to locate. Linda Beck, then archivist at Krauth Memorial Library of the Lutheran Theological Seminary in Philadelphia, helped uncover church records on the ministers who were involved with Howe.

Col. Herbert M. Hart, head, U.S. Marine Corps Historical Branch, searched his files in Washington for an important piece of information which had excaped me. Russell Pritchard, director of the Loyal Legion's War Library in Philadelphia, opened his files to me, and the material occupied me for weeks.

Brother Patrick Ellis, F.S.C., president of La Salle College, an old and good friend, read the manuscript with the eye of an English scholar. Brother Patrick listened to my tale of Howe with the patience of a saint – though I am sure that after a while it became boring. Dr. Russell F. Weigley, another good friend, read the manuscrip with an historian's keen eye and encouraged me to complete the manuscript.

Stuart G. Vogt, historian at Fredericksburg National Military Park, took me around the battlefield and its environs and relived with me Howe's adventures and misfortunes. He also read the chapter on the battle.

I must have ignored someone or another. If I did, please, it was not intentional.

*These are the times that try men's souls. The summer sol-
dier and the sunshine patriot will, in this crisis, shrink from
the service of their country; but he that stands it now, de-
serves the love and thanks of man and woman. Tyranny,
like hell, is not easily conquered; yet we have this consola-
tion with us, that the harder the conflict, the more glorious
the triumph. What we obtain too cheap, we esteem too
lightly; it is dearness only that gives every thing its value.
Heaven knows how to put a proper price upon its goods;
and it would be strange indeed if so celestial an article as
FREEDOM should not be highly rated.*

Thomas Paine
*The American Crisis*

# 1

# The Times

A CRISIS WAS in the air. It could be felt in almost every walk of American life. But William H. Howe, a young Pennsylvania German, did not realize it. Living in Perkiomenville, a small rural community in Montgomery County, Howe was more concerned with eking out a meager day-to-day existence for himself and his family. National, state, and local politics did not interest the young man because they did not touch on his life. But the year was 1860 and soon politics would affect every American. History would prove that these were indeed the times that tried men's souls.

In Washington, D.C., a place of which Howe had heard, but never visited, the president of the United States, James Buchanan, had reached a decision. He would not seek another term. And, as usual, many men lusted after the presidency. Stephen A. Douglas, John C. Breckinridge, Abraham Lincoln, and John Bell were some of the men who wanted to replace Buchanan. Howe had never heard of any of these men, even though each had attained some modicum of national notoriety.

Howe was also not aware that America was divided. The South claimed that if Lincoln were elected president, there would be secession. Lincoln was elected and the Southerners, always gentlemen, lived up to their promise. But the South was a distant land from Perkiomenville, almost another country. Government leaders had come and gone, and life went on in the same way. In the past, when a new leader was elected, party differences were set aside for a while and the country offered a unified front.

The differences of the times, however, did not provide for such unification. Lincoln, a Republican, had been silent during his campaign, even though most Americans felt he should take a stand. Lincoln was determined to wait until he moved into the White House before he made his position public.

Opposition to Lincoln was a typical human phenomenon. He was in office and the Democrats were not. If the Democrats had won the election, the Republicans would be expected to oppose the incumbent administration. American politics had always been that way and always would be. The only difference was that the Southern states had withdrawn from the Union.

With this secession, war came. When hostilities began, national, state, and local politics began to intrude on the life of William H. Howe. The young farm boy became a pawn in the gigantic chess game of the American Civil War.

Though Howe was an aggressive individual, confident of his own abilities, he was not the type of man who would be one of the first recruits in the Union army. He was satisfied to stay at home to farm, hunt, and drink with his boyhood friends. War was going on, but in Perkiomenville there was peace.

Peace, however, was a tenuous thing. As the war between the North and South intensified, both Union and Confederate governments needed men to fill their army's depleted ranks. Enlistments were not what either administration expected or wanted. Something drastic had to be done, and done quickly.

Ever since the French Revolution, nations had called upon their young men to serve in the armed forces through some form of conscription. Theoretically, the rights guaranteed by the government to the individual citizen also imposed an obligation on the person to defend and protect these rights by fighting for the country. The only alternative to conscription, or draft, was to maintain a constant flow of volunteer soldiers. During the early days of the Civil War, the blush of patriotic zeal glowed. Men rushed to recruiting stations to enlist and fight for their country. But, as a result of the losses incurred by the Union forces, the blush wore off. This lack of new recruits placed the Union army in a dangerous position.

Realizing the political implications of forced conscription, federal officials used every means at their disposal to encourage volunteers. Secretary of War Simon Cameron sought an effective program to provide the army with a reservoir of recruits and replacements. He felt, after studying the situation, that the recruiting efforts of the states and private individuals were inefficient and used manpower ineffectively.

Under Cameron's plan, once the existing programs had completely filled a unit, all additional troops would then be requisitioned by the War Department. The secretary's idea was first to fill up those units reduced by sickness and casualty; then, if needed, other regiments could be created. Through this plan, promulgated on December 3, 1861, recruiting was provided for in each state, but administered by War Department supervisors. Recruits obtained in this manner were to be forwarded to central locations, equipped and trained. Later, they would be sent wherever needed.

Cameron's central recruiting system was a good one. But Simon Cameron was ousted as secretary of war and replaced by Edwin M. Stanton, and, on January 15, 1862, the Cameron plan was discarded.

Stanton, always critical of his predecessor, eliminated the embryonic recruitment service in an economy move. He was confident the existing federal army had sufficient numbers to crush the Confederacy. He was wrong.

Five months after his appointment, Stanton instructed military commanders to request the state governors to fill in the ranks of their decimated regiments in the field. The reaction and the recruitment were less than adequate; and, on June 6, Stanton ordered a reinstatement of the federal recruiting service, but not the one conceived by Cameron. Secretary Stanton's plan led to the wholesale creation of new regiments and the almost total ignoring of replacement for existing units.

William Howe had heard rumors about the need for men and had dismissed them. As long as there were men willing to volunteer—and their work could be shared by those at home, with increased income—why should he enlist?

But pressures were mounting. On July 2, 1862, Abraham Lincoln called for 300,000 volunteers. Despite the encouragement of financial contributions to bounties and premiums by prominent citizens, the response of the young American men was disappointing. On July 17, the government returned to the people with another approach: the Militia Act. Under this proposal, the individual states were compelled to upgrade their militia systems and provide the federal forces with the needed manpower. If the states were unable to conform, the act stated in no uncertain terms that the secretary of war would then be empowered to draft men for a period of nine months.

Local businessmen and civic leaders, moved either by patriotism or by self-protection, began to donate large sums of money to the local bounty funds, offering anywhere from $50 to $1000 to any volunteer. Still, the increase in manpower for which the Militia Act was drafted was never realized. Perhaps it was because the American people did not believe Lincoln when he said he would call the militia for a limited time, not to exceed nine months. Rumors circulated throughout the North that, once the men were in uniform, Lincoln would keep them in for the duration of the war.

Frustrated, Lincoln announced on August 4 that any state that had not reached its established quota of three-year volunteers by August 15 would be subject to a draft. In those states without a system of conscription, the War Department called upon the legislators to appoint certain officials to handle the enrollment, consider exemptions, and finally draft the men. The president also indicated that the War Department would appoint civilian provost marshals for the states, nominated by the governors, to enforce the draft.

The threat of the 1862 draft never became reality. State governors protested to Washington that less than two weeks was an inadequate length of time to fulfill the quotas. Besides, they argued, the established quotas were onerous. The people demonstrated their repugnance to the policy by rioting and threatening other forms of violence. Aware of the situation, Secretary Stanton permitted the governors to postpone the draft for a month. Then, because of continued pressure, the draft was permanently delayed.

Very few people acknowledged the postponements as a permanent thing. The spectre of the draft still hung over their heads. To an uneducated man like William Howe, the threat of being conscripted into the army for an extended period of time—with a minimal monthly salary—was very real and frightening.

Many heretofore law-abiding citizens felt the draft concept was Napoleonic in practice and they, as private citizens, really had no constitutional obligation to take up arms in the defense of the nation. If a man decided voluntarily to commit himself to becoming a soldier, his decision was considered noble and excellent. But, to compel him to bear arms was definitely undemocratic. To many, the entire concept of conscription was un-American.

Many government officials, on the other hand, countered that the mere suggestion of conscription would spur men to enlist. Volunteers could be used by the individual districts to fill the quotas and, with this thought in mind, many patriotic individuals launched massive recruiting drives. These people hoped that Amercans would answer the nation's call—through patriotism—rather than through force.

Some of these drives used heavy-handed techniques. That, coupled with a lack of understanding of the entire system, drew a violent and vocal reaction from the people. The states that experienced the greatest problems were Pennsylvania, Indiana, and Lincoln's own Illinois. In Pennsylvania, the major opposition was focused in the coal regions of Schuylkill County, where the residents were politically Democratic. At the outbreak of war, these people adopted a strong antiwar, antiadministration position.

There were other areas with concentrations of opposition to the draft and the war. In Howe's immediate neighborhood, the citizens had been opposed to war dating back to the time of the Revolution. The times had changed, but not the people and their distaste for armed conflict. They were content to live in peace. If others wanted to fight, let them.

With the storm clouds hovering over the North, William Howe continued to farm his land in Perkiomenville and, perhaps because of the war, he took on a part-time job rolling tobacco into cigars. He heard rumors about the draft, but as long as they were only rumors, he was not affected.

HEADQUARTERS, 116th REG. P. V.,
No. 624 MARKET STREET.

*In spite of the flash of their muskets, the roar of their cannon—the assassins of freedom must be crushed.*
*So says the 116th REG. P. V. Young men who desire to win Glory and Renown, as well as performing the duty they owe their Country, will at once FALL IN, under the Flag of the 116th, and tear down the standards of Treason and Rebellion. Apply at the following Recruiting Stations:*
*Capt. Thos. Ewing, Co. A, No. 4 S. Del. ave...*
*Or at Camp, now established at Hestonville, 24th Ward.*
*By order.*

DENNIS HEENAN,
Colonel, Commanding.

Philadelphia *Public Ledger*
August 12, 1862

# 2

# Recruitment

**W**HILE HOWE worked his farm, the battles of First Bull Run and Shiloh proved that the war would not end with the first major engagement. By May 1, 1862, Secretary of War Stanton was forced to reinstate the federal recruitment service. Confronted by strong rumors of a potential Confederate onslaught on Washington and realizing he had made a mistake, Stanton sent frantic messages to the governors of the various Northern states, requesting all the militia they could possibly raise be sent to the capital. What the secretary of war did was create a reserve army, trained by the states, and able to be drawn into the war as the occasion required. The Philadelphia *Daily Evening Bulletin* noted on June 11, 1862, that this was a good idea because "it inspires the people with new confidence in the Government." Regardless of the editorialist's strong feelings, Stanton's plan did not adopt any of the realism of Cameron's program. In practice, Stanton created a mechanism for the wholesale manufacture of new regiments. But, at the same time, the plan totally ignored the need for replacements for the regiments already in the field.

Losses incurred by the army and a lack of recruits caused President Lincoln to ask the nation for 300,000 additional men. Lincoln's call on July 2, 1862, occasioned the composition of the inspirational song, "We Are Coming, Father Abraham," but did not result in what Lincoln and Stanton wanted, an influx of willing volunteers.

7

In Pennsylvania, Governor Curtin answered Lincoln's call and was applauded by the Philadelphia *Sunday Dispatch* on July 13 for what seemed the logical method to fill the required quota. Curtin's plan established a form of support for the volunteers between the time they enlisted and the time they were finally mustered into service. In former plans, this amenity had been lacking. Besides the financial drain on the recruiters, many men who were capable of military service were poor and could not support themselves while waiting to be mustered. The recruiting officers, in order to keep the men, absorbed a great deal of the out-of-pocket expenses. Curtin's plan limited the government's liability "for such support to twenty days' rations at forty cents for each recruit actually mustered into service."

Curtin had also discovered that the time-honored way of conferring the rank of colonel on someone before he had recruited a single man into the new regiment was time-consuming and injurious to the service. "We have had specimens of the working of this system in Philadelphia since April, 1861," the *Dispatch* account stated. "Skeleton regiments and skeleton companies have 'loafed' about town month after month, when the services of the men enrolled were actually needed by the country."

One of the "skeleton" units was Meagher's Guards, under Col. Dennis Heenan. Heenan, a former field officer of the 24th Pennsylvania Regiment, had begun recruiting a three-month unit during the furor caused by the May 1862 cavalry raid into Pennsylvania by Jackson. On June 11, 1862, he was authorized to recruit a regiment of infantry in Pennsylvania.[1] By the time of Lincoln's call, the colonel had mustered only about two hundred volunteers.

In an effort to bolster the strength of his unit, Heenan had selected his own cadre of officers. (In some military units, the officers were elected by the men; in others, they were appointed by the governor because of some prior military service or for political reasons.) The officer selection was clearly not the best. It was the popular contention that in many cases the officers, especially those with higher grades, were chosen not for their skill and experience as military men, but for certain local influences that would be of little value in their new profession.[2] Still, that system was all that was available at the time.

Heenan and his officers set up ten recruiting stations throughout the city of Philadelphia. Advertising played a major role in the efforts of the unit (now known as the 116th Regiment, Pennsylvania Volunteers) to enlist men. Even before Lincoln called for the additional 300,000 men, Heenan's recruiters alleged that the three-month regiment had been "accepted by the Secretary of War" and was under orders to march south.[3] The last in a long series of advertisements, published by the *Public Ledger* and other Philadelphia newspapers, appeared on June 12. It indicated that only a few recruits were needed to bring Company I up to full strength. The ads stressed that the men would be mustered into service on Friday and sent to Washington on Saturday. They never left Philadelphia that day. After Lincoln's call for troops, the duration of the enlistment period was omitted from the advertising message.

Striving to meet the strength requirements, the colonel extended his recruiting dragnet from Philadelphia to far-flung areas, such as Reading, Lancaster, Pottsville. His expanded enlistment efforts were in keeping with Governor Curtin's plans. Previously, the Pennsylvania troops, with the exception of the reserve regiments, represented individual cities and counties, noted a report in the *Sunday Dispatch* on July 13, 1862. Under the new concept, the men would only represent the state. The public was uncertain if this was a good or bad arrangement. Some felt that local pride should be maintained in order to make the men consider the honor or disgrace their actions would bring to the loved ones at home.

State pride was not as strong in the North as it was in the South, and many contended that the men would fight harder for the reputation of their country than they would for their state. The *Dispatch* reporter reasoned that the majority of Northern soldiers would fight for the honor of the United States and its cause. By July 24, Colonel Heenan's efforts were rewarded when, at least on paper, he had over four hundred recruits and had established his camp, Camp Emmett, on the Lancaster Pike near Hestonville in West Philadelphia.[4] In a moment of ethnic pride, Heenan had named his camp for Temple Emmett, a recently deceased aide to the then-Colonel Thomas Francis Meagher. Heenan's acquisition of recruits was further enhanced by his recruiting officers' use, or abuse, of language in the company advertising. The concept of offering large sums of money as a premium or bounty opened the door to many men who heretofore would have been unable to volunteer their services. "The arrangement for recruiting is now more favorable to poor men who join the volunteers than ever it was before," the *Sunday Dispatch* told its readers on July 13: "Previous regiments obtained no bounty and no advance, and many, whose labor was barely sufficient for the support of their families, hesitated about going into the army, leaving those who depended upon them penniless, with nothing to look forward to but the appearance of the regimental paymaster at some indefinite period in the future. This feeling has kept thousands of men out of the ranks." The new arrangement, the article concluded, would make life more bearable for those who enlisted. Each recruit under the new system would receive a $3 premium, the advance of his first month's pay, and one-quarter of the full bounty of $100. The remainder of the payment would be forwarded to the soldier at the end of the war or to his family if he should die. Before a soldier left his home state, he would have $40 for his family. This provision was important for the poor men and aided the recruiting drive.[5]

But a full explanation of the deferred payments was never included in advertising for the 116th or for any other regiment. In one particular advertisement (*Public Ledger,* July 19, 1862) one of Heenan's captains offered a bounty of $250 for ten men. This sum far exceeded that offered by any other unit. But, it must have been a $25 bounty for *each* of ten men. Philadelphia's bounties were the highest anywhere in the country—but never that high!

The recruit had two alternatives: he could join an established regiment that was already in the field, or he could enlist in one of the new units. By joining a regiment in the field, a recruit could immediately obtain a $6 premium from the citizens' bounty fund and a $50 bounty. The same man, according to an article in the *Public Ledger* on August 1, would obtain the $56 from the committee, plus a $25 advance of the federal bounty and an extra $3 premium. This would give him $84, not including the first month's pay in advance. Enlistment in the old regiments was financially more equitable since recruits in the new three-year regiments had to wait until their particular company was full before they could receive half the bounty ($25). It was not until the entire regiment was full strength that the balance was paid. Most recruiters ignored this minor fact in their sales pitch to the men.

Some citizens wondered about this expense to entice men into doing their patriotic duty. "Would it not be better," a concerned citizen wrote to *The Press* on July 26, "to devote the money, contributed by the patriots of our city for the encouragement of enlistments, to the support of the families of volunteers, in case of death or wounds, in preference to squandering it in the payment of bounties, which are nothing more than a premium on idleness and slowness in coming forward. It seems hardly justice to the noble souls, who went at the first trumpet, without any 'bounty,' nothing but love of country for their stimulant. . . . These last, which have not even toiled one hour," the writer concluded, "receive not only 'also every man a penny,' but an additional sum, a 'bounty,' because they are the newest comers."

Regardless, the men did enlist, even if it appeared to have been just for the money. On August 2, one of Heenan's recruiters, Capt. Lawrence Kelly, had "the honor of being the first Captain mustered into the service, his company consisting of the required number. The fact was communicated to the Committee of the Citizen Bounty, and immediately a check for $400 was drawn in favor of the Captain in accordance with the resolution heretofore adopted."[6] The same day, another officer of the 116th, Capt. Thomas A. Murray of Company B, advertised in the *Public Ledger* that he needed "a few more able-bodied men" to fill up his company, with the inducement of a $165 bounty, $12 in cash when the man was mustered in.

Despite Kelly's notoriety in the local press, Edmund Randall, 1st lieutenant in Kelly's company, was, on July 8, the first officer mustered into the 116th. Randall took command of the regiment's bivouac at Camp Emmett on that day.[7]

Heenan now had one complete company. Unfortunately, he still lacked men in the other nine. Without ten full companies, his command as colonel of a regiment was in jeopardy. *The Press* realized that the "business (of recruiting) is not as brisk as it should be. This we are assured is in great measure the fault of the recruiting officers." On July 17, the newspaper charged that these men did not "display the energy they should." There were recruiting offices on nearly every corner of the city, the account continued, "and at some of these places were it not for a few straggling men around, or the presence of a poster here and there, we might pass and repass and yet remain ignorant of the nature of the business conducted therein. At very few of these stations is the sound of the drum and fife to be heard. As for a squad of men with martial music parading the streets in search of recruits, that is a sight seldom met with now-a-days. This good and old habit seems to have fallen entirely into disuse," the newspaper asserted, "and yet all sensible military men admit that this is the only proper way for promptly obtaining volunteers. If officers," the newspaper exhorted, "want recruits, let them exert themselves properly, and they will have no cause to complain."

These comments apparently struck a responsive chord with the recruiting officers because, four days after the charges appeared, *The Press* rejoiced that "the city is now beginning to assume the appearance as in the summer of 1861, when the wartocsin first sounded after the fall of Fort Sumpter (sic)."

Judging from the names on the rolls of the 116th Regiment, Colonel Heenan's unit appealed strongly to the Irishmen in the Philadelphia area. He was active in the Irish–American movement and capitalized on this involvement. There were passionate feelings among Irish-Americans that the Civil War could provide valuable basic training for officers and men—for yet another civil war elsewhere, the one designed to regain Ireland's freedom. Activists and editorialists made strong appeals to national pride, urging the foreign born to love the land of their birth, but to serve their new country. Each ethnic group played this theme and made it almost an obligation on the part of its people to respond as well as, if not better than, other nationalities. This, it was felt, was necessary in order to preserve and protect the name of its native land.

The spark of nationalism, fanned by newspaper pleas, began to take effect. On August 12 the *Inquirer* indicated that "the residents of many towns in the vicinity of Philadelphia are now thoroughly aroused to a sense of the greatness of the emergency, and recruits are beginning to be as plenty as blackberries." As the weeks went on, enlistments increased also for the 116th. By mid-August, Heenan could count almost 500 men. [8]

One of the men recruited into the 116th during that period was William H. Howe. Howe, a young married man with two small children and a third expected shortly, was a farmer from Frederick Township in Montgomery County. [9] He was not a typical recruit in the unit. He was not Irish, but German-American. While English was not unfamiliar to him, Howe was more comfortable speaking German. [10]

Perhaps Howe enlisted because he was inspired with patriotic fervor. "The triumphant response," *The Press* called it on July 17, "which the country is making to the President's recent call for new troops—clear, clarion tones ringing out full, and firm, and free from every Northern State." Or it might have been the fear of being drafted, which the government had threatened on July 4. Howe was not an educated man and might have listened to more-informed citizens who felt that if they were drafted, Congress could very easily hold them for the duration of the war rather than the advertised three months. [11]

It is also possible that Howe needed money. The land on which he lived could not have produced more than an abundant crop of rocks and boulders. The attractive offer of bounty money would have helped greatly in maintaining the Howe family while he was away in the army. And, if his luck betrayed him, his wife and children would be cared for by the government in a better manner than he could ever afford. [12]

Enlistment might also have been a way for the young man to defy his wife and their mutual family. Howe's father had died before he was two years old, and his mother remarried. The man she took for her second husband was Charles Schoener, a neighboring widower with several children. [13] After their marriage, William lived with them. His brother and sister and Schoener's children lived with relatives. [14] In 1860, William Howe married Schoener's daughter Hannah. Hannah Schoener Howe was eight years older than her husband and, at the time of their wedding, brought forth a dowry of $1500 in personal property and $450 in cash. William had nothing. On March 31, 1862, slightly more than four months before he enlisted, Hannah Howe bought six acres of land and the house in which they lived. [15] Is it possible that such an arrangement left William feeling emasculated?

He might also have enlisted as a demonstration of bravado—to show his neighbors that he was as brave as, if not braver than, they were. After all, he was a crack shot—and proud of that fact. "His life in the hills along the Perkiomen Creek had given him," one account said, "a practical use of his gun that made him very good company when there was shooting going on, although his reputation was none of the best until he went into the army."[16]

Based on the time of his enlistment, August 8, it is likely that Howe joined to obtain the lucrative bounty offered by the 116th Regiment before such payments were discontinued. He could not know at the time of his enlistment that the deadline would be extended, and the draft, as such, would not be implemented that year. The threat of draft had accomplished what many people in high places had hoped it would: it had frightened men into enlisting.

While uncertainty regarding William H. Howe's motives for enlistment in the army will always exist, the reasons for his selection of the 116th are even more difficult to comprehend. From all extant information, Howe was not a political activist. He might have been a young man filled with recklessness and derring-do, but he was not active in the political clubs which flourished in the German-American community during that period. There is no indication that he had ever been involved with the Forty-eighters, the German immigrants who saw America as the base for a new German world. Howe cannot be traced to any faction of the club or to the contingent that became a part of the old Pennsylvania Dutch element in the area where he lived. The German population of Pennsylvania, however, was a dominant part of the commonwealth. As late as 1837, Pennsylvania legislation was published in German, as were the governor's messages. In addition, a law was enacted to permit German instruction in the schools.[17] This strong ethnic identity makes Howe's choice of a predominantly Irish regiment even more difficult to understand.

Howe's selection of Company A is also strange. There were very few Germans in this unit prior to August 8, Howe's date of entry. They included: Sgt. Thomas Detweiler (August 4), Musician Philip Clause (July 7), and Privates Freeman Dyson (August 6), Fred Eisenhower (July 31), John Giltman (July 21), Jacob Lick (August 5), and John B. Mickle (July 30). The only other German-surnamed soldiers in this company were mustered in either along with Howe or later. They were: Sgt. Major, later 2nd Lt., George Roeder (August 30); and Privates John S. Altimus (August 24), Augustus Bidding or Bitting (August 12), Jacob H. Deihl (August 21), Peter Engle (August 15), John Geiger (August 13), Joseph H. Hibbs (August 12), Jonas M. Hendricks (August 18), Daniel Hauck (August 23), William Moser (August 22), Samuel Pennypacker (August 23), Charles Rodormell (August 12), and Jonah Strechaboc (August 30).[18]

Of these men, Howe was acquainted only with one (Augustus Bitting, a neighbor) or perhaps two others (Daniel Hauck and Jonas Hendricks, as both names were common in the area). These men joined after Howe had enlisted and might have been influenced by his example.

Although "why" was—and is—a mystery, William H. Howe did enlist in the army. He did throw his lot in with Company A, 116th Regiment, Pennsylvania Volunteers.

Despite the fact that the 116th was drawing men from outside the limits of Philadelphia County, the unit was still deficient in total strength. The minimum number of soldiers mandated by law for most of the volunteer units was sixty-four privates to each company. Ten companies would constitute a regiment. On August 16, 1862, Heenan's regiment had only two companies mustered into the federal service—Companies E and G. The remaining eight contained a low of four men in Company C to a high of forty in K.[19]

By August 6, the 116th Regiment began to bring its mustered men into camp. Captain Kelly, on that date, informed the general public through a notice in the *Public Ledger* that "all men mustered into COMPANY G. 116th REG'T. P. VOLS., are hereby notified to report at Camp, THIS (Wednesday) MORNING, at 10 o'clock." The lack of response indicated that perhaps the men were fiercely independent, or maybe they couldn't read Kelly's notice. A week later, the captain was forced to re-advertise his order, changing the date to Thursday, August 14, and adding, "to receive their Bounty."

The men of Company G finally were brought together and "presented their certificates to Dr. (James) McClintock, City Treasurer, and received the cash (their warrant of $25). The Treasurer," it was reported, "intends to go to camp, and, with the assistance of his clerks, pay out the money as the companies are filled."[20] The fact that the men had actually received their money on August 19—just five days later than advertised—was generously promoted in the Philadelphia area, ostensibly as an inducement to others to enlist. Apparently it worked. By August 23, Heenan's regiment announced it had 671 men, including officers. But more privates were needed to fill the other companies and complete the regiment.

Just when Heenan and his officer cadre thought they had tried everything and still were deficient, Gen. Michael Corcoran was released by the Confederates, thirteen months after his capture at Bull Run. As a first order of business following his release, he visited several Northern cities, including Philadelphia. The "City of Brotherly Love" opened its arms and heart to this stalwart Irishman. His bearing and exploits appealed to the Irish and the public at large. "Corcoran, the brave Irish leader," as the *Daily Evening*

*Bulletin* called him, was met at the Baltimore Depot in Philadelphia. News of his expected arrival had drawn people to the depot early in the morning, and by noon several thousand people lined Broad and Washington streets. Heenan's unit had arrived early and marched into the yard of the station. The city had provided a strong police detachment to guard all the station entrances and keep out crowds.

Corcoran had traveled north on a regularly scheduled train that arrived in Philadelphia on August 21, shortly before one o'clock. As the train entered the depot, the large crowd which had poured onto the platform surrounded it, despite efforts by the police to keep out the people. Several military units, which had formed on Broad Street, led the procession down Washington to the Refreshment Saloon. Preceeding General Corcoran were the mounted high constables, the Reserve Corps of Police, Birgfeld's Brigade Band, and the 116th Regiment. Chief in command of the reception was Col. Dennis Heenan, aided by his assistants, Maj. G. H. Bardwell, acting lieutenant colonel, and Captain Kelly, acting major.[21]

At the Refreshment Saloon, Corcoran responded to the outpouring of public admiration. "I am glad to see here so large a representation of my own countrymen. The war is a holy war," the general declared, "and I believe that this last call of the President will be responded to, as it ought, by every Irishman who has tasted the blessings of life in the land of liberty.[22] Wherever Corcoran stopped to speak, he demanded strongly that the Irish should be part of the war effort and that, after a brief period of rest, he would be back at the head of a brigade, the Irish Brigade.

While Philadelphia feted the general, it was announced that the 116th was to be attached to his brigade. Being part of such a popular organization could only mean an influx of men into his unit, Heenan reasoned. "The acceptance of Col. Heenan's regiment as part of General Corcoran's brigade," the *Public Ledger* reported on August 25, "has stimulated enlistments in this regiment to a wonderful degree." On August 28, the same newspaper confided that Heenan "may be trusted to fill up his regiment by the prescribed time," because of its newly acquired Irish connection.

August 22 was the declared termination date for men to volunteer and still obtain bounty money. On that last day, the 116th was reported to have mustered 30 men, giving them the grand total of 625.[23] Newspaper reports of the total differed slightly. It is possible, however, that one paper used only enlisted men as the basis for their compilation; another, an aggregate total of enlisted men and commissioned officers.

The final day for enlistments came, but was then continued until September 1. Heenan received an additional stay. He was authorized to continue recruiting until September 2, and if the unit was not full by that time, the regiment would report to Harrisburg. "As this regiment has been accepted as part of General Corcoran's Irish Brigade," the *Public Ledger* opined on September 1, "there should be no difficulty on the part of Col. Heenan in securing the required number of men. Two hundred will fill the regiment to the maximum number." Two days, the paper thought, was sufficient to enlist the men. "Let them come forward at once. In New York and Boston, the Irish are rushing around the green flag and Philadelphia should not be behind them." Though the 116th Regiment was attached to the Irish Brigade and would serve with distinction as part of that unit during the war, it never became a "green flag" regiment—a completely Irish-American unit. Throughout its history, "mingled with its Hibernians were many Willauers and Diefenderfers, Pennypackers, Linckes and Laudenschlaegers, from the Pennsylvania German stock." [24]

On September 2, at long last, Heenan published Order No. 1: "The Captains of Companies composing this Regiment will have their commands at CAMP EMMETT THIS DAY, at 10 o'clock A.M., to receive their BOUNTY, and to prepare to march under orders now issued from the War Department." [25] Though he issued the order, enough men still had not been mustered to complete the regiment. Forty-five men were recruited for all the new Philadelphia regiments on the same day. They were distributed, apparently in equal numbers, to the three Philadelphia regiments—those of Colonels Heenan, Chapman Biddle, and Hermann Segarath—which, the *Inquirer* noted, "had not been able to muster the sufficient minimum number of men."

Finally, the time for recruiting ran out. "Once more the seat of the struggle against the rebellion is in front of Washington," the *Daily Evening Bulletin* declared on September 1. "The cannonading of the past few days is said, indeed, to have been heard in the streets of the city. The rebels have gathered all their strength, and are making a last desperate effort to take the capital." No more time could be wasted. All the volunteer units had to start moving south. The men were needed to defend and fortify Washington.

Advancement to the front was not accomplished smoothly. The Zouaves d'Afrique were angry they had not received their bounty, and they demonstrated this disfavor. That unit's dissatisfaction was not an isolated protest.

When the 116th was ready to march, "only a portion . . . got off," the *Public Ledger* reported. "Another portion left yesterday (September 3). Many of the men refused to go until the bounty was paid, and in West Philadelphia gave the policemen much trouble by their conduct. Some of them were locked up in the station houses, and will be transferred to the Provost Marshal."

There was no "reasonable excuse," the *Inquirer* contended, for most of the men to refuse to go to the front until the bounty was paid. There were, however, some legitimate problems. "A case in point," the newspaper noted, "occurred yesterday (September 4), wherein a soldier fully equipped to leave for the seat of war made his appearance at the Mayor's office, to request advice. He was accompanied by his wife and two small children, and stated that the expected bounty was all he depended on to produce the necessaries of life for his wife and children, until such time as he could send them money from his monthly Government allowance." The soldier wanted to leave with his regiment "but had no heart to do so knowing that his family had no means of subsistence."

Regardless of such distressing situations, segments of the 116th Regiment, Pennsylvania Volunteers were reported to have departed in style, complete with several sword presentations. The only ceremonies worthy of newspaper coverage, however, involved Lt. Robert T. Maguire of Company E and Colonel Heenan. Maguire received "a magnificent sword, as a testimonial from the citizens of the Seventeenth Ward, of which he was, for several years, an executive official"; the sword was presented "on behalf of the donors by Thomas E. Harkins, Esq., and briefly responded to by the Lieutenant. Though Heenan received less notice, he was given a "handsome sword by his friends through J. B. Nicholson, Esq." [26]

A reported 688 men marched out of Camp Emmett behind Dennis Heenan. Company A, William Howe's unit, marched out with the fewest men—twenty-nine. The *Inquirer* printed the following list on September 19:

| COMPANY | CAPTAIN | MUSTERED MEN |
|---------|---------|--------------|
| A | Thomas S. Ewing | 29 |
| B | Thomas A. Murray | 80 |
| C | John Test | 83 |
| D | William A. Peet | 80 |
| E | John McNamara | 82 |
| F | Wm. M. Henerson | 42 |
| G | L. Kelly | 80 |
| H | John Smith | 84 |
| I | Thomas S. Mason | 53 |
| K | John O'Neill | 75 |

The regimental command consisted of Col. Dennis Heenan, Lt. Col. St. Clair A. Mulholland, Maj. George H. Bardwell, and Adjutant John R. Miles. [27]

After the men broke camp at Hestonville on September 2, Heenan marched the first detachment of his new regiment through the city to the Cooper Shop Refreshment Saloon, where a few weeks earlier they had cheered for the charismatic General Corcoran. There they were fed their last meal at home. The Cooper Shop had been established the year before to demonstrate to the soldiers that the people of Philadelphia cared for them. Located at Otsego Street, south of Washington, the shop's name was derived from the cooperage firm of Cooper and Pearce, whose building it used. Though it received no governmental assistance—federal, state, or city—the Cooper Shop Refreshment Saloon fed more than 400,000 men during the war.[28] The location, though not convenient to the railroad terminal, was ideally suited for the heavy Delaware River traffic, which brought men and supplies from the North to Union regiments in the South.

Following the meal, William Howe and the men of the 116th marched west to the Philadelphia, Wilmington & Baltimore railroad for their train ride south to "the seat of war."

*DEPARTURE OF TROOPS. – A detachment of new recruits for the Thirty-third Massachusetts Volunteers; portions of Colonel COLLIS' Zouaves d'Afrique and Colonel HEENAN'S Regiment left yesterday. The latter regiment left the city at four o'clock in the morning. A number were left behind, who refused to go for various reasons, principally the non-payment of the bounty.*

Philadelphia Inquirer
September 4, 1862

# 3

# The Journey South

THE SOLDIERS WERE not much to look at as they boarded the train at the depot in Philadelphia. While at Camp Emmett, they had received their first meager issue of military clothing. The uniforms did not make William Howe and his fellow recruits look like dashing, devil-may-care patriots who were going to war to restore the Union. "The ideal picture of a soldier," Abner Small, a private in the 16th Maine, reminisced, "makes a veteran smile. Be a man never so much a man, his importance and conceit dwindle when he crawls into an unteaseled shirt, trousers too short and baggy behind, coat too long at both ends, shoes with soles like firkin covers, and a cap as shapeless as a feed bag."[1] Appearances aside, Howe and the others had been soldiers ever since the time of their muster. They might not have been paid yet, but they were soldiers.

The condition of Company A's clothing at this time was described by its officers as "somewhat worn," and the men's demeanor, though labeled "good" lacked the polish of military discipline and courtesy.[2] But Howe and the rest of the men in the 116th Pennsylvania were not unique in this regard. It took more than a uniform to make a boy or man a soldier. The rank and file were, "for the most part," *The Press* contended on July 29, 1862, "comprised of *raw recruits*," and needed discipline.

But discipline was no where to be found. The captain of Company A,

Thomas Ewing, didn't make the trip. Because of the small number of recruits he had been able to enroll, Ewing was mustered into neither the company nor the regiment. In fact, the company muster rolls indicate that he never received a commission or appointment of rank. Lt. William M. Hobart, off somewhere promoting a new assignment for himself, was theoretically in charge of the unit.

Though Lieutenant Hobart was one of the first officers mustered in — on June 11, 1862 — he was not close to his men. He envisioned himself in a much higher position, a more prestigious role in the operations of the army. He did not fancy himself to be always a lowly line officer. The men could sense this ambition and did not look upon him as their leader. The ideal of the Union army officer was a man with very special qualities. An officer could not lead just because he wore "shoulder straps," the insignia of rank. His men had to get to know him and, through this knowledge, respect him as their leader.[3] Howe and many others like him needed discipline and education in military affairs. Their lives hinged on knowing how a soldier survives. This lack of training festered in many minds until it erupted, often resulting in desertion.

Besides the lack of rapport with their officer, there was resentment in the hearts of the soldiers. "In this hour no man has a right to assign any reason for failing to defend his country." That is what the folks back home believed. "No man has a right to assign an excuse for allowing his wife to drown, when he might have rescued her, or his child to burn, when he could have protected it." After all, "the more plausible excuse a man gives for treason, the more dangerous he is as a traitor." The *Bulletin* on September 10, 1862, cautioned its readers to "beware of men who love the Union — 'but.'" Many young men had believed this and had enlisted, but where were all the others? Company A was sadly understrength. Though publicly listed as having from twenty-nine to forty-seven men, there were actually only thirty-seven names on the muster. And, of these, five were not present for duty. In addition to the absent Ewing, four men had deserted on September 2: James Duffy, Charles Jones, John Vesil, and Charles Michel. Boarding the train were only thirty-two men, less than one-third of the approved strength for a company.[4] Howe's determination to survive must have been jarred by the depleted ranks.

The curious banter and laughter, unique to untried recruits in camp, were gone. Silence now prevailed. "Few, indeed, were they who did not see more clearly the serious and dangerous side of the undertaking," one soldier recalled. "Hope told of easy victory and renown won. But, somehow, the other side would turn up and show a reverse of ugly wounds, of sudden death, of defeat and disaster."[5] The minds of all the recruits were filled with personal thoughts, private thoughts. Except for some of the officers, few of the soldiers had ever served in the military before. Most looked on this train ride as the beginning of a new and great adventure. The country boys, for the most part, had never ridden on a train, and they were silent with awe and wonder. The city fellows were immersed in dreams of the adventures they would have living under the stars in some far-off battlefield. Some dwelt on how they would perform under battle conditions and in the face of the enemy.

It is probable that those men who knew each other in civilian life arranged to be together in this moment of mutual need and silent understanding. Bitting, Hauck, and Pennypacker might have joined Howe. Together they might have sat and reminisced about life at home, their families and friends, and about their roles as soldiers in the army. So the silence of the first part of the journey wavered as whispered confidences were shared. It was finally broken as members of the regiment began singing "Johnny Is Gone for a Soldier" as the train rattled south.

Early on the morning of September 3, the train arrived in Baltimore. After breakfast with some townspeople, the men of the 116th continued their excursion south to Washington, D.C. When they finally reached the nation's capital they found it sweltering. The heat intensified as they marched, virtually unnoticed, through the city and across the bridge that connected the federal city with the rebels' primary state. The heat and the dryness of the city left their mark on the men. "The dust settling on the new uniforms dimmed the bright blue," so that when a halt was called, a staff officer in Howe's regiment remarked, "a dull gray was the prevailing color."

Still lacking the basic accoutrements of the soldier, other than the uniform, the regiment made camp. Lt. Col. St. Clair A. Mulholland wrote after the war of the thrills that he supposed the men enjoyed upon their arrival: "the first taste of camp life, the excitement of getting up the tents, lighting the first camp fire, cooking the first camp coffee, eating the first 'hard tack,' mounting the first camp guard, and the hundred interesting incidents so new, so fresh and so full of charm to the young patriots. . . . Now they were in the enemy's country, among real veterans who had been in real battles and showed real scars and told wonderful tales of hair-breadth escapes and fierce encounters." It is more likely, however, that the tales exchanged centered around money—the lack of payment of bounties, premiums, or monthly pay. Also, the men might have been frightened to be in enemy territory with neither weapons nor ammunition. Although the unit was not armed, Heenan did not hold Howe and the others up to ridicule by issuing them sticks with

*St. Clair A. Mulholland, Commander, 116th Regiment, Pennsylvania Volunteers.* War Library, Military Order, Loyal Legion of the United States, Philadelphia, Pennsylvania

which to protect themselves while on guard duty. Other Philadelphia units had also experienced a great deal of delay in the issue of uniforms and equipment, and some regiments in the Irish Brigade had been forced to drill and mount guard armed only with wooden guns, wooden swords, and cornstalks.

The regiment camped at Fort Craig on Arlington Heights for two days. During this brief encampment, Howe's small company was bolstered by the arrival of four new men mustered in at Harrisburg on September 5. All were of German descent: Sgt. Christian Foltz, Cpl. Jacob A. Coble, and Privates George M. Book and Samuel Foltz, brother to the sergeant. Christian Foltz, according to Mulholland, was "a brave, unassuming, Christian soldier, and though a man advanced in years (35, at the time), he was as full of patriotic feeling, and ever as ready to share in the hardships and dangers as the youngest." Foltz was an important addition to Company A.

The 116th Pennsylvania was then ordered back to Washington, where the men drew weapons, ammunition, and camp equipage. The weapon furnished was the "old pattern musket," designed to fire a 69-calibre ball and three buckshot. Each man was also issued sixty rounds. William Howe's fears lessened considerably; at least he had a weapon with which to defend himself.

On September 7, the regiment marched to Rockville, Maryland, and Heenan reported to Gen. Darius N. Couch, commanding II Army Corps. To their amazement, the men found out the unit had been assigned to the defenses of Washington. With an about-face, they marched back to the capital and reported to the commander of the defenses north of the city. Camping near Tennallytown, the men of the 116th used their talents in the construction of Fort McClellan. They were also schooled in the duties of the soldier in active warfare. The troops drilled and developed "field fortifications" . . . from behind pick and shovel.[6]

There had not been enough time to teach the basics of soldiering at Camp Emmett. Recruitment was the first order of the day, and everything else, including military instruction, came second. What little instruction given was drawn from military manuals and books that some of the officers had obtained. As fast as they could learn what the printed word meant in practice, they would try to convey this to the men. The few officers that were at the 116th Pennsylvania's camp had attempted to drill the men in marching and company formations. But with the small number of recruits in Company A, it would have been extremely difficult for any officer, no matter how skilled or schooled in military science, to drill them. For the most part, such small units were relegated to positions of menials—caring for the horses, digging "sinks" or latrines, and the like. Since weapons had not been issued at Camp Emmett, Howe and other marksmen could not demonstrate

*Christian Foltz, Company A, 116th Regiment, Pennsylvania Volunteers.*
War Library, Military Order, Loyal Legion of the United States, Philadelphia,
Pennsylvania

the prowess that would ultimately make them important as soldiers. Now, at long last, the men had their weapons. They had ammunition. All they needed was a chance to prove themselves.

For the next ten days, Howe and the others worked diligently to acquire the skills of soldiering. The weather was fine and the work was not hard. Changes were made in Company A, which further depleted the ranks. The muster book showed that George M. Book was "detailed" on September 13 as regimental sergeant major; Richard H. Wade on September 16, regimental quartermaster sergeant; and John W. Arms on September 17, regimental quartermaster clerk. The company also discovered that Pvt. John Dobbins had deserted on September 15.

On the eighteenth, the regiment marched to a point between Hall's Hill and Arlington Heights, near the Glebe House, and set up camp within six miles of Washington. When word reached Heenan on the twenty-first that his regiment was now assigned to XI Army Corps under Franz Sigel, they broke camp.

There must have been joy in Howe's heart as he heard this news. Sigel was an idol to the German-Americans. His exploits and personal demeanor had earned for him the highest rank of any German-American in the Union forces. It would be a great honor, many German-Americans thought, to serve under such a fine and illustrious leader. Sigel's name was a rallying cry for many of the Germans who spoke for union in the nation's hour of crisis rather than fragmentation based on political differences.

Heenan's regiment arrived at Fairfax Court House, Sigel's headquarters, on September 23. Upon arrival, the company clerk reported Samuel V. Marshall, a private in Howe's company, as a deserter. The regiment continued drilling and instruction for another week, under the watchful eye of Gen. Adolph von Steinwehr of Sigel's staff. The troops were also assigned guard duty. This time they marched guard with loaded weapons.

While the 116th Pennsylvania was on guard duty, Lincoln delivered his Emancipation Proclamation. The reason men had joined the army now took on a different dimension. Journalist Charles Halpine contended that most white soldiers sincerely believed blacks were inferior beings, and those that had contact with slaves had had their opinions reinforced. The soldiers — especially members of the 69th New York, Irish Brigade — strongly opposed any effort to recruit Southern slaves into the army. At the beginning of the war, the *New York Times* reported that members of the 69th would rather see the Union fall than be saved by Negroes.[7]

A further reason for resentment to emancipation was predicated on purely economic grounds. Howe and the other foreign-surnamed soldiers had faced the frustrations of finding work and the discrimination against immigrants. The fact that they had found work made most ethnic immigrants unpopular. The freeing of the slaves caused great disagreement among the troops.[8] Many men were ready to throw down their arms in disgust at Lincoln's apparently politically motivated edict. Some did. Others felt that the administration had precipitated the draft to force men into the army and out of the labor force. Lincoln, they contended, could then liberate the slaves and fill the jobs left vacant by the soldiers with cheap black labor. This action by Lincoln festered under their skins, and the men needed little stimulation or provocation to explode.

On October 6, the 116th Regiment broke camp at Fairfax. Howe and the others were ordered to move to Harpers Ferry and officially become part of the Irish Brigade. At the same time, Colonel Heenan acquired the services of Patrick V. Carrigan as captain of Company A. Heenan could finally rejoice at the fulfillment of Corcoran's public relations gesture with orders including his regiment in the almost-legendary brigade commanded by now-General Meagher. Many of the men who had been involved in the strong Irish movement in America were associated, in one way or another, with Meagher's brigade. And the units and their commanders making up the brigade—63rd New York (Col. Richard C. Enright), 69th New York (Col. Robert Nugent), 88th New York (Col. Patrick Kelly), and the 29th Massachusetts (Col. Ebenezer W. Pierce)—created a spirit of adventure for all men who sought renown.

As part of the Irish Brigade, the members of the 116th could extend their military education. At the feet of the fighting Irish veterans, some of the recruits could also participate in the fun and games that set this brigade apart from all the others. With the Irish, some of the Pennsylvanians joined in horse racing, all-night partying, scrounging, and other forms of nonmilitary amusement[9] . . . things at which, in his younger days, William Howe had excelled.

The regiment journeyed towards Washington again, camping near Bailey's Cross Roads. The troops entered Washington on October 9 and were issued overcoats. The 116th then marched to Sandy Hook, near Harpers Ferry, arriving there the next day. They set up camp on a cliff overlooking the Shenandoah River, at Bolivar Heights. The ground of this new campsite was still littered with the debris of the battle which had taken place a short time before.[10] So close to the war, Howe could inhale the air and detect the lingering odor of black powder. It would not be long, he must have thought, before he too would be in the middle of the fray.

A regiment from Maine, "green" like the Pennsylvanians, camped nearby. Being resourceful, yet naive, these men found an abundance of 30-pound

*Thomas Francis Meagher, Irish Brigade.* Library of Congress

Parrott shells lying around and decided to use them in the construction of camp fireplaces. "Four or five of the oblong bolts in a ring with the points up," Mulholland remembered, made "an excellent resting place for the coffee pot." What the Maine boys did not know—but would soon find out—was that as the fire heated up the coffee it also heated up the undetonated shells. Half a dozen cooks were slightly injured in the fireworks that followed and everyone supposedly had a good laugh. But the lethal lesson of what these shells could and would do was learned by all.

In the early days of setting up the regimental camp at Harpers Ferry, Samuel P. Bates, deputy secretary of the Commonwealth of Pennsylvania, came south and presented the 116th Pennsylvania with the state and national colors. "The camp at Harper's Ferry," Mulholland thought, "will always be remembered by the members of the regiment with pleasure. The weeks spent there were full of enjoyment."

Besides receiving flags from the state, the Pennsylvanians also received word of the recent elections and the Republican wins. Though the public had voted to reduce the number of Republicans in both the Congress and the Senate, Lincoln's party was still in control. The valiant effort of the Democrats had been felt, but not enough to change the direction of the national government. Lincoln "has reason to be satisfied with the solemnly recorded verdict of the people of the State upon his administration of the Government," the October 25, 1862 *Inquirer* editorialized. The newspaper felt that Lincoln's hand had been strengthened, and he could rely on the majority of the people to support his policies to end the war. "Our gallant Army and Navy will be taught," the *Inquirer* argued, "that the warmest sympathy is felt for them by those who remain at home, and that while they are facing the enemy in front there is no danger of a fire in the rear." The newspaper continued that "it can no longer be a secret that there is at the North a number of this class (traitors) who barely shelter themselves behind the organization of a great party, that they may communicate information to the enemy and sow dissensions and distrust among the people." The same issue of the *Inquirer* also reported that in the 6th Congressional District, where Howe lived, the Democrats were victors by a 320-vote majority.

While in camp at Bolivar Heights, the 116th was particularly fortunate. Very few of the men took sick and no one died. Other Pennsylvania regiments camped near Howe's unit were plagued with almost epidemic fever, and there were many funerals. During the entire war, more men would die from disease than would fall before the guns of the enemy.

Diarrhea and its often fatal effects were caused primarily by ignorance. Civil War officers commanding volunteer units, uncertain of their duties and responsibilities, sought not to offend the men who would be behind them in a line of battle. Thus, many officers never established rules of sanitation and diet, and where such regulations did exist, they were reluctant to enforce them.

Since many of the recruits came from rural areas, they had never been exposed to the diseases common to the cities. Thus, these country boys had never developed the antibodies that allowed them to resist disease. Shortly after exposure, these men would drop like flies. Some citified soldiers used this to prove a point: the countrymen were no hardier than city boys.

But it was more than that. An officer of another Pennsylvania unit, camped near Heenan's regiment, wrote home that "Doctor Fulton today reported Bell's camp among those for bad sanitary arrangements." It was a source of amazement to him that Bell's company, composed of rough and tough backwoodsmen, had five times more sickness than another company nearby, which was made up of delicate city boys. The difference, he reasoned, was based on the great care the city commander took with his men in keeping their tents and blankets clean and in providing drainage in his street. Bell apparently failed to do this. Perhaps because Howe's unit was a melting pot of rural and city boys, it was lucky to have avoided disease for so long.[11]

In addition, the diet supplied to the soldiers was not conducive to fine health. Deficiencies in such nutritious items as fruits and vegetables continued to plague the army. Milk, a staple in any well-balanced diet, was a rarity. But those in command were more concerned with waging war and inflicting wounds on the enemy. They could not bring themselves to realize that the prevention of disease would bolster the strength of the men and therefore maintain the strength of the unit with little need for replacements, except for battle casualties.

Minimal care was taken in the establishment of a camp. Tents were pitched close together and the "sinks," or latrines, were uncovered holes in the ground, oftentimes located upstream of the camp. "The only sink," one camp inspector reported, "is merely a straight trench some thirty feet long, unprovided with pole or rail; the edges are filthy, and the stench exceedingly offensive.... From the ammoniacal odor frequently perceptible in some camps, it is obvious that men are allowed to void their urine, during the night, at least, wherever convenient."[12] Many of the country boys, who at home followed nature's call to the most convenient and closest spot, ignored the latrines. Unfortunately, the example of the rural soldiers influenced the city boys. Even those who in civilian life had been meticulous about their personal hygiene became as nonchalant in the army as the most unsophisticated backwoodsman.

After living in the field for a month and a half, the members of the 116th

Pennsylvania were still hale and hearty. They were indeed fortunate to have survived so well. But there were more days to come and more camps, as well as more exposure to the elements, to disease, and to the enemy.

Heenan received marching orders on October 15. The regiment left Harpers Ferry at daybreak the next day, as part of Gen. Winfield Scott Hancock's division.

The division moved down Winchester Pike on a reconnaissance towards Halltown, Virginia. After passing the town, the brigade was formed into a line of battle, with the 116th Pennsylvania in position on the right. "Then the advance in the clear air. Oh," chortled Mulholland, "it was glorious war at last." For roughly half an hour, Howe, his regiment, and the other units of Hancock's division were under enemy artillery fire. After this baptism, the line advanced and the enemy retired from the field. The division entered Charlestown unopposed.[13]

The advance troops searched out and found about one hundred Confederate soldiers in a church that had been converted into a hospital. They were made prisoners. Lt. Edmund Randall of Company G "was detailed to take charge of and parole them." Following this exciting duty, the regiment returned to Harpers Ferry and bivouacked in "the field where old John Brown had been hanged."[14] It might be boring duty at the Ferry, Howe and his comrades reasoned, but they finally had experienced war and had met the enemy, even if he was only sick or wounded.

"Our troops have returned from the grand reconnaissance," the *Inquirer* reported on October 20, 1862, "and are now busily engaged in spending the money, which they received just previous to the advance. The boys are in the best of humors at the little scrimmage, and are now calmly awaiting the real advance." The newspaper report, however, was not quite accurate. Howe and the men had not seen any money since they left Philadelphia. Not until the end of October did a pay-muster take place for the men of the 116th[15] Company A's muster roll shows the men were paid to October 31, but it also indicates that the men who deserted after that time had not been paid. It is highly probable that regular records were not kept by the unit. Rather they were reconstructed at a much later date when requested by the War Department.

The *Sunday Dispatch*, on the other hand, reported on November 8 that "the army has not been paid for more than four months, and the soldiers have no money. This is a grievous evil," the newspaper felt, "and should be remedied promptly." Officers, the paper implied, were reduced to their last dollars, and enlisted men "almost forget what it looks like. . . . The men in the field have to 'grin and bear it,' but there is some tall swearing done, both loud and deep, at the negligence of the Government in this particular, which promises to pay the troops every two months, but, like lovers' vows, such promises seem made only to be broken. How the families of the soldiers at home make out under such circumstances, God only knows; but there must be a great deal of suffering." Howe's personal files from the War Department indicate the only money he received was a premium of $2!

"I am happy to be able to inform you that the advance of the Army of the Potomac commenced this morning," a telegraphic dispatch from Harpers Ferry announced, "and I have reason to believe that before to-morrow night the movement will be general along the whole line, placing the Potomac in our rear." The men of the 116th Pennsylvania struck their tents on the evening of October 26 and with the army at last left Harpers Ferry. After marching three miles, Couch's corps halted and camped for the night. It was probably during that evening—with all its disorder and rushing hither and yon—that Howe's boyhood friend, Augustus Bitting, found that he could no longer stomach the lies and broken promises. His desire to be with his family was greater than his wish to serve his country. Under cover of night, Bitting deserted the army, his unit, and his friends. [16]

Bitting was not alone. Three other members of Company A were reported as deserters on October 31: Joseph Lynch, Alexander McCarroll, and Samuel Pennypacker, another neighbor of William Howe. [17] Perhaps Bitting and Pennypacker went back to Frederick Township together. There were hundreds and thousands of others throughout the army who were deserting. "The attention of the proper military authorities," a concerned letter-writer told the readers of the *Public Ledger* on November 4, "should be directed to the number of deserters, who, dressed in citizens' clothes, are daily seen walking the streets of the city. . . . One reason assigned for these desertions is that so many of the officers are absent from their companies that the men have become careless and lax in their discipline. While the officers show such dereliction of duty, the men cannot be expected to be much better."

Company A, since the time the regiment was mustered into service, had been disorganized. They did not even have a captain in command. Lieutenant Hobart was supposedly in charge but he never emerged as an effective officer. Sergeant Foltz, from the day he joined the company, had displayed the rare quality that made enlisted men relate to him. On October 25, Christian Foltz was promoted to 2d lieutenant. The company muster roll indicated he had acted in that capacity from September 24, but without a commission. Patrick Carrigan was officially recognized as the company's captain. [18] In the next few weeks, it would be the responsibility of these two officers to take the demoralized men of Company A and mold them into a fighting team. This was the first bright ray of hope to penetrate William Howe's otherwise dismal military experience.

On the morning of October 27, the 116th Regiment marched to Key's

Pass. They rested there a day and were "mustered for pay. The pay-rolls were sent off . . ."[19] and it was time to be moving on. "We jogged on, up hill and down dale," a correspondent who accompanied the troops wrote in the *Inquirer* on November 3, "now on the top of a hill, from whence we could see for miles and miles, away in the dim distance, until the far-off mountains in Maryland looked like blue mist. We could see the Sugar-loaf Mountain, with its autumn-tinted leaves," he marveled, "rearing its tall head up among the black clouds that hung heavy and threatening in the direction of the Maryland shore." But the atmosphere did not bother the men in the least: it was the heavy black clouds from the South that Howe and the others feared most.

On November 2, the unit reached Snicker's Gap and met some elements of Confederate cavalry. By this time, Company A had lost more men: George M. Book had transferred to Company B on November 1; George Roeder had been promoted to regimental sergeant major; John Arms, for the past two weeks detailed as regimental quartermaster clerk, had deserted; and Thomas Butters was recruiting in Philadelphia.[20] At first sign of the rebels, the men of the 116th were deployed as skirmishers, exchanging shots with the rebel pickets.[21] Perhaps Howe, because of his skill, was in the forefront of his regiment. "We moved quietly along," headquarters reported in the *Inquirer* two days later, "until our skirmishers were within something less than a mile of Snickersville, when some half dozen of the enemy's cavalry were seen emerging from the woods, on the hillside, directly in front of us. On observing their proximity to our troops, they at once wheeled about, and putting spurs to their horses, soon hid away in the woods."

After General Hancock surveyed the scene, he positioned the Irish Brigade to the left of Gen. John C. Caldwell. "These were all drawn up in line of battle, the batteries, in the meantime, occupying prominent and commanding positions," the *Inquirer* noted on November 4. "In this position were they advanced until reaching the village of Snickersville. Seeing no sign of the enemy, our skirmishers were pushed through the valley and up the steep surrounding hills, but with the exception of a few cavalry, early in the morning, not a single one of the enemy at that time was discernable."

"The Rebels are in view from the crest of Blue Mountain Ridge," the *Inquirer* reported the next day, "and in considerable force beyond the Shenandoah. Cannonading is going on towards Manassas Plain, and shells are seen exploding. The mounted scouts of the enemy occupy the roads in our front. Everything is advancing in the greatest order. Our troops are in high spirits, the weather and roads excellent."

"After a spirited engagement with the enemy for about four hours," Headquarters, Army of the Potomac, reported at 7:00 P.M. on November 3 that Upperville was occupied by Gen. Alfred Pleasonton and his men. "We had none killed," the *Inquirer* report continued, "but several wounded. The enemy left three of their dead on the field." The next day, the 116th Pennsylvania and the rest of II Corps reached the town. Two days later, November 6, they were in Rectortown.

On November 7, the troops moved into camp at Warrenton. "The valley, as yet, had not been denuded of provisions," Mulholland recalled, "chickens, mutton and pork were plentiful, and fence rails made bright fires." The fires were quite important for the comfort of the men, because a heavy snow began to fall that morning and showed no sign of stopping.

"Warrenton," a correspondent on the advance reported in the November 12 *Inquirer*, "appears to be; just now; the centre of attraction, as everybody is here. General BURNSIDE and staff are quartered at the large hotel back of the Court House. Very few citizens are to be seen on the streets, and almost every house is closely shut up.

"Hundreds of soldiers," the reporter continued, "are parading up and down the principal streets. Many talking to some of the Rebel nurses left behind to take care of the Confederates, wounded at the last Bull Run fight, of which there are at least one hundred and fifty here. Many, or a majority of them will never recover.

"Warrenton is a pretty place, and has some very pretty private residences in the south side of the city.

"The tops of the mountains are clad in snow, while in sheltered spots roses and snow are mixed up together."

At Warrenton, amidst the splendor of nature, General Meagher drew up his brigade and read General McClellan's farewell address. McClellan had just received word that he had been relieved of command of the army, and Gen. Ambrose E. Burnside had been selected as his replacement.[22] The reason for the change of command was simple: Lincoln, Stanton, and Halleck thought "Little Mac" spent too much time rushing here and there, and too little time engaging the enemy. The federal leaders—and the press—wanted a victory, and they wanted it to happen very quickly.

The 116th "enjoyed all the good things [at Warrenton] perhaps with a greater zest than that of the others around us," Mulholland recalled, "for it had not yet lost a man." But those men who had become ill or wounded in the last few encounters with the enemy had little or no opportunity to enjoy the experience. "We are at present in a hospital, if it may be so called," a soldier wrote from Harpers Ferry. "What receptacles, and what attention to weak, sick, and wounded men, who have risked everything in defense of their country! Here is a score or so of miserable, emaciated looking beings, lying upon the damp, bare ground, without any fire, in an old, dilapidated, roofless stone foundry. There, from stables and out-houses, fifty or sixty more may be seen to crawl forth each morning to beg the pittance of wretched food, doled out grudgingly to them, by petty, insulting menials, employed from their capacity to insult and heap all kinds of abuse upon the sick soldiers.

"How long shall this continue?" he asked. "Can these men, who the Government has commissioned as surgeons, and at large salaries, too, be indeed human? The money seems to be all they wish; and they endeavor to shirk the labor and responsibilities of their position. There is no hope; there is no pity; there is no redress for sick soldiers, at their hands. Even if there were better accommodations in our cities for them, they are refused permission to enter them; while here and elsewhere they are ordered about from one place to another, by surgeons, and their assistants, like so many brutes, more than reflective, and in the majority of instances, refined and sensitive human beings. Besides all this," he charged, "too much whiskey and brandy is the bane, rather than an advantage, to our hospitals. The medical corps of these institutions generally help themselves liberally to these stimulants, while the sick must, of necessity, do without, not, however, without feeling its influence in a reflected manner.

"Men—good, brave men—have died by hundreds in barns, stables, and around straw stacks, who, with anything like humane attention, might have now been living. Hundreds and thousands are now doomed to die, by an objectless and inexorable military law, who might be saved—saved to their country, saved to their families, saved to themselves.

"Why are men entirely unfitted for service denied their discharges?" he asked. "Why are sick and wounded men denied even furloughs? To say nothing of the inhumanity of keeping a thing created in God's image in the places called hospitals. The expense to Government is very great in every way. In the first place, it is paying millions to those who are villainously squandering its resources and rendering no service; in the second place, it is creating a vast amount of anxiety and misery at home; lastly, it is losing thousands of brave men, who might, under kind care and treatment, be returned to duty, and thus be a continued source of augmentation to the army.

"Why are our sick, now kept here in lingering agony, to live against hope, to die and be buried in a miserable manner, far away from home and kindred? —we ask why are they not permitted to go home at once? Not a community in our broad land but would rejoice to receive its suffering soldiery. There they would have some chance for life—there, if they lived, they would be the sooner fitted to return, willingly and thankfully, to the army. The soldier would be rejoiced; every home and community would be happy and satisfied.

This course would remove one great cause of gloom and foreboding from the soldier's heart—the continual dread of becoming sick, under the present regulations in regard to army hospitals and army treatment. God, grant that the war, and its concomitant evils and miseries, now desolating our beloved country, may soon close, upon such a basis as may make us in all future a free, happy, and united people." [23]

"Since the army reached Warrenton," a correspondent noted in *The Press* on November 10, "it has been allowed a short breathing spell, but it is not likely that it will remain motionless long at a time." The correspondent's contention was accurate. On the fifteenth, the march south resumed, in the direction of Fredericksburg, Virginia.

Shortly after dark that night, a private in Company C, David E. Major, became violently and unexplainedly ill. Within an hour, he was dead. The men of his company "tenderly wrapped [him] in his blanket and prepared for burial next day," Mulholland wrote. "But at midnight orders came to march at daybreak and so the boy had to be buried at once. . . . The chaplain said a prayer, and so at midnight the first brave boy of the regiment was laid to rest, his blanket marked U.S. his only shroud." The burial rite must have chilled the men of the 116th Pennsylvania. Though death is considered commonplace in wartime, it remains a bewildering experience. When the first death occurs in a unit, the concept of the vulnerability of man becomes more evident—and increasingly more difficult to understand. The sudden death and the just as sudden interment would instill in the soldiers' minds thoughts they should not have had as they marched off.

After the Irish Brigade left the town, Warrenton bore little resemblance to its former appearance. "Hungry soldiers now prowl about," the *Inquirer* reported on November 18, "intruding whenever they get a chance, without fear, except of the Provost Guard. All the fences have disappeared, causing all the yards to look like commons. The ladies fear to walk the streets on account of the number of soldiers. This is," the account declared, "the realization of 'what is war.'"

On November 19, the folks at home read in their morning *Inquirer* that the Army of the Potomac had begun to evacuate the town on Saturday morning. Two days later, the town was deserted and the troops were on their way to Fredericksburg, with Gen. Edwin V. Sumner's corps in the lead.

Under Burnside's reorganization of the Army of the Potomac, the Irish Brigade was now part of Sumner's Right Grand Division. This type of reorganization and the swift movement of the troops created the atmosphere that federal officials had hoped would develop with the ouster of McClellan. "Our army moves with renewed and buoyant spirits," *The Press* chortled on November 18, "and we may look for the happiest results whenever and wherever the enemy is found." Company A moved out with a lighter step than ever before. By this time, its ranks had been further reduced—for various reasons—to a total of twenty-one officers and men.

To increase its total manpower for the major offensive, the War Department issued Special Order No. 338, demanding that all officers, regardless of grade, and part of the Army of the Potomac, rejoin their companies within twenty-four hours. Those who disobeyed would be dismissed from the service.

"While these steps are being taken with regard to the officers," *The Press* observed on November 19, "measures of an equally stringent and effective character are in progress to arrest the immense number of deserters now scattered through the country, and to hold them to the severest penalties prescribed by military law for their offences. It is the determination of the authorities to make examples," the newspaper noted, "which will cause every soldier to consider seriously before exposing himself to the chance of an infamous death, as the penalty for deserting his standard. Many of the men now absent are deserters from the army in the field, and not a few of them lured by the bounty, have enlisted in the new organizations." This reenlistment, *The Press* contended, was no excuse for desertion. Officers of the new regiments, who were aware of such men, and who did not send them back to their original units, would be held responsible.

"Others of those now absent," the article continued, "are men who were discharged from hospitals to return to their regiments, but who have skulked to their homes." All of these were to be classified as deserters, and the military authorities would mete out proper justice to them. "There is yet another class," the newspaper added, "and one to which no mercy will be shown, viz: those who joined new regiments recently recruited, received the numerous bounties given, and then deserted before the regiments had been placed in the field. The country has suffered most deeply from the latter class, various States having paid bounties for their full quotas, while their effective force reported at headquarters of the army is still short by many thousands of the required numbers." Because of these facts, the public was exhorted to become "a great moral police to expose and shame back to duty all officers and men who cannot prove incontestably that they have the authority required by army orders and regulations for their absence from their commands." Most soldiers, however, did not think that the War Department would try to enforce that order.

On November 19, the War Department announced that one hundred officers, absent without leave, were stricken from the rolls of the army, and that their names would be published the next day. "This is the first installment," it was promised, "of the thousand now absent, skulking."[24] The strong move on the part of the War Department was looked on with some distrust by the rank and file. Though it was fine and dandy for the officers to be dismissed and their names published in the newspapers as "skulkers," the punishment for desertion by an enlisted man was death. Besides, many enlisted men felt that the War Department was working in collusion with the class of officers. After all, was not getting out of the army what many of them really wanted?

*All their movements that I have been able to discover took to a concentration at this point, and it appears to me that should General Burnside change his base of operations, the effect produced in the United States would be almost equivalent to a defeat. I think, therefore, he will persevere in his present course, and the longer we delay him, and throw him into winter, the more difficult will be his undertaking. It is for this reason that I have determined to resist him at the outset, and to throw every obstacle in the way of his advance.*

Robert E. Lee to Jefferson Davis,
November 25, 1862[1]

# 4

# Bivouac of the Dead

THE 116TH Pennsylvania made the march from Warrenton, a distance of forty miles, in two and a half days. By November 17, William Howe and his fellow soldiers were within gunshot of Falmouth, Virginia. "This may be set down as very good marching," the *Inquirer* reported on November 21, "as the corps was encumbered with a very heavy train of baggage trains."

Regardless of the speed with which they traveled, soldiers are only men, and men will be boys when an opportunity presents itself. A newspaper reporter on the march was astonished at the eagerness the men showed for frost grapes and persimmons. "A weary, foot-sore, exhausted soldier, staggering under his gun, blanket and knapsack, will run a quarter of a mile to climb a persimmon tree, and taste the rich, unsatisfactory fruit, or to chase a squirrel or rabbit." Having engaged in this slight diversion, the soldier hurries back to the ranks, "and relapses into his old, weary, hapless, woe-begone aspect. Persimmons and squirrels are play; the road is work."[2] The reason for these little excursions was, perhaps, more for sustenance than merely for play.

The road they traveled, "here and from the Junction runs on a ridge and is almost a desert, so far as water is concerned. What few streams there are running," the *Inquirer* noted on November 21, "seem to be nothing but muddy pools. Water is very scarce."

Sensing that his men were "in the very best spirits; their merry echoing voices rang through the forests, raising the spirits of the weary ones in the rear, all hurrying on towards this point," Sumner saw an opportunity to engage the enemy. When near Hartwood Church, he ordered the Irish Brigade to move up the road towards Falmouth to see if any of the enemy were lurking ahead.[3]

The area was reconnoitered, and Sumner's intelligence indicated that the Confederates in the city of Fredericksburg were not firmly ensconced in their position. From his vantage point, he could see only four guns and a scattering of men. The Irish Brigade had begun, by this time, to bivouac in a field "hard by" and were performing an old army rite—"cooking coffee" and resting after the march. At the general's command, the unit "in three minutes . . . was going to the river in a run." But General Burnside, at the last minute, decided against such an offensive move, and the unit was forced to return to their coffee.[4]

The Irish, however, used a certain amount of journalistic freedom in reporting on that encounter. In their official history, they adjusted the truth slightly to provide an interesting campfire story with which they could beguile their children and grandchildren for years to come. The way they told the story, Sumner ordered them to charge upon the enemy battery. "They plunged into the Rappahannock, dashed across it, flung themselves on a battery of the enemy, capturing two guns. As they dashed at it, they gave one Irish cheer, kicked over kettles, frying-pans, coffee-pots, and every thing in their way. The enemy fled without firing a shot," supposedly frightened by the noisy Irishmen. Gen. Winfield S. Hancock, after reportedly seeing this, is supposed to have exclaimed to General Meagher, "I have never seen any thing so splendid."

At dawn, Couch's advance corps was on the road to Fredericksburg. "Howard's division was in want of new clothing," the *Inquirer* reported on the twenty-first, "*but it did not wait.* We marched ten miles; the clothing came up from the railroad after dark; the garments for two brigades were all issued that night, and at daylight the men were again upon the road, clothed and in their right minds." The next day, the rebel pickets "were scattered along the bank of the Rappahannock, and conversed freely with our own," *The Press* confided, "but no firing took place."

Early the next morning, November 18, Couch's corps moved on. The 116th Regiment went into camp in the woods about a mile and a half from Falmouth. The understanding of the troops and their officers was that the year's campaign had come to an end and the establishment of winter quarters was the next order of the day. Soldiers then, as soldiers now, hope against all hope that there will be no battle tomorrow.

Heenan's regiment camped "on a rise of a hill . . . [the surroundings were] generally healthful," Mulholland related. "A few, however, succumbed to the usual camp fever and sickness due to exposure."

While in camp at Falmouth, Lt. William Hobart left the regiment. He had used all his resources—military, political and personal—to obtain a better position. It had finally paid off, and he was "detailed to the staff of General Winfield S. Hancock as Provost Marshal of the division," Mulholland reported. Hobart never returned to the regiment and remained, until the end of the war, at division headquarters.

The army at Falmouth suffered severely. "The little shelter tents (ponchoes) do very well to keep off the dew during the summer nights," an *Inquirer* correspondent noted on November 24, "but when it comes to a winter rain, a man might as well be out of doors, as they do not afford the slightest protection." The 116th Pennsylvania shared in this suffering. By that time at least twenty-seven members of the regiment were sick in Washington's military hospitals. And, due to the diseases that ran rampant through the camp, they suffered their second fatality, Cpl. William E. Martin of Company C.

The desire to do battle was dulled by the waiting and the tent-tales of no battle until spring. Camp life was boring and the men had little to keep them occupied. "What a contrast!" a visitor in camp told the readers of *The Press* on December 1: "I left peaceful Philadelphia a few days ago, to pay a hasty visit to the Army of the Potomac. I am here, and yet it appears that I have come to a still more peaceful spot. What a contrast, I say! At home people appear to wake up simply to read the 'war news'; they stand at street-corners and speculate upon the future; they purchase 'extras' with their hearts in their mouths; they retire at night with fear and trembling lest the morrow's sun should herald bloody news. But what is the picture *here*?" he asked. "Here are nearly 200,000 men in arms, sent here to fight; within two miles is an enemy, perhaps as strong in numbers—we see their guns, we see them walk their posts; we see them plant their instruments of death, and throw up their earthworks, yet there is no commotion, no anxiety, not even *curiosity*, men appear to have resolved themselves into mere machines, and I question very much whether a ten-pound shell would create as much excitement in these animated fields and forests as would a ragged newsboy shouting 'extra' at Third and Chestnut streets. . . .

"There is a sublime stillness surrounding everything here," he noted. "The army seems to care little whether it goes ahead or not. It is no longer an army of enthusiasts—it is an army of tired veterans, who know their danger, and dare to face it.

"I am happy to say that it is generally conceded here that the Pennsylvania regiments cannot be excelled in drill, discipline, health, or fighting qualities."

The other regiments of the Irish Brigade, those who had seen battle before, were reported by their historian as being so "accustomed to encounter death in every shape and form, and hold their lives by so slender a thread, that they soon forget their dearest friends who have fallen." Such men tried to fill their hours and days with diversions.

By now, though, winter had set in, with cold and bleak winds unique to the fields of Virginia. The soldiers, imagining that the war was suspended for the winter, prepared some semblance of shelter.

"We officers had our wall tents, and had them fixed with puncheon floors also," Maj. Frederick L. Hitchcock, adjutant of the 132d Pennsylvania Volunteers, boasted, "and sheet-iron stoves so that as long as we kept a fire burning all were fairly comfortable."[5] The enlisted men were not so lucky. They built rough shelters—nothing more than crude log cabins, chinked with mud, or holes in the ground topped with shelter halfs. To provide heat, they constructed fireplaces of mud, sticks, or stone, which, in many cases, provided more smoke than heat.

Food was another element of camp life which was missing, prior to the battle of Fredericksburg. "Yesterday Lieutenant Colonel Myers, assistant chief quartermaster, viewed the several corps to inspect the amount and condition of supplies," the *Inquirer* explained on December 2. According to the army, "all were found abundantly supplied with good rations. A large amount of fresh vegetables have been ordered for General Sumner's and General Burnside's old corps, the scurvy having made its appearance among them. It is remarkable," the report noted, "that these troops have always been the first to be attacked by the disease when deprived of vegetables." Though the Army of the Potomac asserted there were sufficient rations, the men themselves never saw them. They continued to look about the town of Falmouth and its immediate neighborhood for "forage."

"Great complaint is still made by the soldiers relative to provisions and forage," the *Inquirer* reported from the ranks on December 8. "Yesterday over two hundred wagons were all day at Belle Plains waiting for forage, yet they were compelled to go back to their brigades without any, as there was none to be had. It is very evident there is a screw loose somewhere. From what I can learn there is little or no forage in Washington, and down here in the army, in some of the camps, there is not enough for a day ahead, while in others they have, perhaps, enough to last two days. The indications are that the horses and mules will be short of feed in a day or two, if hay and oats is not hurried up. The greatest drawback to our army since its reorganization," the writer contended, "has been the bad management of certain parties at

Washington. This fact has become so notorious that it is freely discussed by all grades in the army. It is time there was a change."

Colonel S. K. Zook, 57th New York, was appointed acting military governor of Falmouth. A reporter maintained that he "manages to keep it quiet, orderly, and free from despoilation." Most of the credit was given to Zook's order "shutting up the Sutler's stores and compelling them to locate near the regiments to which they belong." This was done, the writer contended, to prevent "the men straggling from camp, under the plea that they desire to patronise [sic] the Sutlers."[6]

These stragglers, the *Inquirer* editorialized on December 5, contributed greatly to the absenteeism of the army: "Absenteeism is one of the most serious evils. . . . Hundreds of officers and thousands of men are almost continually away from their commands. Many of them are really *stragglers and deserters*." According to a report from Secretary Stanton, which the *Inquirer* quoted, these absent men "are not to be estimated . . . by 'hundreds' and 'thousands'; but, if the officials' records are to be relied upon, by hundreds of thousands."

Officers were able to escape the discomfort and boredom of camp life by arranging trips to Washington. Pvt. Warren Lee Goss of the 2nd. Massachusetts Cavalry recalled that "officers in tinsel and gold lace were so thick on Pennsylvania Avenue that it was a severe trial for a private to walk there. . . . Perhaps I exaggerate, but in a half hour's walk on the avenue I think I have saluted two hundred officers. Brigadier-generals were more numerous there than I ever knew them to be at the front. These officers, many of whom won their positions by political wire-pulling at Washington, we privates thought the great bane of the war." He and the other privates felt that these officers should all be "sent to the front rank of battle to pursue the enemy instead of Old Abe and the members of Congress from their district, until they learned the duties of a soldier."[7] What the army needed, an editorialist confided in the *Inquirer* on December 4, was "a few more men; or rather we want that vast army of 'ABSENT WITHOUT LEAVE,' who deserted their posts and are skulking ingnominiously at home."

While some of the men were deserting their posts, or junketing and politicking in Washington, those who remained made Falmouth their home-away-from home. "To keep themselves comfortable in these cold nights, the soldiers have made rude huts or sheds, which has led to the notion that they are making themselves permanently snug for the winter; but this is a mistake," a reporter warned. He prophesied that barring the unforeseen, "the great movements will be soon made, and the great game played out, with the odds in our favor."[8]

During this November, the coldness of the Virginia nights took its toll. Everything was frozen; the wood was wet; blankets few; shoes and clothing worn out. Many men could not stand it. Some went on sick call. "What with previous exposure," a young lieutenant wrote, "and long trying to keep up while really sick, I broke down."[9] Several deaths from exposure were reported; and one night six pickets were frozen to death on their posts. At this time, the 116th was assigned to picket duty—a duty that continued for sixty-eight hours.

By Monday, December 8, the situation had worsened. While Burnside vacillated on a deliberate battle plan, the elements spoke in decisive terms. "It is intensely cold," it was reported at 10:00 A.M., "with two to four inches of ice in the Potomac and Rappahannock. . . . Any movement involving the probability of fighting is considered by our generals impossible during this inclement weather. Every wounded man would die. With great fires, log houses, and embanked palisades under their tents, the troops keep tolerably comfortable. It is reported that two or three intoxicated men froze to death last night."[10]

"Newspaper correspondents like myself," *The Press* writer stated on December 11, "who have no claim on army rations, and eat at farm houses, will not regret parting from this spot. The surrounding people have been robbed by our army of nearly all their provisions, and have not sufficient to last them through the winter." During the 116th Pennsylvania's stay with the Irish Brigade, General Hancock had issued orders to all the men to "respect all private property. . . . This was all well and good, but," the brigade's historian reminded, "hungry men did not relish it."[11] Petty thievery—most times for the sake of their own survival—was rampant throughout the ranks, from colonels and chaplains, down to privates.

"The weather is milder to-day [December 9]," the army reported. "The nights are exceedingly cold. Much sickness prevails. The Rebels are still at work upon their batteries and forts in the rear of Fredericksburg. All [is] quiet. . . ." The report continued that "the very severe weather gives to our army temporary pause. It requires rousing fires, shelter, and numerous layers of clothing to keep the men even moderately comfortable. Those who are exposed suffer greatly, and those who become intoxicated and 'lie around loose,' freeze to death. Huts are hurriedly constructed, and warmth is the greatest desideratum at any expense of labor and trouble. It is too cold to fight, for the gunners would be benumbed, and the wounded would die to a certainty. So to wait a while is a necessary condition of successful movement hereafter."[12]

While that author's wishful thinking was being read in the warmth of many Philadelphia homes, General Burnside was visiting the divisions of Sumner and Hooker. The *Inquirer* reported that "the troops were on dress parade, and uproariously cheered the commander as he passed along the lines." Rumor had it that Sumner had instructed his men to cheer Burnside.

While news correspondents and soldiers breathed a sigh of relief thinking there would not be an encounter while cold weather prevailed, army leaders were hard at work, preparing for the decided eventuality.

"It is a great satisfaction to know," a message from Headquarters, Army of the Potomac, confided on December 12, "that ample arrangements have been made for the reception of wounded men in the forthcoming fight." Army officials allowed two hospital tents for each regiment. A single tent would accomodate twenty men. In addition, division hospitals had enough tents, it was thought, to furnish two additional ones for each regiment. "Considering that many men are wounded in the arms, or slightly in the head, and are not disabled from walking," army officials decided these accommodations to be ample. "Good fires and covering will be provided for all hospital inmates, and no suffering through the cold will be endured."[13]

Following Burnside's inspection, the Falmouth camp was put in a state of readiness since December 11 was the date Burnside had determined for crossing the river. "The roads leading to the front," Mulholland wrote, "were filled with troops marching in silence to the fray. Camps deserted, the camp fires burning dim, the woods pouring out their thousands, everyone, every thing towards the river."

All that went before was minor. Everything the men had done before was incidental—in soldiering. Fighting, to the Civil War soldier, was intimate and unsophisticated. The infantry bore the brunt of each battle, with the cavalry and artillery merely acting in support. Closing with the enemy, in mid-nineteenth century terms, was not a mere figure of speech—it was a statement of fact. Each side would meet the other face-to-face, and most battles ended in a head-on confrontation of shrieking, screaming, yelling, shooting masses of humanity.

The individual soldier, prior to battle, had much to think of, besides the family and friends he left behind. He had to think of how he, as a man, would respond to the stimulus of warfare. The concern for how they would perform was paramount in the minds of the men. In most letters, written after battle, there is a single, common reference by the soldier-writer to taking care of himself, "number one." Sometimes, he ran away to survive; other times, he stayed and fought for survival. The usual thought of death or injury was not so strong as the fear that they would be unable to stand up under the test of the unknown that faced them. Some thought it far more important to be wounded or killed while facing the enemy than to be a coward and humiliate or embarrass the folks at home. Death was something they could respect and accept. As one Maine volunteer put it, "Death is the common lot of all and the diference between dyeing to day and to morrow is not much but we al prefer to morrow."[14]

On December 10, the Irish Brigade received orders to issue each man three days' cooked rations and sixty rounds of ammunition. It was time for members of the 116th Pennsylvania, and William Howe, to face their destiny.

"Now came the so-called battle of Fredericksburg. It was rather a foreordained slaughterhouse," Lieutenant Rusling determined, "and our brave boys the predestined victims. Lee had been given all the time he wanted, to fortify every hill and flood every ravine; and so all he had to do was to sit still and see us march into his traps, or knock our heads against his works."[15]

At last the army began to cross the Rappahannock, an *Inquirer* correspondent reported, "and before this article appears in print [December 11] our gallant forces will have ascertained the true meaning of the smoke which for some days past has 'so gracefully curled' beyond the Rebel batteries at Fredericksburg. Whether their forces were actually there encamped or bivouacked or whether it was a feint with which to deceive our soldiers upon the other side of the river, will then be known."

During the night of the tenth General Couch reported that General Hancock was directed to send two regiments from Colonel Zook's brigade to protect the working parties who were throwing bridges over the Rappahannock, opposite the city of Fredericksburg, and where [II Army Corps] was to cross."[16] That night, the river exhaled a foggy mist, a mist so thick that the opposite shore was hidden from view.

The next morning, December 11, at 8:00 A.M., Couch massed his troops to the rear of the bridges and held them ready to cross. The spans were incomplete and not readily usable because of the strong concentration of musket fire directed at the engineers who were building the bridges. Sumner ordered Couch to send up a brigade in support of the engineers; but, the Confederate sniper fire was too intense. Finally, it was decided to do a more logical thing—send a group of volunteers across the river in boats to dislodge the sharpshooters. The 7th Michigan, followed by the 19th and 20th Massachusetts, used the pontoon boats and, according to the official report, "seized the buildings occupied by the enemy's sharpshooters, took a number of prisoners and advanced into the town. This was a gallant affair." After the beachhead had been won, the bridges were rapidly completed. But because darkness was upon them, only Howard's division was able to make the crossing before the night completely obliterated their view of Fredericksburg.[17]

Meanwhile, Meagher's brigade had left camp and advanced toward the pontoon bridges. "The brigade was never in finer spirits and condition," Meagher wrote. "The arms and accoutrements were in perfect order. The required amount of ammunition was on hand. Both officers and men were comfortably clad; and it would be difficult to say whether those who were to be led, or those who were to lead, were the better prepared or the more eager to discharge their duty."[18]

The Irish Brigade marched to the lower crossing, passing along the south bank of the Rappahannock, arriving within a few hundred feet of Sumner's headquarters. There, they were halted, "countermarched, stacked arms, and in this position, ankle-deep in mud, and with little or nothing to contribute to their comfort, in complete subordination and good heart awaited future orders." All the while they stood there, the Confederates continued their fire, and Meagher noted that "an entire division, crossing immediately on our left flank was compelled to fall back and wait for the approaching night to conceal and protect its advance."

Shortly after 4:00 P.M., word reached Meagher that Howard's troops had begun crossing on the pontoons. "Immediately after this word was brought to me," he wrote, "an order reached me from Brigadier General Hancock to march forward my brigade and take up and hold a position nearer the river."[19] There they spent the night. Couch had issued an order that no fire should be lit after nightfall. "This order," Meagher wrote, "was uncomplainingly and manfully obeyed by my brigade. Officers and men lay down and slept that night in the mud and frost, and, without a murmur, with heroic hearts composed themselves as best they could for the eventualities of the coming day." The "fortitude and endurance" of the men affected the general deeply.[20]

That night, as the men of the 116th lay in the muck and the mire, the city of Fredericksburg became a scene of "pillage and destruction." "Wine cellars [were] broken into and the soldiers," according to Francis Pierce, a member of the 108th New York, were "drinking all they could and then opening the faucets and [letting] the rest run out—boys go to a barrel of flour and take a pailful and use enough to make one batch of pancakes and then pour the rest in the street—everything was upside down. . . . I can't begin," he concluded, "to *describe* the scenes of destruction. It was so throughout the whole city and from its appearance very many wealthy families must have inhabited it."[21]

At sunrise on Friday, December 12, the remaining divisions of Couch's corps began crossing the river, moving toward positions in the streets of Fredericksburg, parallel to the river. The medical officers made arrangements for the care of the wounded as the troops crossed the river. A location in the covered area to the right of each unit position was selected for divisional hospitals. Buildings on the Union right (such as churches and other public buildings) were commandeered for hospital use. Where the ground was open, on the left, many of the unit hospitals were situated in ravines close to the river. This location provided some protection from the direct fire of the rebel guns on the Fredericksburg hills. By that evening, the medical department had completed all arrangements for the transportation and care of the wounded.[22]

At daybreak on the twelfth, the Irish Brigade was under arms, and in less than two hours, its lead elements had crossed to the opposite bank of the river. "It was a cold, clear day," as Mulholland remembered it, and when the 116th Pennsylvania climbed "over the bluffs and began descending the abrupt bank to cross the pontoons into the town, the crack of two hundred guns filled the valley of the Rappahannock with sound and smoke." The order of the troops crossing was: Colonel Zook, the Irish Brigade, and General Caldwell.

As they moved up the bank, the men passed between the bodies of dead Union and Confederate soldiers. "One group [of the dead]," Mulholland recalled, "had an almost fascinating interest to the young men of the regiment, because every one of the party was boyish and handsome." A confederate unit had been fighting in a garden, near the bank of the river. Their position was sheltered from the heavy fire, and they died "just where they had been placed. There was not a sign of struggle near the spot, and, singular to say, no indication of blood or wounds. . . . The bodies were frozen hard, and all retained the appearance of life—eyes were open, faces placid and calm, and one bright looking youth seemed to smile in his sleep."

Back home, the public read in their newspapers that "the troops are in excellent spirits, anxious to receive the command to advance upon the works, and determined that no obstacle shall prevent them achieving a glorious and decisive victory."[23]

It was a "woful [sic] scene of destruction [which] presented itself, which from the opposite shore could not be realized," *The Press* [December 13] announced. "House walls were riddled with breaches, roofs were fallen in, and the interiors were a mass of fallen timbers mingled with broken plaster. The men rushed in like locusts, and finding many objects still unremoved, transferred those of suitable size to their pockets."

As part of the Irish Brigade's duties on its first few hours in Fredericksburg, the soldiers "at once set to work, mopping up, clearing the houses and shops, street by street, of Confederate sharpshooters, and establishing secure bridgeheads for the Federal army. The city was under heavy shellfire from both sides."[24] As to looting, Meagher asserted "the Irish Brigade scrupulously abstained from any act of depredation."[25] But Thomas Galwey, who served with the Hibernian Guard Company of the 8th Ohio, countered that "just after passing the bridge we halt near tobacco warehouses. The men pillage them at once."[26] Many members of the 116th also lined their blouses with tobacco-filled bags. After the battle, many soldiers would be able to tell tales of how a solid plug of tobacco stopped a minie ball, and thus saved their lives.

"The night of the twelfth was exceedingly cold," Mulholland wrote, "and dismal, and, when morning came, the sun had a long struggle with the chilling fog before full daylight filled the valley. The men chewed on their hardtack and resumed their pastime of fishing up tobacco, and listening to the shells that passed over their heads in countless numbers." That night was one of the most miserable ever experienced by the men of the 116th. "The cold was bitter and penetrating. The troops massed so close that there was not even room enough for the men to lie down on the ground, and it was a fortunate man who could secure a cracker box to sit upon during the weary hours. "Sleep," Mulholland continued, "was impossible, it was so cold and chilly. Groups of officers occupied the parlors of the fashionable residences, spending the night in song and story." The men were not allowed to sleep in the houses because "they would not then range themselves rapidly in case of an attack, nor be under the eyes of their officers."

War ceased being fun for the men that night. "It is mere duty, and becoming very wearisome," an eyewitness related. "An engagement is now entered upon without zest, and with an unconcern almost stolid, as the sailor climbs the giddy mast in a storm. The danger has been often met, it is thus far harmless, and has lost its terrors."[27]

The next morning, Saturday, December 13, dawned, wrapped in a dense fog. The brigade was ordered under arms. The order was delivered to Meagher at 8:00 A.M. After forming his brigade, the general addressed each regiment individually, "reminding them of their duty, and exhorting them to do it bravely and nobly."[28] Though Meagher's remarks to each unit were brief, he reminded each and every man that, because they were Irish, the public's attention would be focused on them to see if they lived up to the proud fighting tradition of the Irish. And, because "they were Americans now, it was their duty and privilege to uphold the Union at any cost." The brigade's colors, which had been torn and tattered in previous battles, had been returned to New York to be exchanged for new ones. Faced with the possibility of entering this encounter without colors, the ever-resourceful Meagher ordered the men to decorate their caps—the general himself setting the first example—

with pieces of green boxwood, as a reminder of their homeland.[29]

Even as Meagher was addressing the 69th New York, which was on the right of the brigade, three men of the 63rd were hit by fire. Before he had spoken the last word of encouragement, the members of the brigade watched in horror as "the mangled remains—mere masses of blood and rags—were borne along the line."[30]

The column then moved through Fredericksburg, where the streets were deserted except for the soldiers—living, dead and wounded—and agents for the undertakers. As the soldiers marched, professional embalmers thrust business cards into their hands. The cards were "suggestive of an early trip home, nicely boxed up and delivered to loving friends by express, sweet as a nut and in perfect preservation."[31] At the front of the street, the right of the brigade rested. After a point, the raking fire of the enemy reduced the number of people in the street to the advancing men and "a solitary pussy cat sitting on a gatepost mewing dolefully."[32]

The sight of the cat must have evoked memories in the minds of the rural soldiers like William Howe. Had not many of them kept just such an animal in their homes or barns to keep down the field mouse population? For some of them, that lonely cat would be the last fragment of their more-pleasant past they would ever see.

While the 116th Pennsylvania was going out of the town through Washington Street, it came under fire. A shell struck Sgt. John C. Marley of Company G. He died instantly, his head severed by the shell. Marley's death was bizarre. He did not fall down. Rather, he slumped to his knees, Mulholland recalled, with his musket clasped in both hands and resting upon the ground. A piece of this same missile reportedly shattered Colonel Heenan's right hand, leaving him unfit for duty.

That same shell killed three more men. "The men [of the 116th] were struck by the instantaneousness of the deaths. . . . A sharp report, a puff of smoke, and four men lay stark dead," Mulholland wrote, "their faces calm, their eyes mild and life-like, lips unmoved, no sign of suffering or indication of pain."

"We crossed the mill-race immediately outside the city," Meagher wrote. The entire brigade of 1,200 men at that point had to cross a single bridge, and, veering to the right, form into battle line. The millrace ditch was virtually impassable, "except at the bridge from which the planking had been removed." The men were forced to cross on the stringers.[33]

In actuality, the bridges that had been constructed for the crossing troops had been destroyed by shellfire. The 116th, for the most part, waded through the icy water. "Here quite a number were wounded," the *Ledger* reported on December 17. The men had to exercise extreme caution, the *Inquirer* noted on the same day, "owing to the snow and ice. The danger of falling was imminent; but notwithstanding this and other difficulties, the soldiers stood the hardships bravely. Not one man was heard to complain, and none, either officers or privates, flinched in the slightest. They stood fire like veterans."

"The shells still fell and now the whistle of the minie was heard mingling with their scream." Lt. Robert Montgomery, Company I, was mortally wounded as he stepped off the bridge.[34]

Beyond the ditch, the ground rose, forming a natural protective cover. To get into this position, Meagher explained, "necessarily took some time to execute." The 69th, located on the brigade's right, "was compelled to stand its ground until the rest . . . came up and formed. This ordeal it had to endure for fully half an hour."[35] Behind this barrier, the troops were able to defend themselves roughly 400 to 500 yards in front of the stone wall. Behind them the ground was dotted here and there by houses and fences. It did not make for a convenient retreat because the plain was swept by the Confederates' artillery and musketry fire.

"How different," Mulholland recalled, "is the real battle from that which one's imagination had pictured. Here there was no disorder. The men were calm, silent, cheerful. The commands of the officers, given in a quiet, subdued voice, were distinctly heard and calmly obeyed, and the regiments maneuvered without flaw."

While the 116th was in this protective position, Lt. Seneca G. Willauer of Company C, "a brave boy from Chester County, Pennsylvania," was hit by a shell which stripped the flesh from his thigh and left the bone "white and bare" for four to five inches. He went to Lieutenant Colonel Mulholland, who had assumed command after Heenan had been hit, and asked, "Colonel, do you think I should go on with my company or go to the hospital?"[36] Willauer was sent back to the hospital, but his bravery was not forgotten.

It became quite evident to the military commanders that the "first ridge of hills, in the rear of the city, on which the enemy had his guns posted behind earthworks, could not be carried except by a charge of infantry."[37] The Philadelphia newspapers described this offensive:

"The troops advanced to the works ten minutes before twelve o'clock at a brisk run.

"The enemy's guns opened a rapid fire upon them.

"When within musket range of the ridge they were met by a terrible fire from the Rebel infantry, who were posted behind a stone wall, and some houses on the right of the line. This checked their advance, and they fell back to a small ravine, but not out of musket range. At this time another body of troops moved to their assistance in splendid style, notwithstanding the gaps made in their ranks by the fire of the Rebel artillery."

The 116th advanced a total of 1,700 yards "under a blizzard of shell and musketry." Men fell at every step, sometimes singly, sometimes in groups, Mulholland related, "without any chance to strike back or even return the fire, only to march forward to be crushed and hurled back in defeat. It took," he concluded, "great courage to advance under the circumstances, yet the division line did go forward without a break, the colors flying, and the gaps knocked in the ranks closing up as quickly as the rain of iron made them."

"Line officers ran behind the men," *The Press* said on December 17, "picking up cartridge-boxes from the dead, and replenishing those of the living. Back and forth they went in the rear of their companies, asking men if their ammunition held out, indicating localities where shots might be effective, and encouraging them with helpful words."

"The roar of cannon, the whirr and scream of shells, the crack of musketry," a non-combatant noted in *The Press* on December 17, "is unending. Poor fellows. God help them! What will not the nation owe to men who face these horrors!" The men of the 116th advanced. "The noonday sun glittered and shone bright on the frozen ground and all the batteries opened upon the advancing lines." The men could pin-point the location of the enemy "by the fringe of blue smoke, that quickly appeared along the base of the hills." The regiment "marched into an arc of fire. . . . Fire in front, from the right and left. Shells came direct and oblique, and dropped down from above. Shells enfiladed the lines, burst in front, in rear, above and behind; shells everywhere. A torrent of shells; a blizzard of shot, shell and fire."[38]

While Meagher viewed the heavy fire unleashed upon his men, he directed skirmishers to be thrown out on the right flank. "I had hardly done so before the Eighty-eighth, Sixty-third, Twenty-eighth, and One hundred and sixteenth, coming up, and deployed themselves in line of battle, drew down upon the brigade a still more terrific fire. The line, however, was beautifully and rapidly formed, and then boldly advanced."[39]

The 116th was positioned on the left of the brigade line. It was, Meagher noted, "a new regiment . . . but its conduct from Bolivar heights, where I had the satisfaction of welcoming it to our camp, down to the present moment, when the headlong gallantry is placed on record, it has proved itself worthy of the cause into which with so much enthusiasm it has thrown itself." As the lines of the men went forward, the Confederates "poured in a merciless fire of musketry as the devoted Irishmen came within range, mowing them down by scores at every step." Still they continued. On, on, onward "to within a few paces of the rebel line. The [116th] regiment by this time [had] lost nearly all its officers and half its men. Unwilling to turn back, [the unit] halted, and dressing line on the little rise of ground just under the rebel works, opened fire, pouring in a steady rain of buck and ball."[40]

As the men fell, others moved in to take their place. Lt. Garrett St. Patrick Nowlen, who took Willauer's place, was shot through the thigh. Maj. George H. Bardwell was badly wounded. Lt. Bob Maguire received a ball through his lungs, as did Capt. John O'Neill, Company K. The orderly sergeant of Company H, John Farley, was killed.

Sgt. William H. Tyrell of Company K sat quietly on the crest of a hill, waving the regimental colors defiantly in the face of the enemy. He stopped waving the flag only after five or six bullets entered his body.[41]

"Onwards, still forward, the line withering, diminishing, melting away," every man knew how desperate the situation was, but no one faltered or turned back. "The hills rained fire and the men advanced as when walking against a hailstorm. . . . The struggle was hopeless. The attacking line waved like corn in a hurricane, recoiled, then broke, and the shattered mass fell back amid the shouts and cheers of Cobb's and Kershaw's Confederate Brigades that [lined] the trenches." The men began to realize that they were there "only to be shot down without being able to return the blow."[42] They continued fighting "more from habit than purpose," and only quit when ordered to do so.[43]

"The plains in the rear of Fredericksburg afforded cramped space for the deployment of troops . . . it was cut by fences, ditches and the canal [millrace]. While moving by the flank from the town, these forces," Private Goss recalled, "were exposed to a severe fire from the enemy's batteries on the heights above them." A resident of the town had told Howard's men as they went through the city "the soldiers on those hills are looking down and laughing to see you coming up to meet them. It is just what they want." Goss's disgust and horror were complete. "No commander has a right to expose his men, by desperate attack made upon those impregnable heights partook of the nature of a forlorn hope."[44]

The soldiers reached a point "within a stone's throw of the stone wall. No further. They try to go beyond, but are slaughtered. Nothing could advance further and live. They lie down doggedly, determined to hold the ground they have already taken. There, away out in the fields to the front and left of us, we see them for an hour or so, lying close to that terrible stone wall."[45] Thomas Galwey described the battle: "The air is alive with the concussion of all sorts of explosions. We are kneeling in the soft grass and I notice for a long time that almost every blade of grass is moving. For some time I supposed that this is caused by the merry crickets; and it is not until I had made a remark to that effect to one of our boys near me and notice him laugh, that I know it is the bullets that are falling thickly around us! It is wonderful how a man can live through such close danger. I have made up my mind that I shall not, cannot, escape. Strangely this idea causes me no nervous-

*Defense of Marye's Heights, December 13, 1862.* Painting by Sidney King, Fredericksburg & Spotsylvania National Military Park

ness nor the least bit of inward excitement. I contemplate the prospect of sudden death without flinching. It is not heroism, but cool reason which actuates me."[46]

"But safety," one soldier found, was only possible by "hugging the ground as tight as a human body could be made to hold on to the earth. Darkness was a relief from the stiff and uncomfortable postures, but during those ten or twelve hours of that winter's daylight, there was no safety except with bodies prone and flattened to their fullest length. A raise of the head, or a single turn not unfrequently proved fatal."[47]

From his vantage point atop Marye's Hill, Confederate General James Longstreet recalled, "By that time the field in front of Cobb was thickly strewn with the dead and dying Federals, but again they formed with desperate courage and renewed the attack and again were driven off. At each attack the slaughter was so great that by the time the third attack was repulsed, the ground was so thickly strewn with dead that the bodies seriously impeded the approach of the Federals."[48]

In formation, "under the unabating tempest of shot and shell, the Irish Brigade advanced at the double-quick against the rifle-pits, the breast-works, and batteries of the enemy."[49] Lieutenant Colonel Mulholland was hit, fol-

**Above:** *The stone wall (reconstruction) at the foot of Marye's Heights in Fredericksburg, Virginia.* Photograph by author

**Right:** *The only remaining section of the original stone wall.* Photograph by author

lowed in quick succession by Capt. John Smith, Company H, Lts. George L. Reilly, Company D, and John R. Miles, regimental adjutant. Lt. Francis T. Quinlan of Company B took command and led them back. "And then the few minutes' firing at the base of Marye's Heights while the sheet of fire leaped from [the] stone wall by the sunken road," and Howe's regiment was ordered to fall back. It was all over for them.[50]

Meagher, as he told it, "owing to a most painful ulcer in the knee-joint which I had concealed and borne up against for days," had already returned from the front lines. (The report from the field, however, published in the *Inquirer* on December 15, indicated he was shot in the leg, "and will probably lose it.") After three or four hours of fighting, the general had realized that his brigade's hospitals "were dangerously, if not fatally, exposed" to the enemy fire. Deciding, at that point, that retreat was the better part of valor, Meagher took his command to the opposite side of the river—away from the battle. "I should not, however, [have brought them over], nor dreamed of asking permission to do so, but for the horrible accidents to which the wounded of the brigade were exposed. . . . I was solely actuated by the affectionate and intense concern for the wounded officers and soldiers of my command."[51]

William Howe did not return with his regiment, however. He continued fighting. When he had fired his issue of ammunition—and any other he could find—he discarded his musket and grabbed an Enfield rifle from a fallen soldier's frozen hands and continued fighting. With the skirmishers, he stayed on the field all day and all night.[52]

Shortly after he returned to the Falmouth side, Meagher met with General Sumner and told him that his "principal object had been, after reporting to him and explaining the reason for my crossing the river, to procure rations and ammunition for my men. The rations had been flung away as the brigade advanced to the assault. The ammunition had been exhausted in the field." On towards midnight, Meagher returned to Fredericksburg. On the way to report to General Hancock, he "stopped at the houses that had been taken as hospitals for the brigade that morning, and in them found many officers and privates who had been brought in from the field since I transferred the brigade to the opposite side of the river. Most of them were in great agony, not having had anything to sustain or soothe them since they received their wounds." The brigade's surgeon was called from across the river to minister to the wounded and dying.[53]

That night, "the cries of the wounded were piercing and horrible," Lieutenant Evans wrote, "groans, curses, prayers all mingled together, in the awful surrounding stillness, and the confused buzzing of the battle not yet out of our ears. . . . Now I was shattered and unnerved by sickness. I had eaten nothing since morning. There was not a drop of drinkable water to be had, and my mouth and throat were parched. Hard biscuit tasted like compressed sawdust, and a pebble I used to carry in my mouth on many a day's march had been jerked out or swallowed, I don't know which, in passing over the uneven ground." Evans threw his blanket, waterproofed with a gum coating, over a pile of manure and tried "to shut out the present by borrowing hopefully of the future, but it would not do. Nothing but the past would come and of that all that contrasted most disagreeably with the present. I felt that I should like to die, or be far away or die *and* be far away in the unknown beyond into which human strife and horror do not enter."[54]

General Meagher's concern for his troops did not change the fact that he had left his dead and the majority of his wounded on the slope, where they would "lie in great numbers on the field all of Sunday, the day following the battle."[55] That Sunday, December 14, "no assistance could be given to the wounded who lay in great numbers out on the plains, but after dark . . . many of the men made heroic efforts to bring them in, although the enemy was vigilant and fired at every object seen moving against the sky."[56]

Other units were not lucky enough to have a commander who swept them off the field. Many men slept where they fought. The firing continued, making the removal of the killed and wounded extremely difficult.

A lieutenant from each regiment, with a small party of men, was assigned the task of climbing the hill under cover of night to aid the wounded. Edmund Randall was designated from the 116th, and William Howe joined Randall's small group. They crawled up the hill and went from body to body. In the darkness, it was impossible for them to identify members of the regiment. They had to feel for the fallen men's hats. With cold fingers, they traced the letters and numbers on the caps. The letters would indicate the company; the numbers, the regiment. Whenever they found a wounded member of the 116th, they carried him off. If the man was dead, they took his valuables to return to his family and friends, and left his body where it fell. "They found such all the way up; some not far from the stone wall, a greater number near the corners of the house, where the rain of bullets had been thickest."[57]

"The body of one man, believed to be an officer," Confederate General Lafayette McLaws commented, "was found about 30 yards of the stone wall."[58] Lt. Christian Foltz, Company A, was that man. His life had been snuffed out by a bullet in his brain. Brave and defiant to the end, Foltz had led his men to the brink of hell. "In actual measurement," Mulholland corrected, "[the body was found] within twenty paces of the Washington Artillery."

"Our dead," the army reported on December 14, "which were killed yesterday, while charging the enemy's works, still remain where they fell. When attempting their removal last night the rebels would open with infantry."[59]

After the firing had finally ceased, a Fredericksburg lady looked out her door at the field of battle. "The field was blue—blue with the uniforms of the dead. A few hours afterwards she looked again, and the field was white—the ghastly white of human bodies stripped of their clothing."[60] Under cover of night, the shivering Confederates had taken the clothing—after all, who needed it more, the living or the dead?

Behind the shelter of the stone wall, Cobb's brigade had cut down the Union forces. The army had fallen, Longstreet described, "like the steady dripping of rain from the eaves of a house. Our musketry alone killed and wounded at least 5000; and these, with the slaughter by the artillery, left over 7000 killed and wounded before the foot of Marye's Hill. The dead," he remembered, "were piled sometimes three deep, and when morning broke, the spectacle that we saw upon the battle-field was one of the most distressing I ever witnessed. The charges had been desperate and bloody, but utterly hopeless. I thought, as I saw the Federals come again and again to their death, that they deserved success if courage and daring could entitle soldiers to victory."[61]

General Lee, amidst the shouting, cheering young Confederates, looked over the battlefield. Turning to W. R. Pendleton, he commented, "It is well war is so terrible, or we should get too fond of it."[62]

*All here have again settled down into a quiescent state. The many little personal incidences which came under the observation of this one and that one, during their participation in the late battle, have been related over and over again, until they have now become stale and of no interest whatever; and were it not that we see around us the many new made graves, the many maimed and mangled forms, the many little scarlet flags, denoting that near by is located a hospital, and did not miss so many familiar faces, we would hardly be able to recognize the fact that, within the past week, and within an area of five miles from where we are now located, that a desperate, well contested and bloody battle had been fought; that in consequence of which at least thousands of manly forms had been suddenly whirled into eternity, and twice as many more made helpless, by means of some bad and dangerous wound. In fact, the late engagement is, with us, almost forgotten, and although our troops are not, to use a familiar phrase, "anxious and eager" for another battle, yet they are ready and willing to follow wherever their superior officers may lead.*

*Philadelphia Inquirer*
December 22, 1862

# 5

# A Time to Go Home

THE LENGTHENING shadows of twilight crept across the blood-smeared battlefield, moving with the same determination the Union soldiers had shown in their daylight attack. For Pvt. William Howe and hundreds like him, the aftermath of the slaughter assaulted his senses. But it was not over yet.

Once more, Mullholland wrote, "the hills flashed fire, shook, rocked, roared and belched forth more tons of iron on the red plain, more minutes of senseless carnage." Hooker's men, armed with empty weapons, had been ordered to take the rebels at bayonet point. The silent muskets and bayonets were again repelled and 1,700 more men joined the already weighty list of killed and wounded.[1] Soldiers prowling the streets found more wounded and dying in the city of Fredericksburg than had previously lived there. The Irish Brigade had marched into the morning mist of that southern town with about 1,200 officers and men. The day after the battle, only 280 men were present for muster. The 116th Pennsylvania crossed the river with a complement of slightly more than two hundred officers and men. Only a handful remained. They had met the enemy and they were destroyed.

Winding his way back through the town, Howe could see that it was, as Major Hitchcock recalled, "one vast hospital." Wounded men crowded into every house and maddening confusion reigned.

Fredericksburg resembled a butcher's shop; its large buildings, homes, and churches converted into hospitals. Whichever way Howe turned, he could see the rumbling vehicles crowded with the broken and bleeding bodies of the young men with whom he had marched. Like most of the officers and men, he was sickened by the suffering of his fellow men but was powerless to help them.

There were no camp fires in Fredericksburg, and blankets and overcoats were in scarce supply. That equipment had been stored in a warehouse before the troops moved into the battle. Earlier in the day, no one mentioned the cold; their adrenalin had warmed them. But the warmth waned as word was passed back through the ranks of the death or maiming of a friend. The hospitals, crowded to overflowing, continued to receive new patients.

The surgeons, coats thrown aside and sleeves rolled above the elbows, had their hands full. With all the preparations they had made, the medical department never envisioned such carnage as the troops suffered at the hands of the Confederates at Fredericksburg. Though they would receive criticism for this seeming lack, no one in authority could have thought, not even in the most frightening nightmare, that events would turn out the way they did.

The surgeons and their assistants were inundated with "capital" cases—amputations. Peering into the makeshift hospitals, Howe could see the ever-growing piles of hands, feet, arms and legs, tossed under each operating table. Because of their location, many of the hospitals were in the Confederate line of fire. Minie balls and shell fragments interrupted the ministrations of the wounded. "And in some instances," Capt. Willard Glazier wrote, "destroying the precious lives that had escaped—though not without suffering—the terrible and deadly shock of battle."[2]

While the battle raged on about the hospital tents, the wounded were constantly passing through the ranks of the advancing troops. Not all those going to the rear were battlefield casualties. Some feigned wounds or sickness with such expertise that their appearances would have been applauded if they had appeared on a stage. "The wounded who could travel," Private Goss conceded, "were treated with kindness, the real sick considerately, but those who were feigning, were made to believe 'there was retribution in Israel.' "[3]

As soon as emergency surgery was performed in Fredericksburg, the patients were transported across the Rappahannock River to receiving stations on Stafford Heights. Then they were forced to endure an arduous journey to Acquia Creek. From there they were transported by boat to the Base Hospital at Alexandria. The medical department had requisitioned boats to carry 3,500 casualties on December 14, but only two of these transports had been fitted up for that intended purpose. Slowly, the emergency station in the town emptied.

As Howe wandered through the city trying to find his regiment, the enormity of the Union defeat became apparent. Even worse than a tactical disaster, the battle left Burnside's forces prostrate, too exhausted to carry on any campaign. The emotional letdown following his experiences made Howe's physical exhaustion even worse. For three days he had stood under arms in the mud and cold. William Howe, wasted both emotionally and physically, continued to function more from habit than conviction.

The Irish Brigade had been pulled out from the field of combat, ostensibly to regroup. But despite his "painful ulcer," Meagher was an Irishman to the core. The entourage returning from New York with the brigade's new colors had arrived during the heat of the fight. In anticipation of their arrival and a presumed Union victory, the general had made extensive plans for a grand banquet to celebrate the return of the unit's standards.

Meagher's men had constructed a large hall on the north side of the river, especially for this festive occasion. Because of the course of the battle, he had to alter his plans slightly and move everything to a small theatre in the town of Fredericksburg. At noon on the 15th, two or three hundred officers —including twenty-two generals—arrived for the party. Around the walls of the theatre, the officers of the brigade and their guests were seated. In the center, two rows of tables held an elaborate banquet menu. The food had been prepared in nearby houses. Despite the thunder of Confederate artillery, military waiters calmly served the guests. The rank and file called it the "Death Feast"; its very existence must have chilled the hearts of William Howe and other frightened fighting men who were excluded. They had not eaten during the battle. What little they had consisted of hardtack and raw pork.

While their officers and friends were drinking and laughing and enjoying the give-and-take of conversation, they were being cut down by the Confederate hailstorm of musket balls. They could see the bodies of their fellow-soldiers lying on the plains behind Fredericksburg. While the officers of the Irish Brigade and their friends were eating, drinking, and enjoying life, the men they commanded were dying.

After the colors were presented to the commanding officers of the individual regiments of the brigade, Meagher called for toasts. The general was neither reluctant nor hesitant to betray his bitter indignation at the course of events by calling down the wrath of God on those political criminals who he felt had betrayed the country with the blood of the Irish. One of Meagher's toasts was to a fellow-Irishman, Gen. Alfred Sully, a West Point graduate: "*He* is not one of your political generals," Meagher shouted, "but a brave and accomplished soldier—who attracted his 'star' from the firmament of glory—

by the electricity of his sword!"[4]  For several hours—"two or three . . . the halls teemed with wine and rang with wit and eloquence."[5]

Apparently Meagher forgot to send Lee and his generals an engraved invitation—and they refused to be left out of the Death Feast. With great regularity and gusto, the Confederates punctuated the speeches with artillery. One particular ball passed through the ceiling, splattered plaster among the delicacies, and suggested to all that an early adjournment was in order.

The Death Feast ended on a dramatic note. While in the middle of a tribute to the still-unburied dead and the still-dying soldiers, accompanied by the cacophony of cannon, Meagher was approached by a waiter bearing the final course—a cannon ball which, a few minutes earlier, had demolished a small building several yards from where the men were seated. Taking the hint from the rebels, the party broke up, and each man returned to where he belonged.

Some of the officers returned to their posts—with their men on the battlefield. Others withdrew from Fredericksburg, the scene of the battle, and from the army itself. A few of them never returned. Gen. Thomas Francis Meagher went to New York "on leave of absence."[6]

While the men were still filtering in from the field, Burnside finally acknowledged what everyone else had known before: his battle plan had been nothing more than suicide. On December 16, he evacuated the city of Fredericksburg and returned the men to Falmouth.

Howe struggled through one of the stormiest nights of the winter. The wind pushed him along and tore at the loose edges of his uniform. He was lost in Fredericksburg. On another day he would have heard the steady rhythm of the bridges vibrating as the beaten thousands of Burnside's men crossed, but the noise was drowned in the howling of the wind as it traveled through the river gorge.

While he wandered aimlessly, the other men, discouraged and disheartened, tramped across the Rappahannock with despair. They were used to defeat, but the senseless slaughter of so many good men was beyond their comprehension. The members of the 116th Pennsylvania marched in silence back to the camp they had left just a few days before. But William Howe was not with them; he was still in Fredericksburg. Mulholland indicated that all of this unit's wounded had been brought over the river before the evacuation of Fredericksburg, probably because of the efforts of Randall and his men, including Howe.

After the troops withdrew, the Confederates advanced their skirmishers along the entire line and, by noon on December 16, had established a picket line by the river bank. William Howe had remained to the last. As Burnside moved his men across, the pontoon bridges were taken up for use at a later time. When the battle-worn Howe reached the Rappahannock, he was forced to swim across, apparently dodging the bullets of the advancing Confederate pickets.[7]

When the rebels had positioned themselves, both armies did what their generals could not. They agreed on an armistice. They mingled freely and exchanged the dead who lay on neutral ground. "During the time," a correspondent for *The Press* reported on December 18, "a general of our army rode by, and put an end to these proceedings. The result was that both parties immediately commenced firing, when nine of our men were killed. After the general had left, the friendly relations of the pickets were renewed, and 'butternut' and blue uniforms freely mixed."

Besides his friends who were dead and wounded, Howe missed other familiar faces when he rejoined his company at Falmouth. Col. Heenan, Lt. Col. Mullholland, and Lt. Willauer had returned to Philadelphia, arriving early in the morning of December 16.[8] They had left the battlefield at 8 A.M. on December 15, barely missing Meagher's Death Feast. They might have delayed their departure since Mulholland spoke of the banquet as if he had been there.

Immediately upon reaching Philadelphia, Heenan went to his residence, at the corner of Eleventh and Buttonwood streets. Dr. S. P. Brown, his personal physician, was summoned to care for his wound.[9] Willauer stayed with Heenan, the *Public Ledger* reported on December 17, "his wound being of such a nature as to prevent his reaching home at present." Mulholland presumably went to his own home. That these officers were allowed to return home must have offended Howe and his comrades who had to remain in camp, waiting for transportation to a hospital in Washington . . . or Alexandria . . . or elsewhere. They couldn't go home—no matter how much they wanted to.

Howe had experienced several severe bouts of diarrhea before the battle. Upon his return, his malady struck with devastating effect. He tried to gain admittance to the unit's hospital at Fredericksburg, but the hospital tent had been destroyed by cannon fire.[10] Even if that hospital had been intact, he would have had a difficult time getting in because of the large number of battlefield casualties.

Howe and his fellow soldiers were at the mercy of the officers and local citizenry. Clara Barton wrote: "But you may never have known how many hundredfold of improper, heartless, unfaithful officers in the immediate command of [Fredericksburg] and upon whose actions and indecisions depended entirely the care, food, shelter, comfort, and lives of the whole city of wounded men." She went on to relate one extremely distressing incident: "A little dapper captain quartered with the owners of one of the finest mansions in town . . . boasted [it was] a pretty hard thing for refined people like the people of Fredericksburg to be compelled to open their homes and admit 'these dirty, lousy, common soldiers,' and that he was not going to compel it."[11]

On December 17, Thomas Evans marched with his unit back to the old camp near Falmouth. He reported that, "here for the first time I became seriously anxious about the state of my health. A bad attack of camp dysentery had set in. My feet were almost black, and the skin commenced peeling."[12] The Virginia weather was cold and there was little comfort in the hospitals. The scant attention of the doctors did not relieve the suffering.

Now that the Federals were back in Falmouth, the Confederates humiliated them further by requesting that the Union forces provide manpower to bury the dead. The *Inquirer's* correspondent accompanied one of these burying parties. After surveying the tactics of the battle, he wrote on December 23, that he first located the dead where the advancing lines broke and in "those portions of the ravine and table-land where we lost such frightful hosts of our brave men. The scene was terrible, ghastly, dreadful! Could it be that man had done this? Had the concentrated destructiveness, the engineering deviltry of military genius, so mangled, crushed and destroyed these once animate forms? It is easy to believe how Omnipotent wrath might have accomplished it, but it staggers my credulity in believing that bands of clay, weapons of modern warfare, wielded even by fratricidal hate, could thus deform, disfigure and destroy. Long rows, piles, columns of our dead."

He rode over the battlefield, noting the stone wall where "our men lay in every conceivable shape and attitude; some across each other, some had fallen with outstretched arms, others with hands beneath them, and again some with arms or legs partially upright in the air. I saw two or three with half or more of their heads blown off—one in particular whose body lay half concealed in a ditch, and bore little resemblance to a human being. But the most humiliating and sacrilegious fact is this, *they were nearly all naked, having been stripped by the enemy on the night succeeding the battle; and had thus lain, for more than sixty hours, as naked almost as they came from their mothers' wombs!* Heathen or barbaric warfare has no parallel to this demoniac act of 'Southern chivalry'!"

"Sadder still," he related, "were the cries and groans of the wounded *who had been left on the field,* and which filled the midnight air with dying supplications. . . . Who can tell his thoughts, whether of home or kindred, wife or loved one, when forsaken, bleeding, dying and lying under the enemy's guns, within hearing distance of both exhausted armies, his sounds of life gradually passing away!"

His final remark was echoed perhaps by many of the soldiers who had been on that battlefield: "I will close with the public announcement that *I do not wish to visit another battlefield!"* Perhaps William Howe had the same thought as he suffered in Falmouth.

This reporter and the soldiers on that burial detail were not the only ones to be so impressed. Confederate Maj. W. Roy Mason watched "with pain" the interment of thousands of Federal troops who had died at Fredericksburg. "The ground was frozen nearly a foot deep," he related, and the bodies were cemented to the ground, making it necessary to use pick-axes to free them. "Trenches were dug on the battle-field and the dead were collected and laid in line for burial. It was a sad sight to see these brave soldiers thrown into trenches, without even a blanket or a word of prayer, and the heavy clods thrown upon them; but the most sickening sight of all was when they threw the dead, some four or five hundred in number, into Wallace's empty ice-house, where they were found—a hecatomb of skeletons—after the war." [13]

The Army of the Potomac could not leave behind the memories of the burials in the fields. Howe watched silently as men continued to die from wounds and disease and their bodies were buried near the camps at Falmouth. In the trauma following the battle, the location of the graves may not have bothered the Pennsylvanians but an artist for *Frank Leslie's Illustrated* wrote: "It is remarkable to a stranger when first visiting the army, to notice the proximity of the burial grounds to the tents of the soldiers. Sometimes, as in the present instance [his drawing], it is close behind the encampment, sometimes on the slope of a hill among the pine stumps, the grim remains of a lordly forest. A friend's, perhaps a brother's hand is seen in the homely decoration on the grave—a piece of cedar or a pine bough planted at the head, and a few pine poles placed around, are all that show where a patriotic warrior takes his last sleep." [14] William Howe, by now completely debilitated, could not walk far without seeing the graves of his fallen companions.

Death remained with him constantly. While Howe battled dysentery and relived the disaster at Fredericksburg, the Army of the Potomac tried to allay the fears of the people at home. On December 18, the *Inquirer* indicated that "our troops are in excellent condition and as enthusiastic as previous to the late engagement." On the other hand, Private Goss countered that "there was universal despondency. . . . The moral condition of the army after the battle may be more easily imagined than described. Gloom pervaded every rank. The feeling was deep and universal that it was of but little use to fight, unless the government could find some one to command who would not throw away our lives in useless experiments. It was evident to the most ordinary soldier in the ranks that we were superior in discipline and intelligence to the rebel rank and file, and fully as brave; and that we were constantly out-generalled rather than whipped."

But Goss was not expected to know much. After all, like William Howe, he was only a private. The folks back home knew better. They read the newspapers and, as the *Inquirer* reported on December 18, knew "it is useless to speculate as to what is to be done in the future. Suffice it now to say, that for the present we are repulsed, but are not driven back, and are in no way disheartened. Our confidence in our leader is in no way abated, and our hope is that in another attack it may be a point where we may have ready, if not quite, an equal advantage." A reporter for the *Public Ledger*, on the other hand, sided with the soldiers, commenting that "the unsuccessful fighting . . . and the hardships endured have not only affected the bodies, but also the spirits of both officers and men, and time for mental recuperation seems also to be required. No-one would be gladder to reflect the bright sides of the situation and prospect of the Army of the Potomac than myself yet a sense of truth compels me to state that it is not by any means encouraging."

The soldiers who served in the ranks thought of themselves as intelligent and became merciless critics when they discovered that they had been led to slaughter. The criticism, when allowed to ferment, was more detrimental to the army than any actions of the enemy. No soldiers in the world, after facing constant blunders by their commanders, grow more dissatisfied than Americans. Their hearts were in the war effort, some stated, but they lacked confidence in their leadership. "They were not tired of fighting," Goss reasoned for all the soldiers, "but of useless fighting, which brought them reproaches rather than victories. They clamored for no particular officer, but considered it due to them to have in command some one who was competent to lead them properly. They considered it madness and murder to continue in command one who had demonstrated his lack of ability so plainly as had General Burnside."

The morale of the Army of the Potomac was decimated. Back in camp, the men had time to think and review. They talked about the battle from their own experience. Nothing, not all the newspapers' or politicians' statements, could convince them that their ranks had been wasted for any reason other than Burnside having run them up against that stone wall when he should have used a flanking attack.

Not everyone in the nation, not even members of Lincoln's cabinet, knew how badly the army had been beaten at Fredericksburg. Secretary of the Navy Gideon Welles noted in his diary that "the rumor at the War Department—and I get only rumor—is that our troops have done well, that Burnside and our generals are in good spirits; but there is something unsatisfactory, or not entirely satisfactory, in this intelligence, or in the method of communicating it. When I get nothing clear and explicit at the War Department I have my apprehensions. They fear to admit disastrous truths. Adverse tidings are suppressed, with a deal of fuss and mystery, a shuffling over of papers and maps, and a far-reaching vacant gaze at something undefined and indescribable."[15]

Regardless of their feelings and knowledge of the situation, the entire disposition of the army was outside the realm of the enlisted men. Howe and others were privates who existed only to obey orders . . . even if the men making the orders did not obey them.

The men might have felt better in their old quarters, but while they were fighting, the camp followers had robbed and ruined the makeshift huts, leaving nothing. The feeling of disgust at the useless murder of so many, coupled with the condition of the camp, did not heighten the soldiers' morale. Seizing hope from the bowels of despair, Howe and the others reasoned that because of their depleted ranks, disease, and exhaustion, another engagement was unlikely.

The sentiments of the private soldier, like William Howe, were best expressed by A. M. Stewart, chaplain of the 13th Pennsylvania Volunteers, who wrote, we have "remained quietly for more than a week without any signs of further aggressive movements, the impression has become firmly seated that, at least in the estimation of our generals, we were compelled to turn back. All this is having a depressing influence on our soldiers. They are not mere machines, but intelligent American citizens. So far as conversant with the feelings of the privates in our army, their confident opinion still is, that the fault, if fault there be, rests not with them, that at any time past, and now, they are abundantly able and willing to meet and crush out the power of rebellion in a day. Their hopes and desires being so long deferred, they are hence becoming querulous, uneasy, discontented and homesick." [16]

Within a few days, the Army of the Potomac rebuilt its camp and "two great cities of log-huts sprang up in the dense forests on both sides of the Rappahannock, peopled by more than two hundred thousand men. It was surprising," soldier Charles Carleton Coffin noted, "to see how quickly the soldiers made themselves comfortable in huts chinked with mud and roofed with split shingles."[17] Quartermaster Rusling saw it differently. "The weather is very cold and winterish," he wrote. "The ground is hard frozen up; and our poor fellows have nothing but flimsy 'shelter tents,' under which to lie and shiver. Talk about Valley Forge, and the huts Washington and his army had there! Why, they were infinitely better off than we are. They were but a small army, in the midst of a rich, fertile country, and could easily subsist. Their huts were warm and comfortable. Wood was near and abundant." But the Army of the Potomac was of prodigious size, camped in a land which had been raped by the marches and retreats of the armies. Rusling was not disheartened: "I face things as they are."[18]

But the way things actually were and the impression given to the general public were often entirely different. The *Inquirer's* readers were told on December 22 that the troops had "settled down into a quiescent state." The personal accounts of bravery had been told so many times that "they are now become stale and of no interest whatever; and were it not that we see around us the many new made graves, the many maimed and mangled forms, the many little scarlet flags, denoting that near by is located a hospital, and did we not miss so many familiar faces, we would hardly be able to recognize the fact that, within the past week, and within an area of five miles from where we are now located, that a desperate, well contested and bloody battle had been fought; that in consequence of which at least thousands of manly forms had been suddenly whirled into eternity, and twice as many more made helpless, by some bad and dangerous wound." By now, the writer felt that the battle of Fredericksburg was almost forgotten, and "although our troops are not, to use a familiar phrase, 'anxious and eager' for another battle, yet they are ready and willing to follow wherever their superior officers may lead."

The winter seemed long to Howe and other members of the 116th Pennsylvania. "The cold was not intense," Mulholland recalled (probably from the warmth of his Philadelphia home), "but the atmosphere damp and penetrating." There was little chance for drill or anything else that would break the monotony and the days and nights at Falmouth seemed to stretch into eternity. The only sound to disturb the boredom was the repeated doctor's call.

A further distraction from the boredom was a visit by a number of government officials who came to Falmouth to see firsthand what had happened to the once-great army. Marsena Patrick, provost marshal general of the Army of the Potomac, wrote in his diary on December 19, that "the Committee on the Conduct of the War, 'Ben Wade, Covode & Co,' came down today, bringing with them the Sergt. of Arms of the Senate, who was so drunk he couldn't walk nor work." The futility of the private soldier's lot was underscored by the actions of these government officials. Not only were the military leaders incompetent, but the men who directed them from Washington were drunkards! Who could expect the troops to be less than demoralized?

General Sumner, in response to a reporter's question about the troops' morale, stated in the *Daily Evening Bulletin* of December 24, that he "believed there was a great deal too much croaking. There was not sufficient confidence." It was difficult for the men to believe in a leadership which drove them, like sheep to the slaughter, into the guns of the Confederates. Was General Sumner demanding too much by expecting the men to smile and prepare for battle again when they were so sick, sore, and disgusted with their condition in life? Perhaps it was too much to ask of any man. "A very great deal of the discouragement comes from the North," one Wisconsin colonel told his family, "from Northern papers & from Northern speakers—who to save their own selfish ends would sacrifice all things—scarcely do we read a good hopeful encouraging article in any of our papers, but nothing but howling against the Administration—against our Generals —detailing all the North *has not* accomplished—instead of what it has."[19]

Many soldiers who had been put to the test at Fredericksburg tried various tactics to obtain discharges. John Billings remembered one man who "responded daily to sick call, pitifully warped out of shape, was prescribed for, but all to no avail. One leg was drawn up so that, apparently, he could not use it, and groans indicative of excruciating agony escaped him at studied intervals and on suitable occasions. So his case went on for six weeks, til at last the surgeon recommended his discharge." Following the approval of his discharge, the man was caught kicking up his heels, while in the midst of a glorious drunk. His discharge, at that point, was recalled.[20]

The number of men who feigned illness made it difficult for the truly sick, like William Howe. There were many "well-known shirkers," Galwey commented, who are as equally well-known to the surgeon as inveterate bummers are to a police judge. Our 'invalids' are robust, big-legged, big-armed fellows," he concluded, "whose appetites would create starvation in a badly provided house."[21] "I must hasten to say," Billings added, "that this is not a burlesque on *all* the soldiers who answered to sick-call. God forbid! The genuine cases went with a different air from the shams." As if he spoke of Howe, Billings remembered seeing "some of my old comrades now, God bless them! sterling fellows, soldiers to the core, stalwart men when they entered the army, but overtaken by diseases, they would report to sick-call, day after day, hoping for a favorable change; yet, in spite of medicine and the nursing of their messmates, pining away until at last they disappeared—went to the hospitals, and there died. Oh, if such men could only have been sent to their homes before it was too late, where the surroundings were more congenial and comfortable, the nursing tender, and more skilful, because administered by warmer hearts and the more loving hands of mother, wife, or sister, thousands of these noble souls could have been saved to the government and to their families."[22]

Despite the poor medical attention, Howe's spirits would have been revived with a visit home. Demands were made to return the sick and wounded to their home states. "Those of our friends and relatives who have marched forth to defend the sacred precincts of home," *The Press* editorialized on December 22, "long no less eagerly for the fireside than those whom they have left behind to administer to the sick and wounded, the distressed and dying. The original strength of the armies," the article continued, "would probably be reanimated and reinspirited by a visit, however short, of the brave wounded to their dearly-beloved firesides. . . . Patriotism evinces itself as much in the relief of the suffering as in the sending forth of the strong to battle."

Unfortunately, when base hospitals were set up in the North, men would go there for convalescence. After they had recovered—and were no longer under the orders of their regiment—they would slip off to home, and stay.

There was little a man could do if he were actually sick but didn't look it. If he could not obtain competent medical attention and care, where could he go?

The days at Falmouth were dark, the nights dreary. The endurance and patriotism of the men were tried as they were forced to stand picket duty all night with winds from the north whipping around them, whirling the snow into drifts. The dark days were filled with rain and followed by weeks of mud. Rather than drill in the mire, they were left with nothing to do but to get sick and, in their sickness, increase their despondency and desire to return home.

Like William Howe, Adam Bright had been sick. "I have something like chronic diarrhea and it uses a fellow up pretty fast. . . . We have been on half rations for the last two months . . . I never like to complain but our rations have been 10 small crackers and a small piece of Beef or Pork and a little coffee and sugar for a day."[23] Howe and Bright were not unique. Many regiments, George Templeton Strong indicated in his diary, were " 'asthenic' or worn out. Line of march is traceable by the deposit of dysenteric stool the army leaves behind it."[24]

In statistics developed by the medical department, almost two million cases of diarrhea and dysentery were reported between May 1861 and July 30, 1866. These figures were low, since the soldiers had a tendency not to report bowel disorders until the situation became critical. It has been estimated that nearly 70,000 Union soldiers died of bowel disorders.

Howe's ailment—he called it "looseness of bowels,"—was a frightening and debilitating sickness. In some cases, it was accompanied by as many as forty to sixty bowel movements a day.[25] When symptoms included painful straining and hemorrhaging, it was diagnosed as dysentery. Diarrhea and dysentery—the terms were used synonymously—killed twice as many men as Confederate bullets.

Victims usually had their systems purged and further irritated by large quantities of whiskey and frequent doses of salt or calomel. Doctors used opium to combat dysentery and in some of the chronic cases, strychnine. Other medications included castor oil, camphor, turpentine, ipecacuanha, laudanum, and "blue pills of mercury and chalk."[26] By the standards of the day, the men dispensing these medications were competent. No one knew about germs or causes of infection.

Faced with such remedies, most men tried to cure themselves. Soldiers, like Howe, were frightened by disease, especially one that devoured their bodies. They had seen men shrivel and die from similar diseases. And, they did not want to die in that God-forsaken camp at Falmouth.

William Howe's bowels had bothered him long before the battle. The stimulation of combat and the excitement he felt were enough to push aside any discomfort. But now, in the quiet and monotonous life at Falmouth, the illness intensified and was more than he could bear. Perhaps Howe was unwilling to take his chances with the doctors in camp. Perhaps the doctors were not even present for duty. Perhaps he recalled how Meagher had to summon the brigade surgeon to cross the Rappahannock to minister to the wounded men. And perhaps, if present for duty, they turned him away because he seemed a big, strong man who was trying to fool them. No one knows why Howe was not treated in camp—but he wasn't.

The thought of dying in Virginia must have terrified the young man. According to his own account, he sought help at the hospital that the 116th had established. If this were the case, it is possible that his visit coincided with the troops' withdrawal when a large number of casualties were arriving. If in fact he went to the unit's hospital at Falmouth—which seems more likely—the hospital attendants and assistant surgeons might have been too calloused by the sight of the wounded to even look at him.

Besides his sickness, army life was not all that Howe had bargained for back in August. The army still owed him money, and it did not seem likely he was ever going to collect it. Hannah was at home in Perkiomenville, pregnant with their third child, with no one to care for her. He was sick, but still was required to carry his weight and more in the unit. No one cared. No one would help him. What could he look forward to? Sickness and death?

What could Howe do? He could wait and hope that things would improve with the coming holidays. But even the advent of Christmas did not appreciably change the situation in camp. Howe did not look forward to the holiday. Neither did Chaplain Stewart. "To-morrow," he said, "will be Christmas. No turkey, goose, plum-pudding, or other dyspeptics, are likely to do us either good or evil. Here, however, is an inventory of good things which have been obtained from our Brigade Commissary for my Christmas dinner, and in the discussion of which an effort will be made to feel both thankful and happy: a cutting of fresh beef, salt pork, beans, coffee, sugar and the ubiquitous cracker." [27]

Edwin Sumner ate well, however, as befitted a general officer in the Army of the Potomac. "During the evening," his son-in-law William Teall wrote, "Taylor brought in and gave . . . [General Sumner] as a Christmas present several partridges sent him by his regiment. At 9:30 Sam brought in from Washington our supplies for Christmas dinner: a fine large turkey, celery, cranberries, mince pies, etc." [28]

The enlisted men did not need turkeys or partridges; they had meat enough. The crackers issued were of very poor quality, often stale from age or moldy from damp storage. In many instances, they became infested with worms or weevil. This fact gave rise to a flood of irreverent comments such as the soldier who contended that all the fresh meat he had came in the hardtack and, preferring his meat cooked, he toasted the bread.

Some of the officers planned to escape Falmouth for a big Christmas feast elsewhere. Their exodus added to Howe's disillusionment. Rusling expected to spend Christmas in Washington, "but it is ordered otherwise. My intention was to get off yesterday and to return on Tuesday; but my application for leave of absence has been delayed, at some of the superior headquarters, and I am still here." [29] Major Hitchcock also desired to holiday in Washington. He was lucky! "No leaves of absence other than for sickness or disability were obtainable at this time" the major wrote, "except on urgent business for the officers of a regiment, and for but one officer to a regiment, and three days was the limit." Hitchcock was the one man selected. [30]

There were, however, other ways to visit the nation's capital; and William Howe found one of them. Along with several other purportedly sick men, he went to Washington. They were not going there on "urgent business for the officers," but because they were sick and had nowhere else to turn. They left Falmouth on Christmas Eve when "a great deal of noise [was] going on." [31]

Once in Washington, the men did not find much medical attention available. The lack of such attention led to a critical decision. They knew the state of medical services back at Falmouth, so they rejected the option to return. At the time it seemed logical to continue their journey home to get more personal, and competent, medical attention. The idea that they would be deserting the army never occurred to most of the soldiers. They were more concerned with the state of their health than in fulfilling an enlistment contract. In short, Howe and his companions were more frightened of death than of any punishment by the army. Faced with such heavy mortality among the sick, and with the countless burial parties, each man recognized his own frailty. Neither William Howe nor any other man relished the idea of dying far from home, among strangers in a hostile country. That thought instilled more terror in their minds than dying on the battlefield. Probably without a second thought, Howe and his friends took leave of the army.

In rapidly growing numbers, other soldiers were laying down their guns and returning to their homes. That simple gesture summed up the enlisted man's no-confidence vote in the war and the government leaders. Certain Democratic newspapers provided open justification for desertion, telling their readers that volunteers had been deceived and that the enlistment oaths were dissolved by the Emancipation Proclamation.

William Howe had never expressed a determination to remain permanently away from the army. It is possible that he did not think it wrong to go home to recuperate. Like many of the enlisted men of the time, Howe had little or no understanding of the implications of enlistment or of military discipline. Absent soldiers always meant to go back—but the day for return was always postponed. Ultimately, the army would declare them deserters; but, in their own minds, many of the men were not.

Desertion—or absence without leave—was quite common in the army in which Howe served. By the end of January, 1863, the Army of the Potomac had a total of 85,123 deserted men! That figure does not indicate that 85,000 men had consciously and willfully set down their weapons and gone home. Most of the men listed on the army's rolls as not physically present had not deserted but simply drifted away. The army's own inefficiency was the real culprit.

Desertion was the bane of the armies—both Union and Confederate. During the Civil War, the Union army had a desertion total exceeding a quarter of a million men. Nearly 60,000 returned to duty. The actual number of deserters apprehended and brought to trial is unknown. A report prepared for Lincoln in November 1863 revealed, however, that during the period between July 1 and November 30, 1863, 592 men were tried as deserters. Of these, 291 were declared guilty, 80 received capital sentences, but only 21 were executed. During that same span, roughly 2,000 deserters returned to their regiments.

Desertion was never understood by either the government or the general public. It was—and is—a despicable crime for a soldier, perhaps the worst crime he could possibly commit. As such, it carried the harshest punishment —death before a firing squad. Despite the wholesale desertions of the Civil War, the government reported executing only 141 men. There was no disposition of some cases of desertion, such as the Illinois regiment that reacted violently to Lincoln's Emancipation Proclamation and went home *en masse*. Eventually disbanded, this regiment was never censured nor any of its men punished.

If William Howe had been an officer, he might have done what Lieutenant Evans did on Christmas Day. Evans turned in his resignation. "It was a hard, bitter thing to do," he wrote. "It seemed as if for me the end of all things. I did not expect to live to see it accepted, but the attempt was made, and God speed it."[32] Or, Howe might have followed the officers aboard the mail boats, which carried "from a dozen to thirty or forty officers of different grades ... going home on a leave of absence for six, ten and twenty days."[33]

But William H. Howe was not an officer. He was a private—an enlisted man. He could not resign anything, but could only resign himself to suffer. No, he could do something, and he did. He went home.

Although Howe never stated why he left the army, other than the fact that he was sick, the reasons seem apparent. Howe's inflamed bowels were destroying his body, rendering him useless to himself, his fellow soldiers and the army. And he could see men around him dying from the same malady that afflicted him. The fact that no one would help him—from a medical standpoint—had alienated him from those in authority.

In addition, Howe had not been paid by the army and he had no recourse. He felt cheated. After all, he had signed a contract for three years of his life. He was willing to spend the time, but what about the other side of the agreement? Was the army willing to uphold its end?

Howe also found himself alone at Falmouth. His close friends and acquaintances were either dead or had left the unit. There were no others in either the company or the regiment to whom he could relate. He couldn't turn to the chaplain for counsel: the chaplain was a Roman Catholic; Howe, a Lutheran. Besides, he could not understand the temperament of the Irish. They held big parties while men were dying. They drank and cursed and had little or no feeling for what they had experienced.

Howe had witnessed at firsthand the carnage and destruction of war —and he did not like it. He probably didn't think it was wrong to go home. His own officers, from Heenan on down the line, had gone back to Philadelphia—and their homes—to be properly cared for. Was he really that different?

So, uncomfortable and seriously dehydrated by diarrhea, William Howe left Washington and traveled home to Perkiomenville—unaware of the implications of his action.

*I have the honor to acknowledge the receipt of the President's proclamation, issued in compliance with the twenty-sixth section of the act of March 3, 1863, pardoning all soldiers now absent without leave from the army who report at certain posts before April 1. There are numerous cases in this army of men now undergoing punishment for desertion or awaiting sentence or trial for that crime. As it would seem to be unjust to visit the severe penalty of the law upon deserters who have been apprehended, I have the honor to recommend that the President, by a general order, pardon all persons now undergoing punishment for desertion, those awaiting sentence, and those awaiting trial for that offense, all, of course, to forfeit pay and allowances for the time lost by desertion.* [1]

> Maj. Gen. Joseph Hooker to
> Brig. Gen. L. Thomas,
> March 20, 1863

# 6

# The Night Callers

WILLIAM H. HOWE left Washington D.C., sometime during the Christmas holidays in the company of twenty men.[2] The route they took is unknown although testimony at Howe's court-martial attempted to establish that he traveled back to Virginia before heading north.

If Howe and the others had returned to a point near Falmouth, they might have tried to pass through the Union lines on the road between Potomac Creek, Chopawamsic Creek, Dumfries, and Occoquan. This escape route had been used by so many men that General Hooker demanded the front pickets of the XII Corps be posted to make it impossible for any man to pass through the lines. Orders were also given to challenge all sutlers' wagons, teamsters, and anyone who tried to identify himself as a telegraph repairer. Further, the pickets received instructions to shoot all deserters and persons attempting to pass who would not respond to the challenge of the guards and submit to questioning by the proper authorities.[3] The Army of the Potomac had drawn a tight line. It was needed.

Upwards of 100,000 men had been identified as being absent without leave and subject to treatment as deserters when Simon Draper was appointed by Lincoln to deal with the issue of desertion. The official army returns for January 1863, estimated 2,923 commissioned officers and 82,188 noncommissioned and enlisted men absent from the Army of the Potomac alone. For the entire United States Army, the figures were astronomical: 8,987 officers and 280,073 enlisted men were not available for duty.[4] These figures, of course, were not exact; and apparently no attempt was made to reduce them by subtracting the numbers of men who were sick or on furlough at the time. Notwithstanding, the number of men absent without leave was excessively high . . . and William Howe was included in those ranks.

Some of the people back home realized how disgusted their men at the front were. Though there is no record that Howe's friends and relatives from Montgomery County intrigued to get the young man home, many soldiers like him were aided and abetted by families and friends. Under the guise of sending food and medicine to the men in the army, sympathetic families would pack civilian clothes and mail them to their soldier-kin. An officer of the 132nd Pennsylvania Volunteers learned of this trick through an anonymous letter from a "friend" in Pennsylvania. He immediately ordered that all the mail be searched. His efforts uncovered two packages of civilian clothes, along with one letter advising the soldier which route to take back home.[5] This particular episode was not an isolated example. Together with other successful ploys, it caused the army to address this problem squarely.

Assistant Adjutant General Seth Williams, in a letter to the Washington-based Adams Express Company, established a new policy to stop this practice. Henceforth, he directed the company, no packages would be brought to the army which did not have an invoice fastened to the outside and the contents certified by the sending agent. No longer would civilian attire or alcoholic beverages be allowed. Williams classed civilian clothing as outer garments only. He excluded items that would make the soldier more comfortable, but not disguise his appearance. The order, however, was strictly for enlisted personnel, not the officers.

The main reason for this restriction, he insisted, was to stop "the pernicious practice of treasonable persons sending citizens' clothing to soldiers here to encourage and facilitate desertion."[6]

It did not matter how many hindrances the army created. If disenchanted or malcontented members of the Army of the Potomac wanted to desert, they would find another way. Some soldiers purchased clothing from the farmers and townspeople nearby. If the men did not have money, they were not adverse to stealing what they needed.

Even without a civilian disguise, the soldiers made strong efforts to leave. Under the pretext of helping the wounded and the sick, many able-bodied, disillusioned, uniformed men — and ne'er-do-wells — boarded the hospital ships where, amid the confusion, their presence would not easily be noticed.

Despite what they thought to be strong measures to stop the evil of desertion, military officials bore the brunt of hometown criticism for their leniency. "The sooner strenuous measures for the arrest of the skulkers are enforced; the sooner our cause will be triumphant," the *Inquirer* declared on January 22, 1863. This newspaper estimated that in the counties of the Eastern District of Pennsylvania alone, there were more than three thousand delinquent soldiers.

An editorial stated that no matter how long or how short a period a soldier absented himself from duty, the penalty was the same—death. And, anyone who helped a soldier desert was subject to fines and imprisonment. Enlisted men, the newspaper continued, joined voluntarily and assumed the responsibility to fulfill the enlistment agreement. The government had the right, it was concluded, to make them live up to the agreement for the good of the country and the cause of the Union.

William H. Howe and the others who left with him probably were not aware of these sentiments. They did not have the opportunity to sit quietly and read these articles and editorials. The trip back to Perkiomenville was not an easy one. Howe finally reached home a month and a half after he took his leave of the army—forty-five days of hiding by day and traveling by night, forty-five days of living with sickness, lack of food, and constant fear.

By this time, the 116th Pennsylvania had undergone a complete reorganization. Because of an insufficient number of men, the regiment was consolidated into a battalion. Mulholland remained with the unit, though his rank was reduced to that of major. Colonel Heenan, the founder of the unit, resigned, citing his wound, the ulcerated knee, suffered at Fredericksburg. Other officers resigned; some were asked to remain. Edmund Randall was one of those asked to stay, but he resigned. Though Randall was a young man, inspired with patriotic fervor, the opportunity of relinquishing his commission and returning to civilian life came at a propitious time. Just before the Fredericksburg battle, Randall had received word that he had been accepted as a member of the bar in Philadelphia. He could return to his hometown as a combat-seasoned veteran, no longer eligible for the draft, and begin to practice law—perhaps even dabble in politics. Because of his decision, Randall's path would again cross that of William Howe.

During this period, desertions continued to mount in the Army of the Potomac. In fact, when Gen. Joseph Hooker took command on January 26, 1863, the situation appeared almost hopeless. Hooker found men deserting at a rate of several hundred a day. His records showed about a quarter of his entire command absent.

When William Howe returned home, he did not try to hide. After Hannah nursed him back to health, he went on about his business and lived a normal life. His third child, William Henry, was born February 6, 1863, shortly after his return.[7] Howe was a civilian again. It is possible that he seldom, if ever, thought about what he had done—leaving the army without permission. His mind was preoccupied with making a living and raising a family. His former devil-may-care attitude had mellowed and matured during this short stint in the army.

But the army had not forgotten William H. Howe or the thousands like him. The army wanted all of them back. Lincoln announced on March 10, 1863:

> I . . . do hereby order and command that all soldiers enlisted or drafted in the service of the United States now absent from their regiments without leave shall forthwith return to their respective regiments.
>
> And I do hereby declare and proclaim that all soldiers now absent from their respective regiments without leave who shall, on or before the 1st day of April, 1863, report themselves at any rendezvous designated by the general orders of the War Department No. 58 . . . may be restored to their respective regiments without punishment, except the forfeiture of pay and allowances during their absence; and all who do not return within the time above specified shall be arrested as deserters and punished as the law provides.[8]

Pleading with all patriotic Americans to oppose and resist treasonable acts, Lincoln called for support in prosecuting and punishing all offenders.

By offering pardon to the deserters, Lincoln had opened a "Pandora's box." Throughout the history of mankind, there have always been people who delight in the role of the informer, especially when it is not necessary to confront the accused in a court of law. Such a climate existed in America during the Civil War. During the early days of the conflict, Secretary of State Seward had made generous use of informants to ferret out enemies of the state. In many areas, he contacted prominent citizens—patriotic, of course—to recommend people in their cities who could detect and arrest people who were employed by the insurgents. For this small service, they would be compensated $50 a month. The information derived from these informants was not always reliable, but apparently it didn't really matter. The secretary of state still authorized state officials to pay informants up to $100 for anything of seeming importance. The money could be drawn "on this Department for the amount at sight."[9] While some men were deriving their income in this manner, William H. Howe was trying to eke out an existence on his farm.

Howe renewed many old friendships and never hid the fact that he had left the army without approval. Possibly his honesty betrayed him in the end. The times were such that a person could accuse another of any crime without having to prove the allegation. The burden of proof had to be shouldered by the accused. Such a situation had never been contemplated by the framers of the American legal system, nor was it espoused in the Constitution. American justice had been based on "innocent until proven guilty." During the trying days of the Civil War, however, men were often considered guilty until they could prove themselves innocent. This distortion of the rights of man began on April 27, 1861, when Lincoln authorized Lt. Gen. Winfield Scott "to suspend the writ of habeas corpus in his discretion on any military line between Washington and Philadelphia."[10] By so doing, the president removed one of the basic rights of American citizenship.

The Congress of the United States recoiled at this suspension. At a special session of Congress, July 4, 1861, Lincoln explained the reasons behind his decision to allow the military "to arrest and detain without resort to the ordinary processes and forms of law such individuals . . . as might [be deemed] dangerous to the public safety."

The president had, he said, "given consideration to the use or misuse of presidential power before he acted. The laws of the nation were for all people, both North and South, but in nearly one-third of the states, they were a failure. "Must they be allowed," Lincoln reasoned, "to finally fail of execution even had it been perfectly clear that by the use of means necessary to their execution some single law made in such extreme tenderness of the citizen's liberty that practically it relieves more of the guilty than of the innocent should to a very limited extent be violated?" The nation was in rebellion, Lincoln cried, and the Constitution permitted such a suspension of privileges when the nation was under a state of rebellion or an invasion by an enemy.[11]

Unfortunately, when one citizen's freedom is abridged, the freedom of all is affected. During the period that the writ of habeas corpus was suspended, more abuses occurred than were justified during the emergency.

Citizens—many well-meaning and well-intentioned, but others with malicious intent—wrote to government and military officials with tales of fact, fancy, and conjecture about various individuals. The correspondent was not required to substantiate any of the charges. The accused would be arrested, confined, and then made to prove the charges were false. Many upstanding American citizens were imprisoned for long periods of time, without hope of a trial or their ultimate freedom.

Lincoln's administration became a party to these injustices by encouraging such action. For example, General McClellan directed Maj. Gen. John A.

Dix, at Baltimore, to make any arrests he felt necessary, even if he did not have direct authorization. McClellan's memorandum displayed his confidence in Dix's judgment and took it for granted that the officer would use discretion.

Officialdom knew what was happening, but could do little to change the direction. To reinstate the writ would be an admission that the wrong course of action had been taken. So, the government tried to mitigate the situation by asking that the constitutional rights of all be respected, to the degree that military necessity would permit.

Newspapers that tried to bring the matter to the public's attention were closed. The *New-Yorker Journal* was shut down because its editors commented that most Northerners deluded themselves by thinking that the most important task of the day was to bring back the secessionists "whilst in truth we have to watch over, first, personal liberty; second, the supremacy of our own race throughout the continent; third, the welfare of millions of all races." The *Franklin Gazette* in Pennsylvania was also closed and its publisher arrested. The newspaper expressed the sentiment that "we are fighting by peaceful discussion and lawful agitation the old battles of the Revolution over again. The liberties then won are now prostrate under the heel of a military despotism."[12]

There is no evidence to show that William Howe was aware of the dark clouds hovering over the North—or over him. He was probably unaware that newspapers were being closed and certain rights of Americans abridged. Even if he had known, it is possible he would not have thought they would ever affect his life. At the same time, there is no certainty that Howe was aware of Lincoln's promise of pardon.

William Howe, the deserter, was at home and thoughts of the army and the battle of Fredericksburg were nothing more than memories of the past. But his actions and those of other deserters were not just a memory to the government; it was a grim reality and efforts had to be made to retrieve these men. As early as 1861, anyone who apprehended a deserter could expect a $30 reward. As the number of desertions increased, the government, in an apparent economy move, reduced the reward on September 7, 1861, to $5. This small amount, in addition to serving as a reward, was also intended to cover the expenses of capture and delivery of the prisoner to the proper authorities. This reduction cooled the "ardor" of some of the arresting officers, since it was more trouble to capture a deserter than it was worth. The adjutant general's office increased the reward on July 16, 1863, to $10. Finally, in September of that year, it was returned to the original $30 amount.

Civilians were expected to do their part in the detection and apprehension of deserters, as were enrollment boards, federal marshals, mayors, police chiefs, constables, and sheriffs. Even postmasters and justices of the peace were authorized by Washington to arrest men and officers who were absent without leave and return them to the nearest post.

Secretary Stanton took the first major step toward arresting the spread of desertion when, on September 24, 1862, he created the office of provost marshal general. Previously, the provost marshals had functioned as military policemen. Their sole duty, prior to Stanton's action, was to preserve and protect the property of citizens along a line of march. The provost marshal concept grew by the appointment of regimental provost marshals with a small detachment of enlisted men. Their role increased in importance as they became responsible for controlling the troops and enforcing discipline wherever the army might be. Later, they were charged with checking the passes of troops and civilians as they attempted to pass through the lines.

The duty of the newly constituted provost marshal general was to appoint one or more special provost marshals, acting assistant provost marshal generals, in each state. Because of their large populations, both New York and Pennsylvania were assigned more than one. On October 1, 1862, the special provost marshals were empowered to arrest all deserters and spies and escort them to the nearest military commander.

Stanton's creation took some time to become effective. It was not until the Enrollment Act of March 3, 1863, that a system was established to attack the core of the desertion problem—the identification of the men. The provost marshal general's bureau in Washington was to act as a general clearing-house for all information on deserters. The raw data was to be culled from the field commanders' reports. When compiled, collated, and interpreted by a staff of clerks, all pertinent information dealing with deserters would be communicated by the provost marshal general to the district marshal. The local provost officers would then attempt to locate the deserter, capture and return him to a military command. The provost marshals could also request additional manpower from the local military commanders.

Reports from the field began to filter into the provost marshal general's office early in April. But because of the busy field operations of the generals (they were soldiers, they contended, not clerks) the reports were never prompt, complete, or accurate. And, the clerical staff in Washington was understaffed and untrained. It consisted of twenty to thirty clerks, mostly incapacitated soldiers drawn from the Veteran Reserve Corps, whose principal function was to copy the numerous descriptive lists.

As a large number of desertion reports began converging on Washington, and amid the confused and inaccurate information, a report on William H.

Howe was relayed to Capt. John J. Freedley, the provost marshal in Pennsylvania's 6th Congressional District. (All provost marshals had been given the rank and pay of a cavalry captain whether they had military experience or not.) Freedley did not have a large staff of assistant marshals and deputies, even though his area included a great deal of what was called "deserter country." During the month of June, 1863, Freedley's staff included two deputy provost marshals, Edward D. Johnson and W. W. Hammersly; a chief clerk, Lloyd Jones; three clerks; four special guards; two assistants; one special officer; and fifty-eight enrolling officers. Of these, only four men were employed the entire month: Deputy Johnson; Chief Clerk Jones; Clerk William H. Griffith; and Assistant Special Guard Albannis Lare.[13]

The employees of the provost marshal's office—especially the enrolling officers—were men who knew their own neighborhoods. But, consequently, they themselves were also known to area residents. In areas where the draft was unpopular, such as the 6th Congressional District of Pennsylvania, hostility on the part of the people made the enrolling officer's job extremely difficult. In other areas, such as in nearby Camden, New Jersey, well-qualified people were deterred from seeking such employment because the enrolling officers were unpopular and poorly paid. In his final report, Provost Marshal General J. B. Fry indicated that his officer had experienced "much difficulty in obtaining the services of reliable men to make the enrollment, this duty in some parts of the country being dangerous to life from the disaffection of the inhabitants." Fry's statement was quite accurate. During the war years, the provost marshal general's bureau suffered a loss of thirty-eight men killed and sixty wounded in the performance of their duty.[14]

If one considers the salary of the Civil War soldier, the provost marshal's men were well-paid. As an assistant special guard, a man could earn $1 a day. Private soldiers, like William Howe, were paid only $13 a month—when the paymasters got around to paying them.

Notwithstanding the danger and supposedly low pay, there were men who wanted to be on the provost marshal's staff. Though political affiliations did not enter into the selection process, the provost marshals would ask the advice of "prominent, loyal men," if they did not know the applicant personally. Though the methods used in obtaining these men were not always the best, Fry contended that the enrollment boards "took great pains to obtain reliable and competent officers."[15]

Unfortunately, not all the men were either reliable or competent. Some, like John K. Clement, provost marshal of Pennsylvania's 10th District, were politically ambitious. Others, like A. W. Bolenius, 9th Pennsylvania District, were accused of controversial behavior not to the "good of the party."

Charges against another Pennsylvanian, Henry S. Kupp, of the 8th District, caused him to resign. He was labeled as "probably a tolerably hard drinker and may be loose in his morals." The Pittsburgh *Daily Commercial* leveled accusations against the enrollment board in the 22nd District, charging the members with inefficiency and unjust conduct.[16] The system had many loopholes. Where loopholes exist in a governmental situation, persons of low moral integrity will gravitate to positions of authority and reap the benefits.

In the late afternoon of June 20, 1863, two men, David Y. Eisenberry, an assistant special guard from Freedley's office, and Michael Wagner, ostensibly on orders from Captain Freedley, unsuccessfully attempted to arrest William H. Howe at his home in Perkiomenville.

It must have been difficult for them to accept the fact that Howe had been within their grasp, and they were unable to capture him. Besides, with only a $5 reward, including expenses, they were losing money by not apprehending him. Perhaps the decreasing amount of reward entered their minds and reinforced their resolve to try once more. On the other hand, there could have been personal grudges involved.

The next day, Eisenberry went to the home of Abraham R. Bertolet, an enrolling officer but not a regular employee. Though Eisenberry was still on Freedley's payroll, Bertolet was not. He had completed his tour of duty on June 19, two days earlier. Bertolet had not been involved with Eisenberry in the June 20 attempt to capture Howe. Bertolet lived in the Swamp Creek area (now New Hanover) with his wife, the former Elmira Sands. They had no children.[17]

That Sunday afternoon, Eisenberry asked Bertolet to accompany him in making an arrest. Bertolet decided against going, however, when told that the man was William Howe. But Elmira Bertolet turned to her husband and said, "Yes, Abe, go with him."

Bowing to his wife's suggestion, Bertolet left with Eisenberry "after tea." The day was dark and threatening, with stormy gusts of wind. As they were leaving, Bertolet's "colored man" approached. Bertolet told him to come along and bring a horse, jokingly adding that it could be used to bring his body home if he were shot. The men then journeyed to the home of Michael Wagner, who was to join them. Wagner, the enrolling officer from nearby Frederick Township, had completed his enrollment June 15 and was off the payroll. It was too early in the day, Wagner decided, to attempt an arrest . . . after all, Howe would not yet be in bed. Perhaps Wagner was not so eager to try again as was Eisenberry. So they whiled away the time, waiting for dark. Some reports indicated that they spent this time drinking either at Wagner's place or at a local inn.

Finally, when the night had sufficiently darkened or the spirits had made them giants, the men started out for Howe's home, arriving sometime before midnight. Within a hundred yards of the house, the small band dismounted, leaving the horses with Bertolet's hired man. Though the night was cloudy and dark, they were extremely cautious in approaching the house for fear of alerting the sleeping residents. Eisenberry stationed Wagner at the northwest corner of the house and Bertolet at the southeast, so that together they could see both ends and sides of the house. When in position, Eisenberry lit a fluid lamp and set it on a garden fencepost, about fifteen feet from the house. With the light shining from this lamp, Eisenberry felt they "could see objects in the house." He then knocked at the door.

A woman he supposed to be Hannah Howe answered and asked who he was. Eisenberry responded, "Augustus Bitting." As "Bitting," he told her that the provost guard was after them and he wanted Howe to come out or they would be captured.

But Hannah Howe knew Bitting. "No," she answered through the closed door, "it ain't Augustus Bitting." Eisenberry claimed he then told her his true identity and what he wanted. Go away, he was told, go away because one of the children "had fits." If Bill surrendered, Eisenberry told her, they wouldn't disturb the children.

Bill, Hannah Howe told them, was in the house but he would not be taken. Eisenberry ordered her to open the door or they would be forced to break it down. She ran upstairs, he said, and blew a horn out of the window. The sound of her call was responded to by other horns from neighboring houses. The small posse, hearing this, anticipated trouble. Eisenberry drew his revolver—they were all well armed—and went around the house intending to fire a warning shot to frighten her. Wagner remembered hearing Mrs. Howe tell them she had a loaded gun and would shoot.

As Eisenberry told it, before he could fire, a shot came from the window and went past his head. He moved around to the front of the house, hoping to break open the door, when Bertolet came up to the front near him. "Break open the door," Bertolet commanded, "for I hear him talking, and let's take him out." Eisenberry said he warned Bertolet that he'd better go back or else he'd get hurt, but Bertolet wouldn't move. He apparently wanted to be in the midst of the action.

Eisenberry shoved at the door once or twice. The door stood firm. Then another report was heard. A bullet, fired supposedly from the window above, whizzed by the guard and, as he reported, passed through the tail of his coat. Without a second's delay, another shot was fired, allegedly from the same direction. This one lodged in the breast of Abraham Bertolet. Clasping his hands to his chest, Bertolet cried out, "I am shot." Acting quickly, Eisenberry declared that he looked up to the window and from the flash of the weapon's muzzle and the light on the fence, he could see Howe withdrawing his rifle.

While Bertolet staggered to the corner of the house, Eisenberry fired again and again at the upstairs window. After perhaps a minute's wait, the guard again saw the rifle emerge. This time he fired directly at it. After he pulled the trigger, he heard Hannah Howe scream, "Bill, are you shot?"

Wagner, since he was at the back of the house, did not see Howe, or anyone else, fire.

Eisenberry left his position after hearing Hannah's cry and went to Bertolet's side and found him dying. The guard yelled to Wagner and asked him to help carry Bertolet's body over the fence. He died, they said, while they were carrying him up to the side of the road. Eisenberry then got a wagon and took Bertolet's body home. The party reached Swamp Creek about three o'clock in the morning.

A neighbor of the Howes, Richard Bolton, heard the shooting. He got up, opened his bedroom window, and heard shots coming from Howe's house. Then, he saw Bill Howe running down the road towards him, shouting, "Murder!" Bolton remembered that Howe cried, "For God's sake go and get my children away." Howe was afraid, Bolton noted, that the children would be murdered. Bolton rushed to a nearby house and got the neighbor to accompany him to Howe's place. As they approached the house, they saw Bertolet in a wagon. They demanded that Eisenberry tell them what was happening, the reason for all the shooting. Eisenberry didn't answer then but asked if the two neighbors would help him and Wagner turn the wagon around.

Shouldn't something be put under Bertolet? Bolton asked, since he might die bouncing along the road. Bolton told them to get straw, but they did not. They wanted to put some manure under him. While the neighbor went to get some straw, Bolton asked Eisenberry if he had seen Howe. "Yes, [I] saw him at the Second Story window, and shot after him," Eisenberry explained.

"Why," Bolton exclaimed, "the house is just one story high." Eisenberry dismissed that fact and said "[I] heard some one groan inside, and . . . thought [I] had shot Howe's wife."

"Eisenberry and his friends," Bolton recalled, "seemed to me to be drunk; they did not seem to know what to do; they smelt strongly of liquor." Eisenberry, Wagner, and the body of Abraham R. Bertolet left Howe's property. Neither Eisenberry nor Wagner made any further attempt that night to look for William Howe.[18]

Conflicting reports circulated throughout the community about the events of Sunday night. No one was absolutely sure what had transpired.

Rumors ran rampant and gained credibility. "One rumor," the *Montgomery Ledger* reported two days after the incident, "has it that Howe was arrested several days ago by Bertolet, but escaped, and that he had since threatened the life of Bertolet should he again attempt to take him."

Evaluating the facts of the incident, the *Montgomery Ledger* announced that it was impossible that Bertolet and the others had been mistaken for burglars, regardless of the fact that they had arrived at such a late hour on Sunday night. "If it should be ascertained," the account concluded, "that Bertolet was acting under orders issued by a proper authority, and gave sufficient warning as to who he was, and what was his errand, or if it can be shown that Howe and his family knew Bertolet and the object of his coming there, without warning, then the shooting was deliberate murder and the perpetrator or instigator of the act should suffer the severest penalty of the law." [19]

An inquest was held on the body of Abraham Bertolet on June 22. The funeral took place at Faulkner Swamp Church two days later. Bertolet's body was buried in the church cemetery.[20] There is no headstone.

Abraham Bertolet was dead and William Howe was running.

*And be it further enacted, That it shall be the duty of the provost marshals to arrest all deserters, whether regulars, volunteers, militiamen, or persons called into the service under this or any other act of Congress, wherever they may be found, and to send them to the nearest military commander or military post; to detect, seize, and confine spies of the enemy, who shall, without unreasonable delay, be delivered to the custody of the general commanding the department in which they may be arrested, to be tried as soon as the exigencies of the service permit; to obey all lawful orders and regulations of the provost marshal general, and such as may be prescribed by law, concerning the enrollment and calling into service of the national forces.* [1]

General Order
Adjutant General's Office

# 7

# Escape to Doom

WILLIAM H. HOWE ran away from the scene of the crime, but not for long. After Eisenberry and Wagner had carted off Bertolet's body, Howe returned to his home. He was still in Perkiomenville on Monday morning, June 22, when District Attorney Enoch A. Banks, Sheriff Kile, Deputy Provost Marshall Johnson, and Eisenberry returned to arrest him.[2]

The entire township knew by an early hour what had happened at Howe's farm on Sunday night, and the residents were frightened. They, and many others in the Union states, did not completely support the administration's draft policies nor did they relish many of what they considered to be oppressive techniques used by arresting officers. In the month previous to the arrest attempt on Howe, several instances of draft and enrollment resistance cropped up in Pennsylvania and elsewhere.

The mountainous areas of western Pennsylvania were considered "deserter country." During the winter of 1863, a member of the secret service confided to General Halleck that he could identify a large number of deserters all throughout Pennsylvania, "as well as an immense lot of government property, which had been carried off by those renegades and by absconding settlers." He stated in no uncertain terms that "almost every man in the State has a rifle, saddle, or some piece of government property."[3]

The resentment of the public was not focused solely on the issue of desertion. The people were much more concerned with the draft, its enforcement, and how it affected them. The Enrollment Act of 1863 had brought that problem to the fore. When confronted with wide-scale public resentment and opposition, Lincoln countered with the statement that "the Constitution declares that 'The Congress shall have the power to raise and support armies.'" That is what they were doing, the President concluded. "There is nothing else in it."[4]

But average citizens did not see it that way, and they expressed their dissatisfaction. There was so much confusion and misunderstanding that the *Public Ledger* on July 22 called for the government to explain the conscript law in language the ordinary citizen could understand. The newspaper considered this necessary in light of the contradictory orders emanating from the provost marshal general's office and the difficulties that some citizens experienced in trying to obtain substitutes. All this, the editorial declared, tends "to add to the unpopularity of the conscription law, and to increase the difficulties of its enforcement."

Some Americans looked at conscription as yet another attempt to erode their rights as citizens of the United States. One Philadelphian challenged the constitutionality of the draft. William Francis Nichols contended that the act of Congress which enrolled and drafted him for military service was done "without his consent, and contrary to his will, [it] is in derogation of the reserved rights of the citizens thereof, and that the same is unconstitutional and void, there being delegated by the States and the people thereof to the Federal Government no power to enact such a law."[5] The Enrollment Act, predicated on Nichols's suit, was reviewed by the federal circuit court in Philadelphia in the fall of 1863.

Yet some people believed that the mere consideration of the question was near treason. "No court of law, at a time like this," *The Press* cried out on July 25, "ought to permit such a question to be raised. No loyal and law maintaining judge can sanction it." Despite this outspoken view the act was declared unconstitutional by a vote of three to two. Two months later, in January 1864, the case was re-argued and this time the law was upheld; it should be noted that this affirmation took place after the composition of the judges sitting on the bench had been changed. In June of 1864, the same law was again tested in Illinois. That court also upheld the Enrollment Act. It was never brought to a test, however, in the U.S. Supreme Court.

Many felt that the draft was politically motivated. When Philadelphia's City Councils met in July 1863, Edward C. Quinn, representing the 2nd District, suggested "that the draft is made to get Democrats, as only Republicans have enlisted. The Republicans are at home holding fat offices, and at the same time they are calling all Democrats traitors."[6] Comments made by the

Republican factions were equally as partisan: "If they [the Democrats] will not serve this country, they should not become the enemies of those in the country's service. They should, at least, do brave and good men the justice of being silent. . . . It is worse than treason for them to go out among the people sowing dissatisfaction and grief."[7]

In Berks County, Pennsylvania, William Hoover (or Huber), a German, was arrested for telling people at a Democratic meeting held in support of the Union and the Constitution that "the Confiscation, Emancipation and Conscription laws were . . . unconstitutional, and, therefore, could not be carried on in the way prescribed by the law laid down for their enforcement." A man who had attended the meeting testified at Hoover's court hearing that the accused had said: "Lincoln would never settle the war, that the common people would have to do it, that the object of the meeting was to carry out a settlement of the war; a curse had been put on the negro, and that Lincoln had desired to place himself above God, and do what the Almighty did not desire."[8]

Closer to Howe's home, *The Age*, a new Democratic newspaper, was the object of a citizen protest. Its offices at Third and Chestnut streets in Philadelphia were mobbed by a crowd of more than 1,200 people on May 8, 1863. The crowd protested posters in *The Age*'s windows, which alluded to the actions taken by the government in the arrest of former U.S. Congressman Clement L. Vallandigham. Philadelphia's mayor rushed to the scene and calmed the crowd, preventing bloodshed.[9]

Vallandigham, an Ohioan, was an outspoken critic of the Lincoln administration and its conduct of the war. His main contention was that the war was being waged, not as the administration stated, to preserve the Union, but to stamp out personal liberty and to establish a despotic form of government. The continuation of the war, Vallandigham declared, was for one purpose and one purpose alone: the freeing of the slaves and the subsequent enslavement of the whites.

After one particularly heated speech in which he called his listeners to action, Vallandigham was arrested. He continued protesting, saying that the action taken against him was "without due process of law, without warrant from any judicial officer, and now in military custody, I have been served with a charge and specifications as from a court-martial or military commission. I am not either in the land nor the naval forces of the United States, and, therefore, not tryable for any cause by any such court, but am subject, by the express terms of the Constitution, to arrest only by due process of law, or warrant issued by some officer of a court of competent jurisdiction for trial of citizens."[10]

Vallandigham's cause was not without supporters—or opponents. A sympathy rally was held for him in Philadelphia on June 1. Commenting on the event, the June 1 *Inquirer* regretted that politicians used such "flimsy pretexts" as the radical's arrest to arouse opposition to the administration.

In reality, the senator's supporters were fighting for more than the fate of one man. That night, they expressed their belief in speeches and passed a formal resolution that "the people of the United States have been insulted, and the laws of the land trampled on by the military arrest, trial and exile of [Vallandigham] . . . for words spoken at a public meeting." This was not the same as shouting "Fire" in a crowded theatre. Vallandigham's words were an example of freedom of speech, as espoused in the Constitution. His supporters, many of them respected members of old Philadelphia families, had fears that if *"military necessity"* could prevail in Ohio, and supercede the laws of a state whose borders were not endangered by the war, where the inhabitants supported the Constitution, and where law and order were judiciously maintained until overwhelmed by military power, this same *"necessity"* might invade Pennsylvania and "reduce us to a vassalage infinitely more intolerable than that against which we revolted when we declared our independence."[11]

Opponents of Vallandigham's philosophy made themselves known following the rally. At first, their expression was vocal. The cheers and jeers of the crowd quickly disintegrated into a running battle. The fight might have had disastrous results, but the Philadelphia police took charge of the situation and made several arrests. "Some of our loyal people," the *Inquirer* editorialized, "are very much annoyed by the exitence of opposition to the Government, and manifest want of sympathy with its efforts for self-preservation."[12]

The administration's actions against Vallandigham were strong, even though he was a prominent citizen. If such an arrest could be made on a person of his standing, a former elected official, what kind of treatment could be expected if the victim was an ordinary man, like William Howe? And, at the same time, could such a common citizen expect the support and assistance, such as Vallandigham received, from the antiadministration forces?

The government continued to move ahead, enforcing the law—and the draft—despite the groundswell of opposition. Two men were arrested, it was reported on June 15, in the "first resistance to the enrollers . . . in the neighborhood of Philadelphia . . . in Rockhill township, Bucks county." Because one of the men to be enrolled would not let the officers in, his door was broken down. Bells sounded from house to house, and the angry protesters began to converge on the enrollers. The man had a gun and, before he could fire it, it was knocked from his hand. "Another one of the guards fired, [and] the crowd, most of them being armed, threw down their weapons, which were taken." The arrested man was injured in the melee but his wounds were "not dangerous."[13]

By this time, the first reports of the Confederate invasion of Pennsylvania's borders, which culminated in the battle of Gettysburg, were announced. Resistance to the draft followed the announcement in Higgins Township, Schuylkill County, resulting in the arrest of three men. In nearby Hubley Township, resisters shot at enrolling officers and scared them away. The local provost marshal sent a force to arrest the supposed ring leader, Abraham Bressler. In a midnight raid on his home, Bressler escaped, though one of his hired men was wounded in the shoot-out.

Several days later, the situation in Hubley Township worsened. A common pleas court ordered the arrest of the assistant provost marshal and all the others connected with the attempted arrest. Pennsylvania's governor sent guns into the area to help maintain the peace, but these weapons were quickly put into the hands of two county commissioners and the sheriff—all of whom were antiadministration. The provost marshal could not complete his enrollment in that district, he wrote, because of the opposition of the civil authorities. He was fearful of the antidraft factions because they were organized and armed. The protesters appeared in large numbers and boasted that they could amass fifteen hundred to two thousand men at a moment's notice. They threatened to do everything and anything to prevent the enrollment and draft.

Furor in the community erupted into violence at Chambersburg, Pennsylvania, when the enrolling officer's saw mill was burned to the ground on June 4. Three days later, a barn belonging to an enrolling officer from the same district was destroyed. On June 10, another officer was shot and killed. Federal troops were ordered into the area two days later to quell the disturbances and apprehend the perpetrators of these crimes.

In other areas of Pennsylvania, enrolling officers were being warned by the residents to stop doing their job. Provost marshals, in view of the smattering of violence, felt they were faced with a clandestine subversive group, organized to resist the provisions of the Conscription Act.[14] The fears of many of these officials added credence to the contention, and they classed every act of resistance—even those isolated, individual cases, such as that of William H. Howe—as the work of well-organized underground organizations.

Pressure was put on the provost marshals to make arrests, thereby setting examples to the other resisters. This fact was underscored earlier in the year when Lincoln's cabinet met on February 3, 1863. At that meeting the question of making such an example of a deserter was seriously debated. "One case, thought to be a strong one," Gideon Welles wrote in his diary, "was unanimously assented to as a necessity to check the rapidly increasing evil."[15] Halleck reported at the close of 1863 that with an aggressive pursuit of deserters he was able to show a considerable decrease in straggling and desertion. But the decrease did not stop the evil. At the same time, the cost of this aggressive action increased the load on Union taxpayers. For the year ending June 30, 1864, the quartermaster's department reported paying $157,031 in bounties alone for the arrest of deserters.[16]

While government leaders attempted to find an ideal case to use as an example, William H. Howe's case was rapidly emerging as the right one to use in Pennsylvania. When the small posse arrived in Perkiomenville on Monday, June 22, the men did not immediately arrest William Howe. District Attorney Banks did see him and talk with him. Banks's suggestion to Howe was simple: give yourself up. Howe was about to do just that when the other men arrived; something frightened the young man, and he ran off. The arresting officers told reporters that Howe's friends had helped him escape.

The aid of friends and neighbors made the apprehension of deserters a difficult task. Well known to local residents, the deserter's presence was kept secret from the authorities. Small detachments of troops in these areas served only to excite the contempt of the organized malcontents and, at the first sight of troops, fugitives fled to the hills or were hidden. A simple alarm system was devised: bells or horns were sounded to alert the hiding deserters. This early-warning system frustrated the soldiers and caused them to vent their frustration on the citizens, whether or not they had helped thwart the arrests. A citizen could do little more than complain in attempt to protect himself from such harassment.

General Order No. 4 from the War Department established a system to deal with such complaints regarding the provost marshal. All complaints, the order read, about improper arrests, searches, or seizures made by the military were to be sent to either the brigade commanders or provost marshals. These officers were assigned the investigation of the charges, and to make reports to the War Department. The ironic part of this recourse was that complaints concerning actions of the provost marshals' men had to be forwarded to that same office. Thus, chances were good that the allegation could be investigated by the persons accused, although the charges were sometimes aired with the provost marshal. The number of citizen complaints decreased as time went on, mainly from lack of action and frustration on the part of the people.

On Wednesday, June 24, 1863, Provost Marshal Freedly sent twenty soldiers to arrest Howe, but they could not locate him. Not wanting to return empty-handed, they arrested John Wampole, the town's storekeeper, Charles Hauck, and Henry Graff. These men were charged with aiding and abetting Howe's escape the previous Monday. They were escorted to Philadelphia for a hearing before U.S. Commissioner Aubrey H. Smith, who, on the next day, listened to their story and held them for a further examination.

At the second hearing held a few days later in Philadelphia, Commissioner Smith questioned three witnesses: Edward D. Johnson, deputy provost marshal, and citizens Samuel D. Rudy and Mary Ann Shup. These three testified that Wampole was trying to persuade Howe to surrender himself to the civil authorities. But because the arresting party could not understand German, the language Wampole used in speaking to Howe, they arrested the shopkeeper under a misunderstanding of his intentions. All three men were released, but the provost marshal told the commissioner that he had found weapons on the other defendants two days after he had tried to arrest Howe. The guns were loaded and one, he declared, was a rifle belonging to Howe.[17]

The soldiers, the *Montgomery Ledger* reported on June 30, remained in Perkiomenville and the surrounding area watching and searching for Howe, but unsuccessfully.

Even before he was arrested, William H. Howe was being tried . . . in the newspapers. The *Montgomery Ledger*, in its issue of June 30, announced that Howe had admitted that he saw and recognized Bertolet before he fired. The *Inquirer* went even further by reporting June 25 that Bertolet had told someone (perhaps Eisenberry, since the unattributed statements in the press bear a striking similarity in content and phrasing to his sworn testimonies at Howe's courts-martial) that Howe had bragged to his friends of the large bounty he received on enlistment. Further, Bertolet was alleged to have said that Howe was proud that "he was the first man to put down his name for the purpose of effecting an organization to resist the draft, and no six men could take him." William Howe was guilty, the newspapers declared. The only thing left for the authorities to do, it was implied, was capture the desperado and have the courts seal his fate by rubber-stamping the newspapers' verdict.

District Provost Marshal Freedley's men continued their attempts to locate Howe. On July 7, Freedley wrote to Provost Marshal General Fry that he had hired John M. Stauffer, the ex-sheriff of Montgomery County, to track down the fugitive. Freedley believed that Howe was being harbored by some of his neighbors.

But William Howe was not in Frederick Township. The presence of the large contingent of soldiers—all looking for him—had made life uncomfortable, not only for him but also for his neighbors. Howe remained a free man, a fact that did not please the government. The local newspaper, the *Montgomery Ledger*, reminded its readers of the situation. Although Howe had not yet been arrested, the paper noted on July 7, "It is hoped that Justice may not be cheated of her dues."

On July 13, 1863, shortly after nightfall, William H. Howe was captured in Allentown, Pennsylvania. He was reported to be accompanied by "one of his cronies" and prepared to leave for New York.[18] Howe had stopped at a cigar store where he was immediately recognized by someone who knew him. That informer told the police, and policeman Franklin Taylor made the arrest.[19] It was fortunate for the officials that an acquaintance had recognized Howe; there had been countless cases of mistaken identity, which only served to further embarrass the provost marshal's office.

Once the arrest was made, there was a question about who was responsible for the prisoner. In the early days of the war, state courts had issued writs of habeas corpus and, in many instances, the provost marshals turned over their charges to civil authorities. Often, during this exchange, the prisoner escaped. The jurisdictional problem was rectified by the federal government. The provost marshals were ordered to resist state interference by force, if necessary, after making due answer to the writ. As early as August, 1861, General Scott informed Lt. Col. Martin Burke in New York City that due to the current political unrest, he should not turn over his political prisoners despite the presentation of a writ of habeas corpus. On November 11, the writ was suspended "as far as it relates to officers and soldiers in the military or naval service of the United States, or marshals and their deputies within the State of New York."[20]

It was, in reality, a contest between the military and civil authorities. If a person were arrested by the military, the military officials considered him to be their prisoner and would not turn him over to the civil authorities. Prisoners, realizing their rights under the Constitution, tried—usually without success—to avail themselves of their rights and privileges. The reaction of the military was exemplified by the instructions issued to the commander of Fort Lafayette by the secretary of state: "The Department of State of the United States will not recognize any one as an attorney for political prisoners, and will look with distrust upon all applications for release through these channels, and that such applications will be regarded as additional reasons for declining to release the prisoners."[21] This practice, for the most part, continued throughout the war. Some lawyers, despite such warnings, still believed in the right of representation and continued their attempts to secure the release of prisoners.

When arrested at Allentown on July 13, William Howe did not resist and no weapons were found on his person. Howe, the arresting officer stated, was unarmed because his revolver was in his carpet bag, and his partner had escaped with the luggage, leaving him defenseless.[22] Accounts of Howe's actual arrest varied. One report stated that he had been apprehended in an Allentown saloon and identified the man who turned him in as Milton Richards, an acquaintance. The man accompanying Howe was reported by Richards to be Augustus Bitting.[23] Since Bitting was never located, a positive identification of him, or a confirmation of his presence with Howe, can never be determined. Even though William Howe made no effort to escape once captured, the police took no chances. When Franklin Taylor put the deserter in the Allentown jail, he fettered him with a ball and chain.[24]

The next day, July 14, in the company of Deputy Marshal Hammersly and a police officer, Howe was transferred by train to Norristown, arriving there at noon. After Captain Freedley conducted a preliminary hearing, William Howe, guarded by a sergeant and a detachment of men, was sent to Philadelphia where he was confined to await his trial. He did not struggle or make any further attempts to escape. William H. Howe was, according to the *Norristown Republic*, "on his way to that country whence he will never return to tell the mysteries thereof."[25]

While the provost marshal was taking William Howe into custody, New York City erupted into an inferno of rioting. Opposition to the draft and the enrollment was at the root of the problem. "The whole city," an eyewitness remarked, "seems to be turned loose in the streets." Mobs patrolled the city, looting and burning. Mingling with them and "acting as leaders and promoters, one sees *strange faces that nobody ever saw on the surface of New York before.*"[26] *The Press* reported that "the elements that composed this mob recall Paris and the worst days of the French revolution. The most degraded inhabitants of the great city—the refuse population . . . adventurers, thieves, the ignorant classes of the foreign population, laboring men without labor, abandoned women, prize fighters, traitors and sympathizers with the South—all headed by a few adventurous politicians, combined together to create these disturbances." The draft riots in New York, the bloodiest disturbance ever to take place in America, lasted four days. Protesters, innocent bystanders, and soldiers and police trying to restore order died during that long weekend.

According to one report, William Howe admitted that he was heading for New York at the time of his arrest. Dutifully published in the newspaper, this disclosure served to incense the Republican factions against him and to increase support—if support it was—among the Democratic members of his community and elsewhere.

Once in Philadelphia, the provost marshal's office placed Howe in its headquarters at Fifth and Buttonwood streets. Philadelphia's Provost Guard—250 men and 14 officers commanded by Capt. J. Orr Finnie—was kept busy arresting stragglers, deserters, and others. But there were not many prisoners confined at the headquarters, since the procedure after the arrest was to either release them on oath of allegiance or send them back to their regiments. Because of the "peculiar circumstances" of the case, Howe was confined at the headquarters of the provost marshal, where he would be detained until U.S. District Attorney George Alexander Coffey decided what to do with him.

At the barracks, Howe was interviewed and interrogated by several men, including Deputy Provost Marshal Johnson. "I had an interview with him at his cell," Johnson said. "He told me then he had killed Bertolet, and that he had been badly advised; and that he was sorry for it."[27] Capt. John H. Jack also visited Howe. "I asked [him] whether he had shot Bertolet; he said he did, that he shot him because his neighbors put him up to it."[28] Both Johnson and Jack indicated that Howe's confession was given freely and without threats, promises or other forms of coercion. Howe denied ever making such a confession, but hinted at his court-marshal that his lips were sealed concerning any pressures that might have been brought to bear while he was confined at Fifth and Buttonwood.

After William Howe's arrest, the enrollment movement felt the effects of yet another protest, this time from one of the nation's strongest centers of resistance—Pennsylvania's 10th District, composed of Schuylkill and Lebanon counties. In late July, several thousand miners organized near Pottsville. These men were drilled daily by veterans, and possessed two to seven artillery pieces. By early August, Gen. William D. Whipple decided that positive action must be taken to correct the lawless state which had existed there for several years and struck terror into the hearts of law-abiding citizens. Three months later, the intimidation and violence against the draft movement culminated near the Schuylkill-Luzerne county lines. The provost marshal sent in a fifty-man force of cavalry to serve the draft notices. While there, the unit was entertained by George K. Smith, a well-known mineowner. For his gesture of courtesy and hospitality, Smith was killed during an attack on his home November 5. Some of the culprits were arrested, but were released after the sheriff's life was threatened. (It was not until the celebrated trials of the Molly Maguires in the late 1870s that Smith's murderers were tried, convicted, and hanged.) This murder was not an isolated case. According to one local resident, the murder of Union men was "almost a nightly occurrence."

But William H. Howe was far removed from being identified with the disturbances in western Pennsylvania. He was in custody, and the authorities focused on the problem of what to do with him. Congress had enacted legislation providing that soldiers charged with capital offenses were to be remanded to the civil authorities for trial. The army wanted to court-martial William Howe, and the civil authorities felt it was their duty to try him.

Meanwhile, Howe was taken to Fort Mifflin, in southwest Philadelphia. Fort Mifflin—a military installation that had seen service during the Revolution and had been rebuilt before the War of 1812—was currently in a state of decay due to military negligence and the effects of nature. It had been vacant for several years before the Civil War. Not until 1863 did the provost marshal decide to use the facility for a prison camp, mainly for deserters, bounty-jumpers and political prisoners.

*Fort Mifflin.* Photograph for Historic Buildings Survey by Jack E. Boucher

On December 12, 1863, W. Hoffman, commissary-general of prisoners, reported to Secretary Stanton that Fort Mifflin was not a large installation and had no place to confine prisoners "but three bomb-proofs, which have no other ventilation than by the doors, one in each, and small openings through the arches overhead. They are all entered through one door opening into halls which lead to them, and of course are dark and the air is very foul." Seventy-five Army prisoners were housed in one bomb-proof, fifty-eight political prisoners arrested for draft resistance in another, and eighty-two Confederate prisoners in the third. "They sleep on straw laid on the stone floor on each side of the room or vault, the arch springing from the floor. There is a fireplace in each room at the end opposite the door, which enables them to have a fire that gives them light and heat and assists greatly in purifying the air. These bomb-proofs are unwholesome places for prisoners, and it is impossible to keep them in a proper state of police, but from necessity they may be used during the winter. . . . The bomb-proofs need be used only for the worst class of prisoners."[29]

The bomb-proofs at Fort Mifflin were dark, damp, and dirty. During the heat of the summer, the walls would sweat and any piece of clothing would rapidly disintegrate. In wintertime, the moisture turned to icicles and, even with fires, the cold dampness was less than tolerable. And the men confined at Fort Mifflin were, by government definition, "the worst class of prisoner." William H. Howe would spend the next several months in their company in the horrid bomb-proofs of Fort Mifflin, awaiting trial by court-martial for desertion and murder.

*Proceedings of a General Court Martial convened at
Philadelphia, Pa., by virtue of the following order.*

SPECIAL ORDERS    HEADQUARTERS DEPARTMENT
No. 166               OF THE SUSQUEHANNA
                           Chambersburg, Pa.
                           December 22, 1863.

*(Extract)*

*I . . . A General Court Martial is hereby appointed to meet
at Philadelphia, Pa., at 10 o'clock, A.M., in the 26th day of
December, 1863, or as soon thereafter as practicable, for
the trial of such prisoners as may be brought before it.*

### DETAIL FOR THE COURT

*Lieutenant Colonel H. A. Frink*
            *11th Regiment Pennsylvania Vols.*
*Captain James McCann*
            *13th Regiment Pennsylvania Cavalry*
*Captain John C. Dobleman*
            *72nd Regiment Pennsylvania Vols.*
*Captain Charles Fair*
            *147th Regiment Pennsylvania Vols.*
*1st Lieutenant A. Morin*
            *90th Regiment Pennsylvania Vols.*
*1st Lieutenant C. A. Clarke*
            *27th New York Battery*
*2d Lieutenant B. F. Evans*
            *55th Regiment Ohio Vols.*
*Captain Charles P. Clarke*
            *99th Pennsylvania Vols., Judge Advocate*

*No other Officers than those named can be assembled,
without manifest injury to the service.*

The Court will sit without regard to hours.
*BY ORDER OF MAJOR GENERAL COUCH.*
            *[signed] John S. Schultze,*
                 *Assistant Adjutant General.*[1]

# 8

# Court-martial

WILLIAM H. HOWE rotted at Fort Mifflin, awaiting news of when he would be tried. His lengthy purgatory violated the spirit, if not the letter, of the Articles of War. Military law called for brief confinement and speedy justice. The accused was not to be imprisoned for longer than eight days—or until enough officers could be mustered to fill a court-martial panel.[2] Authorities on military jurisprudence indicated that a delay in finding suitable jurors might be misused to the detriment of the prisoner; but, for every wrong, they countered, there was a remedy.[3]

William Howe waited patiently to see if the philosophy of the architects of military justice could stand its own test. A court-martial board was appointed and scheduled to convene in Philadelphia by mid-November, 1863. This board included: Lt. Col. Henry A. Frink, 11th Pennsylvania Volunteers; Capt. James McCann, 13th Pennsylvania Cavalry; Capt. John C. Dobleman, 72nd Pennsylvania Volunteers; Capt. Charles Fair, 147th Pennsylvania Volunteers; Capt. Samuel Comfort, 20th Pennsylvania Cavalry; Lt. L. J. Hume, 19th Massachusetts Volunteers; Lt. Robert Bell, 73rd New York Volunteers; and Lt. Liliburn Harwood, 147th Pennsylvania Volunteers. It might have provided some comfort to Howe that the majority of his judges were fellow Pennsylvanians.

Harwood was appointed judge advocate by the court. Beginning on

November 16, the group, with one exception, sat in judgement of William Howe. Lt. B. F. Evans, 55th Ohio, who replaced McCann, was unable to attend. He had been arrested for neglect of duty and disobedience of orders.

Meeting at 1207 Chestnut Street, the panel rushed through several other cases before coming to William Howe. The panel was sworn in in his presence, following a reading of the order convening the court. It was the usual protocol — a dry, determined formality much of which Howe could not comprehend. He did understand the statements that were next read to him:

> William H. Howe, you are charged with
> Desertion
> Specification — in this, that the said Private William H. Howe, having been regularly enlisted on or about the eighth day of August, one thousand eight hundred and sixty-two, in Company A, 116th Pa. Volunteers in the service of the United States, to serve for the period of three years or during the war, did desert the same at or near Falmouth, Virginia, on or about the twenty-seventh day of December one thousand eight hundred and sixty-two, and did remain absent until arrested on or about the fourteenth day of July one thousand eight hundred and sixty-three, at Allentown, Pennsylvania.
> Murder
> Specification — in this, that Private William H. Howe, Company A, One hundred and sixteenth Regiment Pennsylvania Volunteers, on or about the twenty-first day of June one thousand eight hundred and sixty-three at or near his [Howe's] residence in Frederick Township, Montgomery County, Pennsylvania, did wilfully, deliberately, and of malice aforethought, shoot, kill, and murder Abraham R. Bertolet, Enrolling Officer of New Hanover Township, when he [Bertolet] in company with David Y. Eisenberry, and Michael S. Wagner, lawfully attempted to arrest the said Howe as a deserter from the Service of the United States.

The reading of the charges against him seemed interminable. Howe requested a delay so he could try to locate a lawyer to represent him. Considering the magnitude of the indictments, the court agreed and adjourned for a week.

But it was not enough time. Howe wanted Philadelphia lawyer Charles Hunsicker to plead his case, but the attorney declined. In his letter to the court, Hunsicker indicated that a lawyer could provide no service to Howe because if an unacceptable decision were reached in a civil court the lawyer could appeal to a higher authority. That was not, he felt, true in a military court. Leaving the fate of the young German to the military tribunal, Hunsicker washed his hands of William H. Howe.

The frightened, bewildered ex-soldier was left to defend himself with his own meager resources. When asked, he pleaded guilty to the charge of desertion, but not to murder, never to murder. With a plea entered, the court was ready to begin.

Harwood, as judge advocate, called Edward D. Johnson as his first witness. Former deputy marshal of the 6th Congressional District, Johnson testified he had first seen Howe shortly after Bertolet's death when he, the sheriff, and district attorney went to make the arrest. At that time, as Johnson remembered it, no attempt was made to apprehend the man. In fact, the district attorney spent some time talking to Howe. What he said, Johnson didn't know. The sheriff, however, had to be reminded that the purpose of this visit to Perkiomenville was not a social one; they were there to arrest a man suspected of murder.

The sheriff suggested that perhaps if they went around the schoolhouse and surprised him, they could effect the arrest. Since the sheriff hung back, Johnson took the lead and approached Howe. Suddenly, one of the neighbors, John Wampole, yelled something in Dutch. Unfamiliar with the language, Johnson thought it sounded as if Wampole were telling the suspect to escape. Wheeling at the sound of his friend's voice, Howe saw the sheriff and the deputy marshal. Fearing for his life, the young German fled.

Under examination by Harwood, Johnson remembered returning to the house of Hauck and Graff with a detachment of soldiers and searching it from top to bottom. They found a rifle and a double-barreled shotgun. Both were loaded. Going then to Howe's home, they found nothing.

Johnson did not see Howe again, he testified, until Howe was arrested. He walked into Howe's cell and listened to the young man tearfully tell him that he was sorry for what he had done but, as Johnson remembered, "he had been advised to do so."

Sensing the condition of the prisoner, Johnson questioned him. Did he own the rifle found in the house of Hauck and Graff? Was it the one he used to shoot Bertolet? Under the barrage, Howe confessed, or that is what Johnson thought. Interestingly enough, Johnson tried to get Howe to admit knowing Bertolet before that night. He did not know Bertolet, the young man cried, had never known him and thought the group of men had come to his house only to rob him.

Having no further questions, the judge advocate turned to Howe. The young man, unfamiliar with legal procedures, didn't ask any questions.

Based on Johnson's testimony, it was apparent that, though frightened, Howe indicated to the deputy marshal that he had shot Bertolet, but only in the defense of his home and family. This point was ignored by the court.

The next witness was David Eisenberry, the man who led the attack on the Howe homestead. The board looked forward to hearing his eyewitness account.

On June 19, 1863, Eisenberry told the tribunal, he went with Michael Wagner to help him conduct the enrollment in Frederick Township. Wagner, the witness indicated, had been threatened several times by residents who opposed the draft, and he was afraid to do it alone. He had heard tales of the murder of enrolling officers elsewhere and didn't want to suffer the same fate.

On the twentieth, Eisenberry overheard a conversation indicating that the defendant was at home. As officials of the government, it was their duty to arrest him. They went to Snyder Road and, along the way, stopped a neighbor and asked if Howe had been seen recently. He had, the man said. In fact, he was at home. Driving their wagon faster than normal past the house to avoid suspicion, Eisenberry stated he could see Howe sitting inside the house on the ground floor. Jumping from the moving wagon, Eisenberry rushed in the back door.

His unannounced entry frightened Hannah Howe, he admitted, but he pressed on. Was William there? No, she told him, he had not been home. Judging that she was lying, he demanded to know whom he had seen in the window. That was her cousin, Hannah said, but he had left. She wouldn't say anything else, Eisenberry testified.

Since the officer didn't have a warrant, Hannah refused to accompany him on a search through the house. This didn't stop him. After a frenzied search, he found nothing, even when he went into the stable and ripped up the straw. A frustrated Eisenberry returned to the wagon and told Wagner that they might as well go.

Before leaving, he searched the underbrush surrounding the house. Still no Howe. But Eisenberry saw a bootprint in the soft ground and decided it was Howe's. As they rode away, they looked back and saw Hannah talking with a man. That man, Eisenberry stated, was William H. Howe.

On the return home, Eisenberry told Wagner that they would have to go back again. This time, they would go at night. Still frightened, Wagner suggested the next time they bring along a couple of men, just in case.

The next attempt took place that fateful Sunday. Eisenberry went to Abraham Bertolet's home and asked him to join in the arrest. Bertolet apparently did not want to go along; but Eisenberry persuaded him by saying it was his duty as a subenrolling officer of that district. They discussed the problem at great length and, after drinking tea, departed on horses that Bertolet supplied. Traveling about a quarter of a mile, they reached Wagner's house. Wagner hesitated as he did not want to go to Howe's house again. "It's too early in the day. Let's wait until it gets dark," Eisenberry remembered him saying.

Leonard Lynch, Bertolet's "colored man," was at Wagner's place. "You come along too," Bertolet ordered his servant, "to help bring me home after I am shot."

The four men remained at Wagner's, Eisenberry related, until it was quite dark, about nine o'clock, then rode to Howe's residence, arriving there about 10:30 P.M.

Once at the house on Snyder Road, the small posse dismounted, leaving the horses with Lynch about fifty yards from the house. Eisenberry indicated that he stationed Wagner at the northwest corner and Bertolet at the southeast corner, the rear of the house in from the road. He then struck a light and set it on the fence nearly opposite the front door. He knocked on the door and a woman, whom he thought was Mrs. Howe, answered, asking who was there.

Recounting that he disguised himself as Augustus Bitting, Eisenberry told her the provost guard was after them. When she refused to believe him, the enrolling officer told her who he was and that if Howe came out, he would be treated well and even given a horse to ride.

The woman told him to go away because one of her children was ill. "Open the door," he told her. "I would not disturb any of the children."

Howe was there, she told him, "but you can't take him."

"Yes I can and if you don't open the door I will break it in," he responded.

The woman ran from the door up the stairs and began sounding a horn. "It was answered all around through the hills," Eisenberry stated. After a little while, he drew his revolver and circled the house. Reaching Wagner's position, he heard a shot fired from an upper window. "The ball passed my head," he said, "and I do not know what direction it took."

Eisenberry then stated that he returned to the front of the house and knocked at the door once more. Bertolet reportedly came up urging him to "break in the door, I hear the man talking inside, let's take him out." Eisenberry said he told Bertolet to return where he was or he would be hurt. Almost immediately, he heard a second shot which passed through his coat, grazing his leg. And then the sound of a third shot startled him. This one struck Bertolet in the chest. Eisenberry remembered that with the flash of the gun and the light on the fence "I saw the prisoner plain, drawing his gun back. I fired through the window twice without any effect." In a minute or so the gun emerged through the window again and Eisenberry fired a third shot. This time he heard Howe's wife scream. He went to look after the wounded Bertolet who had moved to Wagner's position.

When he found Bertolet, Eisenberry said, his friend was dying. He did not speak and lasted but a minute or two. Unable to find Wagner to help him carry the body, Eisenberry alleged that he carried Bertolet to the fence. There

Wagner appeared and helped him. They carried the body about one hundred yards and laid it by the road side. By this time, Bertolet was dead. They commandeered a wagon, placed Bertolet's body in it and drove away. Eisenberry concluded his testimony by saying that he reported the entire chain of events to Captain Freedley in the morning.

As an afterthought, Eisenberry added, "I heard the prisoner say to Capt. Freedley he had shot Abraham Bertolet, that some of the neighbors had offered him five dollars for every Abolitionist he would shoot. He also said to the Provost Marshal that his neighbors said he had done right, that he ought to have shot me too." This conversation reportedly took place in Freedley's office in Norristown the day after Howe was apprehended.

Eisenberry's statements, though damaging, did not elicit any questions from the defendant. The true story would emerge, Howe thought.

Michael Wagner then took the stand as a witness for the prosecution. Wagner acknowledged knowing Howe for several years and related how he and Eisenberry had tried to arrest the man on June 20. Then he related how the two of them, and Bertolet and Lynch had gone to Howe's home around midnight on June 21.

His account was similar to Eisenberry's. But he added that Hannah Howe threatened Eisenberry that if they did not leave, "she had a loaded gun and she would shoot." Wagner also testified that the first shot was fired from one of the upper windows. Eisenberry, he reported, told the Howes to stop; he only wanted the deserter to give himself up. They were there to arrest him, nothing more. Bertolet, Wagner declared, was shot by someone in the house. Bertolet cried "My God I am shot," staggered forward and, when a few steps from Wagner, fell down. Picking him up, Wagner stated that he and Eisenberry carried him to the wagon and took him home. The witness added that "before Bertolet was shot there was two shots fired and after he was shot there were two more."

Though a discrepancy existed between the two testimonies regarding Wagner's whereabouts at the time of the shooting, as well as the number of shots fired (Eisenberry said six; Wagner, five), Howe did not question him. On this note, the court adjourned.

At eleven o'clock on November 24, the court-martial continued. The proceedings of the previous day were read before the next witness, Capt. John H. Jack, Company B, 2d Regiment, Pennsylvania Reserve Volunteer Corps, was called. The captain detailed how he, with a guard of twenty men, went to Perkiomenville shortly after daybreak to "effect the arrest" of William Howe. His unit went to Graff's house, where Howe was supposedly hiding. Jack ordered his men to surround the house to prevent the fugitive's escape. The captain recalled that "I approached the house with a guard, searched it, and in conversation with some females there I discovered Howe had left the house during the night. During the search of the house I found a double barreled and single barreled rifle both charged with Minie cartridges. I found also these two cartridges which are similar to those which the rifles are charged." Captain Jack presented these items to the court for inspection.

The double-barreled rifle, the witness asserted, was Graff's gun; the other, Howe's, "which he had brought to the house the night of the killing of Mr. Bertolet." Not finding the defendant there, Jack went "to a house where his mother and I believe his wife and child were stopping." The Howe family would not tell him where the fugitive was, except for suggesting that he might be in the woods. Jack searched the area until the next day. He scoured the woods and placed guards at homes where he thought Howe might go. In one of these homes, he found "a rifle charged with powder and sheet lead, which the occupant of the house assured was the property of Howe."

In conclusion, Captain Jack recalled seeing Howe shortly after his arrest. "I asked him what made you shoot Bertolet, what did you shoot him for. He said the neighbors made him do it, they put him up to it."

At this point, Howe surprised the court by asking the officer one question: "Do you know if I brought those Cartridges from the army?" Captain Jack responded, "No, I do not." The court adjourned to meet the next morning.

When the court-martial resumed at 11:00 A.M., November 25, the prosecution called Jacob Sassaman as its first witness. Sassaman, who lived about a quarter-mile from Howe's house, recalled talking to Howe the morning of the day Bertolet was shot. Howe threatened that he had eight barrels loaded and that he would shoot as many men as he could if they came to arrest him. As the witness was leaving the stand, Harwood asked him if Howe had named anyone who might be chasing him.

"No, he did not," Sassaman declared. "He said there was somebody after him Saturday afternoon but that he was not ready for them. His gun was up stairs and he was down stairs and run out." Howe "declined asking any questions" of his neighbor.

The next witness for the prosecution was Franklin Trexler, who had been subpoenaed by the court, but he did not arrive on time. After waiting forty minutes, the court adjourned to meet again at one o'clock. But Trexler still did not arrive, and the court remained in session a little more than an hour. Then Harwood was directed to insure Trexler's attendance at the court on Friday morning. No session was scheduled for Thursday, the ' day of National Thanksgiving."

Franklin Trexler finally arrived at court eleven o'clock on Friday morning and was sworn in as a prosecution witness. During the summer of 1863, Trexler stated, he was an Allentown police officer. Sometime during the summer, he did not remember when, he had learned that someone named Bertolet had been shot by William H. Howe. Obtaining Howe's description, Trexler testified that he arrested the man near the Lehigh railroad depot. He then took him to Provost Marshal W. H. Hamersly, who conducted a hearing. Following the preliminary hearing, Howe was taken to the Allentown jail. Later, the prisoner was escorted to Norristown. "While in jail," Trexler asserted, "the prisoner acknowledged to me his name was William H. Howe and that he had shot Bertolet. The prisoner said that Bertolet and some others had come to his house at night to arrest him and that he had fired out of the window."

"Did you, or did the Sheriff in your presence, make any promises or threats towards the prisoner previous to this conversation?" Harwood asked. "No sir," the witness responded. The judge advocate then asked Trexler if Howe had told him what weapon he used to shoot Bertolet. "He did not," was the answer.

The next question was posed by Lieutenant Colonel Frink, who asked Trexler, "Under what circumstances was this confession made?"

"The Sheriff and myself," Trexler began, "went into the cell where the prisoner was confined to put a ball and chain on him and it was at that time that he made the statement." Howe could think of no questions to ask Trexler.

Harwood announced at this point that the prosecution's case was closed and that he had no further witnesses. Howe was now permitted to enter on his defense. His first witness was 1st Lt. William M. Hobart, who testified to knowing Howe. "I recruited him," the lieutenant said, "and saw him mustered into the service . . . as a private . . . about the eighth of August 1862."

Harwood asked about Howe's character as a soldier. "His character," Hobart asserted, "with the company was very good. He did his duty as a soldier and was in the battle of Fredericksburg December 13th 1862." Harwood had no further questions and Hobart was permitted to leave the stand.

The next two witnesses, Henry Croll and Nathan Reninger, both neighbors of Howe, offered little in his defense. "Do you know David Y. Eisenberry?" Harwood asked Reninger.

"I never knew him before the killing of Bertolet," he replied. "I have no knowledge of him further than seeing him several times."

Howe then turned to his neighbor and asked if Eisenberry had said who fired the first shot on the night Bertolet was killed. "From the way Eisenberry talked," Reninger offered, "I believe he did. He said there was three shots fired and then Bertolet got killed." This answer raised a crucial if largely unnoticed point in the trial. If Howe could establish that he had fired in self-defense, the murder charge could be dropped. But, in his ignorance, Howe did not press the issue. Harwood, representing the prosecution, did not question him further.

William Shankland was called next. Because he could not speak English, Reninger was recalled and sworn in as an interpreter. Shankland admitted to knowing William Howe for ten years. When asked if he knew anything about the circumstances surrounding Bertolet's death, Shankland replied that he only knew that he was taken away dead, "but I don't know who killed him." Shankland denied knowing Eisenberry, stating, "I saw him the night Bertolet got shot and he asked me to get a wagon and help take Bertolet away." Finally, Shankland maintained that he did not know who fired the first shot.

Having no further witnesses, Howe requested time to prepare a written statement of his defense. The court permitted this and ordered him to return the next morning, Saturday, November 28.

During the night, Howe prepared his statement in his cell at Fort Mifflin. Saturday morning, he read it aloud to the court. Admitting that he had deserted as charged, Howe insisted that he had every intention "to again return to my Regiment but through the influence of friends, I did not return." Then, he told his side of the story and the events of the night of the murder.

Unknown individuals, he asserted, came to his house in the middle of the night. One of the intruders alleged to be Augustus Bitting. Knowing it was not her husband's friend, Howe's wife told them to go away. But they would not. One of them, in fact, ordered Hannah to open the door or he would break it open. She rushed to awaken Howe who recalled he "went to the window and raised it and as I looked out to see who was outside they fired at me three times." Jumping out the back window crying "murder," he ran to his neighbor and told him that men had come to his house, tried to break in and then had fired at him. The neighbor went to get help to find out who the people were and to see what they wanted. Howe's friends returned and said that four men were after him. They had fired to scare him. Someone, they told Howe, "had fired out of the house and shot Bartlett [*sic*]." The excited prisoner suddenly interrupted his story to state that "if they had come peaceably and waited until I came down which I would had done as soon as I was aware who it was there would of been no blood spilt and I would of accompanied them wherever they chose to lead me."

Howe continued his statement, relating how shortly after the incident the sheriff and district attorney came to his house and asked him to surrender. He was about to do so when someone shouted, warning him to be careful of the sheriff. Frightened and increasingly suspicious, Howe evaded him. The next day several guards came looking for the deserter and remained three or four days. Finally they left and Howe fled to Allentown for work but was arrested by the constable there that same evening and was then brought to Philadelphia.

Lieutenant Colonel Frink cleared the courtroom for the panel's deliberation. With little delay, the board returned and delivered its verdict, finding Pvt. William H. Howe as follows:

> Of the Specification of First Charge in confirmation of the plea of the prisoner, "Guilty."
> Of the Specification of the Second Charge, "Guilty."
> Of the Second Charge, "Guilty."
> And the Court does therefore sentence him Private William H. Howe . . . "to be hanged by the neck until he be dead at such time and place as the Commanding General may direct."
> Two thirds of the Court concurred in this sentence.

There being nothing further to discuss in the case of William Howe, the court adjourned.

Howe was shocked by the decision. Reninger had told the court that he had fired in self-defense. Did no one believe him? He hoped that a review board would overturn the verdict.

By the end of November, Maj. Gen. George Cadwalader, commanding the military headquarters at Philadelphia, had reviewed the court-martial proceedings and approved the action of the board. Cadwalader recommended that Howe be executed at Fort Mifflin on Friday, February 19, 1863, between noon and 2:00 P.M.

But the matter was not settled. The papers were forwarded through channels, and the judge advocate general's office was not happy with the manner in which the trial had been conducted. As a result, the verdict was overturned due to "informality." Howe's spirits soared, because military law prevented an officer or a soldier from being retried for the same offense. He was not aware, however, that in cases of overturned verdicts, the prisoner might be recharged and tried again.

Unbeknown to Howe as he waited in the bomb-proofs at Fort Mifflin, Gen. Darius N. Couch, commanding the Department of the Susquehanna, appointed another court-martial board in December. On February 15, 1864, this new group met to begin its thirty-eighth case, that of Private William H. Howe.

SPECIAL ORDERS   HEADQUARTERS DEPARTMENT
No. 17           OF THE SUSQUEHANNA
                 Chambersburg, Pa.,
                 January 25, 1864

*(Extract)*

*VI . . . Lieutenant Charles A. Clarke, 27th Battery N. Y. Artillery, is hereby relieved from duty as a member of General Court Martial appointed in paragraph 1, Special Orders No. 166, Head Quarters Department of the Susquehanna, dated December 22, 1863.*

*VII . . . 2d Lieutenant Thomas P. Chambers, Co. L, 20th Pennsylvania Cavalry, is hereby detailed as an additional member of General Court Martial, convened in accordance with paragraph 1, Special Orders, No. 166, Head Quarters Department of the Susquehanna, dated December 22, 1863.*

*BY ORDER OF MAJOR GENERAL COUCH.*

*[signed] John S. Schultze,*
*Assistant Adjutant General.*[1]

# 9

# Justice Revisited

THE NEW COURT convened on February 15 at 709 Sansom Street, a converted house which had been one of Philadelphia's original row houses.

Before his arraignment, Howe asked the court's permission to obtain counsel. His request was granted and though the newspapers reported him to be represented by Lewis C. Cassidy and Edmund Randall,[2] only Randall's name appeared on the court testimony. Edmund Randall was a man whom Howe knew, having served under him during the battle of Fredericksburg. Their relationship was built on mutual respect and trust. Nonetheless, the attorney faced a difficult task because at military courts-martial, a lawyer's presence is tolerated merely as a friend to the prisoner. A military lawyer could only assist the prisoner, but could take no active role.[3]

After the board had called him into court, William H. Howe listened to the order convening the court-martial. As a formality, he was asked if he objected to being tried by any member of the panel. Through his counsel, Howe challenged Lt. Col. Henry A. Frink, who was presiding, because that same officer had prepared the charges and specifications against him. The rules of courts-martial state that one cause for challenge was prior knowledge of the case which could prejudice the judgment of the officer.

Frink agreed that his name was on the charges and specifications against Howe but that he knew nothing of the case. The officer left the courtroom leaving judgment to the remaining members of the board. During their informal discussion, no mention was made that Frink actually knew the substance of the case, having been president of Howe's earlier trial. When the court reopened, Howe's objection was overruled. Frink was permitted to preside —again.

The court was sworn in by Capt. Charles Percy Clarke, judge advocate, in the presence of the prisoner. After Clarke was given the oath by Frink, Private Howe was arraigned on the same charges and specifications for which he had been tried in November.

How did he plead? Rather than commit himself as he had done in November, Howe pleaded not guilty to the charge and specification of desertion. To the charge of murder, he argued that the military court now had no jurisdiction since he was accused of murdering Abraham R. Bertolet, "Enrolling Officer of New Hanover Township." Bertolet, the defense stated, "was in no wise an officer or soldier in the military service of the United States." Howe was agreeable, he told the court, to stand trial under "the laws of the state of Pennsylvania, and the Court of Oyer and Terminer for Montgomery County, in the State of Pennsylvania within the territorial limits of whose civil jurisdiction the crime is said to have been committed."

Frink cleared the courtroom so that the board could discuss the propriety of admitting Howe's plea on the charge and specification of murder. After several hours of discussion in closed session, the court adjourned, to meet the next day to deliberate further.

The next morning, February 16, the court read the proceedings of the previous day and then rendered its decision: Howe's objection was overruled because The Enrollment Act, as the court understood it, called for general courts-martial or military commissions to deal with capital crimes "when committed by persons who are in the Military service of the United States and subject to the Articles of War."

Howe was asked by the court to enter his plea. If he did not the trial would proceed as if he had pleaded not guilty. At Randall's suggestion, Howe pleaded not guilty to the specification.

Captain Clarke cleared the courtroom of all witnesses who were to testify. They would have to wait until they were called. Though they would not be allowed to hear each other's testimony, they could discuss the case in the corridor.

The preliminaries accomplished, the panel got down to the serious business of determining Howe's fate. Clarke called his first witness, 1st Lt. Daniel W. Burke, 2d U.S. Infantry, a mustering officer. After Burke was sworn in, Clarke showed him a document and asked, "Is this the original muster roll of Co. A, 116th Pennsylvania Volunteers?"

*Henry A. Frink, 11th Regiment, Pennsylvania Volunteers.* Library of Congress

Burke replied, "It is." The document was shown to the court and offered as evidence to prove that William Howe had been enlisted and mustered into the army on August 8, 1861.

Burke was permitted to leave and the second witness, Capt. John H. Jack, was called to the stand. "I was Adjutant of the Provost General in June last," Captain Jack said, and then proceeded to retell his November testimony.

Though Jack was not cross-examined, the defense objected to his entire testimony. Howe's objections were based on good legal advice. Evidence in a military court was to be confined to what the witness actually saw and heard first-hand. Hearsay was not admissible.[4] Even though Captain Jack's testimony lacked personal knowledge, except as it related to his going to arrest Howe, the objections were overruled.

Deputy Provost Marshal Edward D. Johnson, now a civilian, was called next. Johnson recounted his experiences in Frederick Township with the sheriff and the district attorney. "I saw him," Johnson testified, "at the house of Hauck and Graff; but he eluded us." Johnson neglected to tell the court everything he had related three months earlier. "I did not see him again until after his arrest at 5th and Buttonwood Sts." Johnson acknowledged that, like Jack, he had "interviewed" Howe in his cell. "He told me," the witness said, "he had killed Bertolet, and that he had been badly advised; and that he was sorry for it. I asked him if the gun we took from . . . Hauck and Graff was the one he killed him with; he said it was. I asked him why he reloaded it; he said to shoot birds with." Johnson concluded his remarks by stating "there were no promises or threats made to induce the prisoner to make this admission to me to which I have testified."

Randall jumped at that comment. "The evidence," the defense contended, "is not in issue." Johnson's statement was not based on firsthand knowledge and, further, his comments were inadmissable because the confessions attributed to Howe were made while he was in custody.

Again, the board overruled Howe's objections.

"I know the prisoner," the next witness, David Y. Eisenberry, stated. Eisenberry recounted his unsuccessful attempt to arrest Howe the previous June and then related his second attempt, in company with Bertolet, Wagner and Lynch. He repeated Bertolet's reluctance to join in the arrest and his relenting as his wife urged, "Yes, Abe, go with him." Eisenberry repeated that Bertolet told Lynch to go with him so that the hired man could "carry his body home if he was shot."

Eisenberry's testimony continued as it had three months before, but with more flourishes. He indicated that when Hannah Howe refused to open the door, he warned her that he would break it down. Then, hearing the horns, he drew his revolver "intending to fire past the windows to frighten her." The witness described what next happened:

> Before I fired there was a shot fired from the window and went past my head. Then I went around to the front of the house, intending to break open the door, and Bertolet came up to the front where I was standing. Bertolet said to me, "Break open the door, for I hear him talking, and let's take him out." I told him he had better go back or he would get hurt, but he would not. I made a thrust or two at the door, when there was another shot fired from the window, which passed through my coat. Almost immediately after there was another shot fired from the window which took effect in Bertolet['s] breast, and from the flash of the gun and the light on the fence I saw the prisoner at the window drawing his rifle back. Bertolet then exclaimed "I am shot," clapping his hand to his breast. Bertolet then walked to the corner of the house. I then fired two shots at the window with my revolver. I waited perhaps a minute, when I saw the gun again thrust from the window, and fired a third shot at the window. I heard his wife scream and exclaim, "Bill, are you shot?" I then went to see after Bertolet.

Eisenberry did not repeat his contention that Wagner was nowhere to be found but stated that he came and helped carry the body over the fence. "I did not," Eisenberry concluded, "see the prisoner again until arrested and brought before Capt. Freedley about July 4th, 1863. He then admitted to Capt. Freedley that he did shoot Bertolet, and that his neighbors said he had done right, and ought to shoot me too, and every other abolitionist. This is all I know of this affair. He made his admission to Capt. Freedley in my presence."

"What time in the night did you attempt to arrest me," the defense asked, "the second time?"

"About 11 o'clock at night," Eisenberry answered.

Eisenberry also, under cross-examination, declared that they had used a fluid lamp, not a lantern, for light. In addition, he pinpointed the location of the door at which he had tried to gain admittance: "the back door, the only door there was in the house, I think."

Captain Clarke asked for the opportunity to reexamine the witness. Apparently, the defense's questioning about the light triggered something in his mind. "Did the light you placed on the fence enable you to see distinctly objects around the house?" he asked. "Yes, sir," was Eisenberry's response.

Following this clarification, Howe entered an objection to Eisenberry's comments about what Hannah Howe had said and done, since Howe did not consider himself responsible for his wife's acts. The defense also objected to Eisenberry's comments on Howe's intentions "or what he had heard of Howe's being a desperate character, and . . . what he heard from Howe while under arrest." The court did not rule on that objection. References to Howe's character, however, do not appear as part of Eisenberry's testimony.

Michael Wagner was the next witness. After being sworn in, he testified that he "was an Enrolling Officer for Frederick Township, Pa. I know the prisoner. I was ordered to arrest him on June 20th, but he escaped. . . . On the 21st of June, Eisenberry, Bertolet and myself went at night to arrest [Howe] between 11 and 12 o'clock." The witness continued, substantially repeating his earlier testimony. But in the passage of time, Wagner had become more specific. "There were three shots fired; the third took effect in Bertolet's breast. There was a light on the fence and we could see objects in the house. I was at the back part of the house, so I did not see the prisoner fire. I saw Bertolet fall. He walked towards me and said, 'My God, I am shot.' Then Eisenberry and I took him to the side of the road. He was dead, when we carried him out."

"Did any persons visit the spot," the defense questioned, "in answer to the horn that was blown?"

"No," Wagner responded. "Not any that I saw."

"Was the first shot from a revolver?"

"It sounded like a musket," Wagner thought.

The defense continued. "Was the first shot that was fired, from the side of the house where Eisenberry was stationed?"

"No Sir," the witness countered. "As near as I can tell it was from the inside of the house."

"Did not Eisenberry fire the first shot up at the window," the defense asked, "to frighten Mrs. Howe?"

Unshaken, Wagner responded, "No Sir. It came from the house."

"Did the ball from the first shot fired come near striking you," he was asked, "and in what direction was it fired?"

"It did not come near striking me," Wagner answered. "It came from the end of the house."

Pursued by the defense, Wagner admitted that he hadn't seen Howe fire the shot. "I was at the back of the house at the time."

Well, if he were at the back, how did he know that Eisenberry was not the one to fire the first shot? Wagner said, "It did not come from the direction that Eisenberry stood. Eisenberry had the front of the house."

The final question directed by the prisoner—"Did you see Mrs. Howe with a gun in her hands through the window, about the time Bertolet was killed?"—was responded to in the negative. There being no further questions of Wagner, the next witness was sworn in.

Franklin Taylor told the court that he knew the prisoner. "I was informed he was the man that murdered Bertolet, and I arrested him at Allentown." Taylor recounted how he took Howe to the deputy provost marshal at Allentown, and talked with the accused in jail while putting a ball and chain on him. "He told me and the Deputy Provost Marshal, that his name was William H. Howe, and that he shot Bertolet. He said he fired out of the window. He (Howe) asked me if I had arrested a citizen that was with him, saying that man was a deserter and that I had better keep him as he and him had deserted from the Service together."

Captain Clarke asked if the prisoner was coerced to confess in any way. "No Sir," was the reply.

Disgustedly, the defense entered its objection to the testimony of Taylor as it related to what Howe said in custody.

Since there appeared to be some question as to evidence that would substantiate the desertion charge, the court adjourned, awaiting the arrival of a transcript from the adjutant general's office in Washington, D.C., to confirm the date of Howe's desertion.

When it reconvened on February 19, the court found it had not yet received a response from Washington. Being unable to continue without the transcript, it again adjourned, to meet on Tuesday, February 23, at eleven o'clock.

At the next meeting, Captain Clarke told the court that he had sent a special messenger to Washington to get the transcript; but he had received no reply. The court also learned that Captain William Hobart was being summoned to appear to verify Howe's identity. Since it would be impossible for this important prosecution witness to arrive before Friday, February 26, the court adjourned until that date.

Hobart did not arrive on the twenty-sixth or the twenty-seventh, and court was adjourned, to meet on Tuesday, March 1.

On that date, after the proceedings of the previous session were read, the judge advocate informed the court that he had finally received the long-awaited documentation from Washington. Clarke at once offered in evidence the statement which read: "It appears from the records on file in this office *that William Howe* . . . deserted December 24th 1862." It added that there was no evidence that Howe had ever returned.

As part of the general administration of a court-martial, any public written evidence is accepted when it has been proven that the signature is authentic or the document is a sworn copy. Official military papers, reports, returns, and the like, are admitted without the strict rules required in civil courts. Such copies are accepted when they bear the mark of the adjutant general or his duly authorized subordinate.[5]

Through his counsel, Howe objected to the introduction of this paper because it was neither certified nor authenticated as genuine, "nor is it signed by the officer within whose custody the original should be, if there is any such."

Secondly, the defense continued, even if the paper were genuine, it was nothing more than a written statement of something contained in an original document. The prisoner, the defense stated, has the "right to inspect the original document if any exists, as it must be in the possession of the prosecutor (the Government) and he may test its genuineness and originality as he is informed and believes, if his name appears on the list of deserters [from his regiment] it would be in the handwriting of his counsel Edmund Randall who at the time of the alleged desertion was 1st Lieut. and acting Adjutant [of the unit], and has no knowledge or remembrance of having transmitted such a document to the Adjutant General's office."

Finally, the objection stated, the document alleged that a William Howe deserted, but the prisoner's name "is not *William Howe* nor was he ever known by such name and that the desertion referred to can not refer to him."

Frink cleared the court to ponder this objection in closed session. When the panel emerged, the officers refused to sustain the objection. The document was admitted as evidence.

The prosecution then called Capt. William M. Hobart to the stand. Randall probably expected Hobart to testify on Howe's reputation as a soldier—as he had in November. The lieutenant stated that he knew the prisoner, having "recruited him, and know his having been mustered into the service about the eighth of August 1861." Hobart stated that Howe deserted before Christmas, 1862, "while the Division to which the Regiment was attached was being reviewed by Major General Hancock. He was reported as a deserter and dropped from the rolls. I cannot say exactly when. He has never been with the Regiment since the date of his desertion."

When asked by the defense, Hobart responded that he first saw Howe "a day or two previous to his enlistment. The last time," he said, "was before a General Court Martial in this City."

The defense worked on the witness, making him tell the court that he was not on duty with Company A at the time of the alleged desertion and that his knowledge of this act came secondhand from a review of the muster rolls. Under pressure from the defense, Hobart could not say how or when he learned of the desertion, or who told him. Later, he admitted "the Orderly Sergeant reported it to me. This was my first knowledge of the desertion."

Captain Hobart's testimony, under the unrelenting questioning, revealed that all his knowledge on the alleged desertion of William H. Howe came from government documents or from other individuals, and "also from admission made this morning of the prisoner himself. He also made an admission two months ago, giving me an account of his trip, and that he walked all the way through Maryland." The prisoner objected to Hobart's testimony, indicating that any information obtained from him since his arrest and confinement was not admissible as evidence.

Sensing that Hobart's testimony differed from that given before, the defense tried to establish the first-person knowledge of the orderly sergeant, who had regularly informed Hobart of activities in the company. Where was he now? "He is," Hobart answered, "a prisoner in Libby Prison, Richmond, Va."

Changing the line of questioning, Randall suggested Hobart's statement that Howe had traveled through Maryland was unlikely, as this state was in the opposite direction to the prisoner's home.

"I know," Hobart replied, "that he could travel that way and reach his home, though it is not a direct route."

"Would it not take me," the defense asked, "several hundred miles out of my course?" What route did Howe tell him he took?

Howe told him, Hobart recounted, that he paid a man eighteen dollars to row him across Acquia Creek to Maryland. Then he could travel home. "He did not give me the exact route."

The defense countered that Acquia Creek was in Virginia. "Did you not think it strange at the time [Howe] told you that [he] could get into Maryland by crossing Acquia Creek, as both sides of it are in Virginia?"

The witness did not think it strange. "I presume he thought it policy to cross in that way," Hobart added.

Randall finished his questioning without asking Hobart if Howe was a good soldier. The judge advocate then began his interrogation of Captain Hobart. "Were you often at the Head Quarters of the 116th Regiment, while you were on detached duty?" Clarke asked him.

"Yes Sir, frequently."

"Did you," Clarke queried, "have an opportunity of knowing the condition of affairs in your Company?" At Hobart's affirmative response, the judge advocate announced the prosecution closed. The prisoner was now permitted to begin his defense.

The first witness called by Howe was Richard Bolton who told the court what he remembered of the night Bertolet was killed. "I was laying in bed at my house on a Sunday night last Summer, when I heard shooting. I got up and opened the window, and I heard it was at Howe's house. I heard Howe come running and he hollered 'Murder.' Then he said to me for 'God's sake go and get my children away.' He was afraid they would 'Murder' them. I went to one of my neighbors and told him to come with me." When they arrived at Howe's house they saw Bertolet on the wagon. What was going on, Bolton asked Eisenberry. His only response, the witness recalled was, "I must help him to turn his wagon around." Bolton asked Eisenberry if "he intended to move the wagon off without putting something under the man Bertolet, as he would die. I told them to get some straw, but they did not, but wanted to put some manure under him. My Neighbor got some straw. I asked Eisenberry if he saw Howe. He said 'Yes.' He saw him at the Second Story window, and shot after him. I said to him, 'Why the house is just one story high.' He said he heard some one groan inside and he thought he had shot Howe's wife."

The defense asked Bolton at what Eisenberry was shooting. "He shot," Bolton responded, "up through the roof." Then he added that "Eisenberry wanted me to go with him to drive the wagon home. I did not go. Eisenberry and his friends seemed to me to be drunk. They did not seem to know what to do. They smelt strongly of liquor."

On further questioning, Bolton admitted hearing Eisenberry say that he could not drive the wagon. To enlarge on the statement that the men were drunk, the defense asked, "Were they so drunk as not to know what they were about?" The witness answered that he believed so.

To further discredit the testimonies of Eisenberry and Wagner, Randall questioned Bolton on the lamp that was used to see into the house. Bolton replied that he asked Eisenberry what the light was doing on the fence, only to learn that it was there when they arrived. When shown the lamp in question, the witness admitted it was the one "on the garden fence about thirty feet from the house on the side." The defense then asked whether the lamp, located on the garden fence, provided enough light to distinguish any person or thing in the house. "No," Bolton opined. "I think not."

Captain Clarke now asked the witness, which window did the light on the fence shine into? Bolton answered that it was the first-story window, which was screened by a curtain or papers.

Was there, the judge advocate wondered aloud, "a window in the Gable end of the house above the first floor?"

"Yes Sir," Bolton stated, "a little one with four glasses." That would be, in the prosecutor's mind, the second-floor window.

"Have you any idea," Clarke asked the witness, "what the lamp was put on the fence for, and do you know who it belonged to?"

Bolton responded, "It belongs to Mr. Awhl," from whom Eisenberry said he borrowed the lamp that night. "I don't know what it was there for."

Continuing, Captain Clarke wanted to know how the witness knew the curtains were drawn.

"When the party went away with Bertolet," Bolton said, "my neighbor and I went with the light up to the house and saw they were down."

"Could the light have shown in the window that was shattered by a gun or pistol shot on the left side of the door?" the defense asked.

"No," Bolton responded, "it was too far off on the side."

Under further reexamination, the defense asked Howe's neighbor how many shots he heard fired that night. He reported hearing what he thought to be three shots. "I thought they were pistol shots."

Frink interrupted at this point and asked if the light was on the same side of the house as the broken window.

"No," Bolton answered, "it was not."

Judge Advocate Clarke now asked the witness how far from Howe's place he was when he heard the shooting.

"About three hundred yards. . . . I heard the Second Shot with my head out of the window." (Previously he had stated that he heard the first shot while he was still in bed.)

"How could you tell the difference," the court asked, "between a pistol and a Gun shot at that distance?"

"The sound," Bolton recalled, "was not loud. I judged it was a pistol."

"Do you know," Howe asked, "who fired those three shots; did Eisenberry tell you?"

"Eisenberry told me," Bolton averred, "he fired three shots after Howe."

At this point, the defense moved that the court adjourn because a material witness to Howe's case had not yet arrived. The court agreed to the adjournment motion. They would meet the next day, March 2.

Howe's important witness still had not arrived the next day, and the defense requested additional time. The court granted the plea and adjourned, to meet at the same time on March 3.

Howe's witness, Patrick Carrigan, had arrived when the court reconvened. "I was Captain commanding Co. A," Carrigan stated, "from about the middle of October to the Middle of January 1863. I was on duty with the Company most of the time. During that time I knew [the men of the company] all intimately. The Company was small."

Randall then turned his line of questioning to an entirely different area in an attempt to discredit the damaging testimony of William Hobart. "Did you," he asked Carrigan, "identify the prisoner now before the Court positively, and without doubt, as William H. Howe, who was a Private in your Company and who deserted in December, 1862?"

Carrigan could not. "I only knew of his being that person by having been told so this morning. I did not know him from the orderlies in the room."

"Do you know Captain William M. Hobart?" the defense asked. "Was he with the Company A . . . and had he an opportunity of knowing all the men of the Company?"

Carrigan admitted knowing Hobart but he "was not with the Company more than a week during the time I was with the Company. He was sick and detached from the company most of the time."

Under cross-examination by the judge advocate, Carrigan admitted there had been a William H. Howe in his company but "I could not swear whether it was the man before me or not." The last time Carrigan saw him, he testified, was "about three days before the battle of Fredericksburg."

Under further interview, Carrigan denied knowing where Howe had lived before joining the army. "I did not recruit him. He was with the Company when I joined it." When asked if Hobart had recruited Howe, he told them he thought so. To the best of Carrigan's recollection, Howe was dropped from the rolls as a deserter "some time in the month of December, 1862."

Howe was now given permission to question the witness again. "Did not Captain Ewing recruit most of the men in Company A?"

"Yes Sir," was Carrigan's response. "He recruited all the men that were recruited in this City for that Company."

Randall then made written application of the court for a further postponement until Monday, March 7, so that the defense could locate an important witness and have him appear in Howe's behalf. Frink cleared the court for deliberation and, because of the magnitude of the charges, granted the defense's plea. The important witness was Nathan Reninger, Howe's neighbor, who had witnessed the incident. Unfortunately, he met with an accident on the way to the court-martial and was killed. Randall also indicated that he would call Thomas Ewing as a defense witness at the same time.

The court-martial resumed at eleven o'clock on Monday, March 7, 1864, and Randall called his next witness, Thomas Ewing.

"I was," Ewing began, attached to Company A "as acting Captain from June to October 1862 . . . . I did not know [the men] intimately."

The defense asked if Ewing thought Hobart had a good or better opportunity to know the men. "I do not think he had as good an opportunity as the Captain," Ewing stated.

Under further interrogation, Ewing admitted he did not recognize the prisoner as the man who had been mustered into the company.

"Was there any peculiar circumstance about the Howe of your Company by which you could remember him?" the prisoner requested.

"Yes Sir. I remember the Howe of my company," Ewing recalled, "being badly poisoned, while with us, and of seeing him at his tent with his eyes closed from the effects of it."

Captain Clarke then asked who had recruited the Howe he remembered. "I don't know," the witness answered. "I think Hobart did."

Perhaps in an attempt to reduce the effect of the former company commander's testimony, the judge advocate asked him what rank he held when mustered. "I was never mustered into the United States Service at all," he said.

There being no further questions, the defense was permitted the opportunity to reexamine the witness. "What was Hobart's general reputation either as a soldier or a man of veracity?" Randall requested.

"I do not know anything of his reputation for veracity," Ewing began. "He was never considered a soldier by the Company."

Jumping back to a previous question by the judge advocate—ostensibly to reinforce the integrity of his witness with the court—Randall asked Ewing why he wasn't mustered into the service. His response was a simple one: "My Company was not full."

The defense closed its case at that point and presented to the court a written statement, which was then read aloud.

"My trial is now at an end," the defense began, "and I might rest here without a further effort in my own behalf, so weak is the evidence against me. But as the charge is to me and my family a serious one, I feel it a duty to those who in this world are dependent upon me, that no effort that I can use should be spared to make my acquittal sure.

"In reviewing my case, I beg leave to present before this Court, and more particularly for the careful examination of the reviewing authority, the many gross irregularities and illegalities which transpired on the trial, and, which I am confident will alter an earnest consideration of the premises by the reviewing officers, be adjudged sufficient to overturn the trial and the finding of the Court."

First, the defense contended, Frink had no right to preside, "as he was my prosecutor, therefore, could not be my Judge." The defense admitted, however, that Frink had performed his work well.

Secondly, Howe felt that the testimony was clearly illegal, especially that of Captain Jack. "It was the duty of the Court to have ruled out the irrelevant testimony or have distinctly admitted it. This was not done. The Court never passed upon it. They were silent as to all my objections." Frink, the defense contended, took it upon himself to admit or rule out testimony without first consulting with the Court. "The only instance in which my objections to testimony was considered by the Court was the objections filed against the admissions of the Paper from the Adjutant General's office." It was further claimed that no authority in either military or civil law gives the presiding officer the right to admit disputed evidence.

"I would also, while upon this subject," the defense continued, "offer my objections to the remark of the President to the Judge Advocate when I objected to the admission of Captain Jack's testimony, 'to take down all the evidence and let it go for what it is worth.' Testimony is worth just that, and all that weight which the law gives it. And, if testimony is admitted at all, it is as evidence going to prove or disprove, a fact material to the issue. It is never allowable to prove an irrelevant matter outside of the issue in order to create grounds for presumption against [the] prisoner."

Further, Howe stated he was tried on two charges—desertion and murder. He and Randall reasoned that the not guilty plea to the first charge and "to the jurisdiction of the Court," to the second would provide him legal leverage. "For inasmuch as an acquittal of the first charge would have substantiated my plea to the second charge, it was imperative upon the Court to have tried me upon the charge of 'Desertion' first." Had they convicted Howe of desertion, "the second one would have then been properly in order. But in pleading 'not guilty' to the Desertion, I denied ever having been in the United States service." It was up to the court to prove he was ever a soldier. They should have, the defense demanded, "extended to me the benefit of that great fundamental principle of Law 'that every man must be presumed innocent until he is proved by evidence guilty.' " But no, the court was indifferent, "but before the last evidence was before me, they presumed me guilty of the first charge when they overruled my plea to the Court's jurisdiction upon the second. Because when I denied being a soldier in the United States service, the Court could not try me. My denial of being in the Service was conclusive upon the Court under the principle of law referred to, until the evidence had contradicted me."

At Randall's urging, the defense, in a desperate move, contended that the court's use of the name William Howe, as opposed to William H. Howe, provided them with the proof that this court was trying the wrong man. To prove his desertion, the prosecution even produced a letter from the adjutant general's office, stating that William Howe, not William H. Howe, "was reported as a deserter from the 116th P. V. from Dec. 24th, 1862."

The defense then summarized the evidence as Howe and Randall viewed it. Captain Jack's testimony was only admissible in that he went from Philadelphia to Montgomery County to arrest the defendant. What some of the people told him regarding the weapons and cartridges was gossip or hearsay. "How am I to be affected by such testimony?" the court was asked. "How am I to be made responsible for the Statements of third parties? If they know anything in reference to the matter, why were they not Summoned by the Judge Advocate to attend the trial and testify to what they knew, that I might cross question them and test the truth of the Statements?" When Captain Jack produced the three Minie cartridges, the defense stated, he did not say where he obtained them. But he did say "the gun and rifle were loaded with the Same kind of balls. Now it is manifest to this Court that the Cartridges he produces will not enter the Rifle. They are 1/8 of an inch too large. They cannot be driven into the bore. Whether they will enter the double barrel gun I cannot say, as it was not for some reason or another produced on the trial."

One other answer of the provost officer bothered Howe. "He told this Court when he produced the three Minie cartridges that they were the same that Howe brought with him when he deserted and the double barrel gun of Mr. Groves had been loaded with them for the purpose of resisting his arrest. How did Captain Jack know what was brought by William Howe from the army thirteen months ago? Was he present at the time? If not, where does he get his information?" No one recalled Jack's contradiction to his earlier testimony. "How does Captain Jack know the purpose for which the gun was loaded? . . . could [he] read the secret workings of a man's mind and judge his intentions and pronounce them murderous?" If he had such supernatural powers, "he could as well have done the same thing on the twentieth of June and have prevented the crime. What venomous motives prompted Captain Jack to give such testimony I cannot conceive."

Realizing that the most important prosecution witness was David Y. Eisenberry, the defense directed its attention to discounting his statements. According to Eisenberry's own testimony, the defense argued, "he disguised himself and when asked who he was replied that he was Augustus Bitting." Why did he disguise himself, the court was asked "if his purpose in coming to my house was legitimate? Why not come in his proper character? Why come armed to arrest a peaceful citizen buried in sleep in the middle of the night in the midst of his wife and children? He further testifies to Mrs. Howe blowing a horn out of the window and as he was about to fire up at her to drive her away, a shot was fired down at him." Who fired the shot? Eisenberry did not say. Though if the defendant's wife was at the window with a gun "it is fair to presume that she fired the shot. If so why then admit the testimony? I conceive it was done for the same reason as the testimony of Captain Jack . . . to excite the feelings of this Court against me by the passion than the reason of the members of this Court. Of the justice of such a course I say nothing."

Eisenberry, the defense continued, had testified that he was "in front of the door pushing against it when a shot was fired out of the window—the ball going through the skirt of his coat." As he jumped back, another shot was fired which hit Bertolet. It did not require too much to dispute this portion of Eisenberry's statement, Howe thought. First, the door to Howe's home was set in the building, "some twenty inches from the out-side line of the house." As he was pressing against the door, it would be "impossible for a shot to come near him." On the other hand, a shot fired from the window beside the door would have made it "necessary for the person firing to have stood directly on Eisenberry's right flank (such is the relative position of door and window) and have fired through a portion of the building or else he would have been obliged to have put the gun entirely out of the window and held it on a line parallel with the house, with his left hand and then fired it from that position. In no other possible way than either of these could Eisenberry have been shot at in his position. That he was shot at in the one way is proved by the evidence of any bullets in the house by the side of the door and that he was not shot at in the Second Story is evident from the fact that the window was down and I could not have drawn the gun back through the broken light quickly enough either to avoid him seeing me or to reload it. Second. 'I jumped quickly back and another shot was fired.' Such is the evidence. Now I put the question to the intelligence of this Court: how was it possible for me to load, prime and fire again in an instant of time?"

No evidence, Howe continued, indicated that a double-barreled gun was used; in fact, a single-barreled rifle was produced in evidence. "There was no double barrel gun found in my house. There is some irrelevant testimony of Captain Jack that he found [one] in Mr. Groves house a double barrel shot gun, belonging to Groves. Even were this testimony admissible it rather assists me than otherwise because if I had such a gun and fired the first barrel at Eisenberry, and instantly fired again I must have shot Bertolet with the other barrel. But, Gentlemen, Eisenberry swears he saw me with this single barrel rifle in my hand when Bertolet was shot."

"Try," he asked the court, "to reconcile Eisenberry's statement with a possibility and I am sure you will agree with me in the manner I will hereafter mention of reconciling it. 'From the flash of the gun and the light on the fence I seen the prisoner in the window and draw his Rifle back.' Here is the gist of the case." A rifle, he explained, "makes no such flash such as comes from a gun or musket. Like its report, it is scarce perceptible. Even in the brightest flashes from the explosion of powder you can but see an act that is done never an act doing. Yet he says I was drawing my Rifle back. It is evident then that if the aid by the Rifle's flash Eisenberry could see nothing but for the lamp on the fence." Eisenberry had maintained, Howe continued, that "it was 15 feet from the house. In either the front or at the side . . . he does not say." On the other hand, Richard Bolton had testified "it was 30 feet from the window and at the side of the house. The difference in these statements," the defense reasoned, "is attributable to the fact that Bolton was sober, and Eisenberry drunk.

"Touching this part of the case, there are few material points in evidence. First, the lamp was a small uncovered fluid lamp. 2nd, It was placed on the fence at the side of the house 30 feet from the window from which Bertolet was shot, which was in the front part of the house.

"3rd. It was upon a very dark stormy night.

"4th. The light did not shine on the window in question and it was impossible to distinguish an object in the window by it."

Was it possible, Howe asked, for Eisenberry to see accurately "when the light did not shine on the window but was 30 feet from it and the night was dark and stormy? His powers of recognizing me by the light of the lamp is as impossible as by the flash of the Rifle. But let us follow him further and if we must suppose ourselves gifted with the same miraculous powers as Captain Jack and divine his motives and intent. Eisenberry, you saw, was rather an ignorant kind of man and supposing it would not bear the aspect of possibility if he told this Court that he saw me by the flash of the Rifle alone or by the light from the lamp, he hit upon (to him) the capital idea of throwing both lights upon the scene, thinking that two lamps will make more light than one and therefore if you doubted the possibility of his recognizing me by one, your doubts would be dispelled by another. How grossly he was mistaken in his supposition. Like the inhabitants of Africa, he supposed what he did not know, did not exist. He never saw a magic lantern and therefore supposed you never did. The flash of a gun is similar in effect to the concentrated rays of light thrown on an object from the lens of a magic lantern. The darker the surrounding space, the more brilliant will be the light thrown on the object. And if the surrounding space be light, the concentrated light will make the object no lighter. In the night time the flash of a shot gun makes a light though not a steady light. In the day time it makes no light at all, but the reverse—a black Smoke. To apply this to the present case, to the discomfiture of the witness, the light on the fence instead of increasing the light from the Rifle must have destroyed it altogether."

Wagner's testimony was unimportant, the defense determined, except for one point. Wagner had sworn the light was placed on the fence and, because it shone on the window, he could "plainly distinguish objects in the house. Admitting for arguments sake, though we deny it—that the light did shine upon the window. Still it was an utter impossibility to see in the window by it. If the light had been in the house you might distinguish objects within the window. But from the fact of the room being dark, a light from without would only shine on the surface of the window glass converting them with respect to those outside into a mirror reflecting themselves. You will readily comprehend, gentlemen, my argument. No doubt you have all witnessed the fact that by the light of a lamp outside of a window you cannot see in a house, though those within can see out. Mr. Wagner then must simply have been mistaken or he was under an ocular delusion."

As to the witnesses who testified that Howe had confessed, the defense objected because the witnesses stated having received the information while Howe was confined. " 'Verbal confessions of guilt,' says Mr. Greenleaf in his work on evidence, Vol. I, paragraph 214," the defense announced, " 'are to be received with the greatest caution for besides the danger of mistake, the failure of the party to express his own meaning and the infirmity of memory. It should be recollected that the mind of the prisoner himself is oppressed by the calamity of his situation and is often influenced by motives of hopes and fears to make an untrue confession. The zeal too which so generally prevails in the pursuit of evidence to detect offenders and the character of the persons necessarily called as witnesses all tend to impare the value of this kind of evidence and often causes its rejection, when in civil cases it would be received.' The weight observations of Mr. Justice Foster is also to be kept in mind that 'this evidence is not in the ordinary cause of things to be disproved by that sort of negative evidence by which the proof of plain facts may be and often is confronted.' "

Citing Greenleaf's work again, the defense countered that " 'where the least inducements are made by an officer having the prisoner in custody, or by any one in authority over him, will render the confession null and void and it must be ruled out.' Again . . . he [Greenleaf] puts a number of cases where the confessions were ruled out because they were elicited from the prison[er] by raising his hopes as well as his fears. For instance, where the prosecutor said 'tell me where my goods are and I will be favorable to you' and another 'there is no use of you denying it, a boy will swear he saw you do it' and again 'I only want my money and if you give me that you may go to the devil if you please' and in another case where a party said to the prisoner, 'If you would tell me all about it I would be obliged, if not we can do nothing' and in another case, where the prisoner's superior officer said to him 'now be cautious in the answers you give about this watch.' In all these cases the admissions which followed the remarks quoted were ruled out."

The circumstances surrounding his own confessions should be enough to rule them out, Howe contended. "Does it not seem strange to you gentlemen, that all the witnesses who testify to my confession were officers who had me in custody? Captain Jack, Trexler and Eisenberry. How come they to receive the confession from me? Why did they not tell all the circumstances of my confession? Had they been my bosom friends and confidants or my wife and children, you might suppose I would open my mind to them voluntarily and confess guilt. But here are three people, perfect strangers, and it is probable that as soon as I saw each one, without any request, promise or desire, that I would at once correct myself by confessing my guilt. They wrung it from me unsuspectingly of consequences in long conversations by the hour by their authority of me whilst in my gloomy cell, hampered with chains and surrounded with guards. Not a being was present—but ourselves. Thus, it is utterly beyond my power to prove the promises insinuatingly held out to me to confess. When the witnesses testify to the confessions they were asked by the Court if any threats were made to get me to confess. Of course, the answer was 'no.' But the law rules out confessions made after promises as well as threats, as is illustrated in the cases I have above mentioned."

Then, in a strange move, the defense stated that it "could not cross examine the witnesses on this point. My mouth was eternally sealed from asking them any question in reference to the matter. That might have brought a full statement of the circumstances and have shown what promises were made. Because I had objected to the admission of the testimony altogether and to have cross questioned them would have been an admission of its legality. I am confident, gentlemen, when you look at the circumstances surrounding these alleged confessions and consider well, you will discard them from the case altogether.

"So much for the evidence adduced by the Prosecution in support of the charge of Murder. How have I rebutted it from the nature of the case? My defense is limited." Unfortunately, the court was told, one of the eyewitnesses to the alleged murder, Reninger, was now dead. "I am left then with but one Richard Bolton. He testified to hearing but three shots fired that night and they were pistol shots. He went over to [my] house and there saw Wagner and Eisenberry with Bertolet in a wagon. Eisenberry and Wagner were so drunk that they could neither turn the wagon around or drive it home. They talked wild and incoherently and were too drunk to know what they were doing. Eisenberry seeing the eave of the roof about four feet above his head, thought it was the prisoner and he fired at it with his revolver." The two bullet holes were still visible in the roof, the defense claimed.

"Such, gentlemen, is the evidence of Bolton and is there any circumstances about him that would lead you to discredit his statement?" Believe him, the court was told, and you must doubt Eisenberry and Wagner, "for if both of them were so drunk as not to know what was going on, what credit is due to their testimony, especially when they go into details? Eisenberry himself testifies to having fired three shots, the marks of two of them are on the house. Where did the third one go?" Bearing down on its own hypothesis, the defense suggested that the third bullet had hit Bertolet "when the drunkard jumped back with his revolver in his hands. This hypothesis is a natural one, and it was the duty of the Judge Advocate to have rebutted it. Why did he not do it? Why did he not summon the Coroner and his Physician who held the Post-Mortem Examination on Bertolet to testify what kind of wound killed the deceased, whether a large Rifle Ball or a small pistol ball; what direction the ball took in his body, and from what direction must it have been fired and was it fired in close quarters or from a distance?" The prosecution should, the defense demanded, have determined in court what type of bullet killed Bertolet. But it did not.

With reference to the first charge, desertion, the prosecution had tried to prove that Howe was a soldier by producing the muster roll of Company A, which showed that a William Howe was in fact mustered into the service. But, the defense noted, "there is a great discrepancy between the date stated on this Roll and the date of muster testified to by Capt. Hobart." William Hobart had testified that he could identify Howe as a private who deserted on Christmas Eve, 1862. Further, Hobart had sworn that "he enlisted me at Perkiomenville in August 8, 1862. Now the Roll above alluded to shows William Howe to have been enrolled in Philadelphia on another date." In addition, Hobart had stated that the defendant "deserted while the division was being reviewed by General Hancock." But, the defense argued, he could not determine what time of day the young man deserted. "Then how did he know what particular event was transpiring at the time? If he could know one thing he could also know the other." Hobart was not even with his company at the time of the alleged desertion and, based on Captain Carrigan's testimony, Hobart was with Company A only "one week from the beginning of October 1862 to the end of January 1863." The rest of the time, he was either on sick leave or with the army "on the Staff of the First Division, 2nd Corps, one half of [a] mile away from the Regiment." Where did he get such intimate knowledge, the defense cried. "From the report of the orderly Sergeant who came to him for advice when there was trouble in the Company." He was nothing but a meddler, Randall and Howe concluded. "He was advising a noncommissioned officer over the head of his commanding officer. Though he was so precise in this information, yet he was forgetful of other matters, as he could not remember whether the Sergeant came to him to report or he went to the Sergeant."

The defense continued its summation, commenting on another critical statement by Hobart.

"Capt. Hobart says I acknowledged to having deserted [and] that I told him all about my going home on foot through Maryland, that I crossed Acquia Creek into Maryland, &c." Under cross-examination, Hobart had been asked if he thought it strange "when I told him I journeyed by the road he stated and if it would not take me several hundred miles out of my way and if he did not know it was impossible to get into Maryland by crossing Acquia Creek, as both banks of the creek are in Virginia? He replied that he was not surprised, that it would take me several hundred miles out of my course and that he did know both sides of Acquia Creek were in Virginia. Yet, forsooth, he was not surprised at my impossible statements, perhaps and very likely nothing would surprise him ... even if I told him I went to South America by the way of Canada."

Hobart, the court was reminded, "also stated that I confessed to him this very morning. Gentlemen, what credit would you give to the man who in the hour of peril, a prisoner with his doom of life and death before him, would go to him under the guise of charity and converse with him and ask questions on collateral subjects and from his answers to them construe his words into a confession of guilt? I might produce evidence to attack Capt. Hobart's character, but I will let him pass in peace and it is my fervent wish that remorse may never trouble the quiet of his conscience, but rather let oblivions veil cover the memory of his course on this trial, as it has hid what little he once knew that might have benefited me now.

"To rebut Capt. Hobart's testimony, I produced Patrick Carrigan," who served with Company A from October 1862 to the end of January 1863, who testified that "he mixed freely with his men and know them all well, that the Company was a very small one. I stood up before him in the presence of the Court and asked him if he recognized me as ever being in his Company. He said he did not ever remember having seen me before; did not know me at all —that he looked at me a half an hour before in the back room and could not tell me from the other orderlies about this Court. If, gentlemen, the Captain of Company A ... never saw me or knew me to have been in his Company, the conclusion is I was never there and the testimony of a detached officer now on duty with the Company to the contrary is of no avail. As one had the full opportunity to know the truth, the other had no opportunity at all.

"But to make the matter more certain, I called Thomas S. Ewing ... who recruited the men [and] took them to be mustered in to the Service."

Ewing, the defense continued, could not recall seeing Howe "before today, though he commanded the Company from July 1862 to October 1862" when he was relieved by Carrigan.

"The evidence on my behalf on this point is too conclusive.

"I submit to the consideration of this Court four Propositions which I respectfully ask them to consider and pass upon:

"First. I cannot be convicted by evidence proving William Howe guilty of an offence which I am not *indisputably* identified as being the same person.

"Second. I cannot be tried by this Court for the second charge if found not guilty of the first. If I am found guilty of the first, then

"Third. As no malice has been proved, I must be considered as having been justified in committing the alleged act in defence of my home and family. As the undoubted evidence shows the deceased and others came to my house in the middle of the night in disguise and attempted to break in.

"Fourth. If this Court do not consider me justified they can only convict me of manslaughter, as no other grade of crime can be proved by the evidence and under the 30th Section of the Conscript Act, they are bound to give the same punishment for a crime as is given by the laws of the State in which the crime is committed for a like offence."

The defense concluded its remarks by thanking the court for its "consideration in my behalf and the many favors they have granted me." And, to Captain Clarke, the judge advocate, "my Sincere acknowledgements for his leniency towards me. I scarce knew he was prosecuting the case against me. With the hopes, Gentlemen, of a speedy release from my confinement and a fervent trust in the providence of God I here end."

The courtroom was then cleared and the board "after having maturely considered the evidence," returned to address William H. Howe, Private, Company A, 116th Regiment, Pennsylvania Volunteers.

> Of the Specifications of the First Charge – "Guilty."
> Of the First Charge – "Guilty."
> Of the Specifications of the Second Charge – "Guilty."
> Of the Second Charge – "Guilty."
> And the Court does therefore sentence him Private William H. Howe. . . .
> He shall be hung by the neck until dead at such time and place as the Commanding General may direct, two thirds of the members concurring therein.

The court adjourned.

*HEAD QUARTERS*
*Department of the Susquehanna*
*Chambersburg, Pa. April 9th, 1864.*

*The proceedings, findings, and Sentence in the case of
Private William H. Howe Co 'A' 116th Regt Pa. Vols, are
approved; the sentence will be carried into effect on Friday
the 24th day of June next at Fort Mifflin near Philadelphia
Pa.*

*By command of
Major General Couch,
[signed] Jno. S. Schultze,
Assistant Adjutant General.*[1]

# 10

# Out of the Depths

THE SOUND OF Colonel Frink's voice intoning "shall be hung by the neck until dead," echoed through the head of William H. Howe. For a moment, he did not fully understand what he had heard. Howe could not immediately comprehend that he had reached the end of the road. The court's decision was, he and Randall agreed, a bad one, based on faulty, inadmissible testimony.

But, as in all military courts-martial, there was no right of appeal. In those cases involving the death penalty, however, an execution could be suspended until the military authorities obtained a statement of the president's pleasure regarding the matter. After a court-martial board had rendered a decision, a copy of the entire proceedings would be forwarded to the judge advocate general for review and recommendations. Following this, it would be presented to the president of the United States for final disposition.[2] Randall had good reason to feel that he had a chance to reverse the court's decision. On February 26, during the court-martial, President Lincoln had directed, through General Order No. 76, that all deserters sentenced to die be reprieved and sentenced to imprisonment at Dry Tortugas, Florida, for the duration of the war. If Lincoln could remove the death penalty from deserters, he might show clemency to William Howe and, at least, commute his sentence to life imprisonment.

Following the trial, Howe was returned to Fort Mifflin where he had been confined during the court-martial. During that time he had been kept in one of the dirty, damp bomb-proofs, which had been reserved for the worst prisoners. Military records do not provide an insight into what life was like for William Howe as a prisoner there. The local papers, unsubstantiated by official documentation, attempted to relay one story—the mass escape attempt of February 24, 1864.

Newspaper accounts alleged that as many as two hundred men—rebels and deserters—using iron spikes, attempted to pierce the five-foot-thick walls of Mifflin's bomb-proofs. One of the guards reportedly overheard a conversation among the prisoners about the escape. He alerted Capt. J. Orr Finnie, who posted guards to prevent an exodus. William H. Howe, credited as the ringleader, led the attempt. The guards waited in front of the exit hole for the young man to emerge . . . then, at Finnie's command, fired. One bullet, the accounts stated, went through Howe's leg.

If Howe had indeed attempted to escape from Fort Mifflin during the court-martial, it seems odd that this fact was not brought out by the prosecution to reinforce its contention that he was, in fact, a desperate man. Also, if he had been shot, as the accounts contend, it is highly unlikely he would have been in court the next morning at eleven o'clock. In addition, when the judge advocate general's office reviewed his case, this flaw in his record probably would have been mentioned—even in passing. But nothing was ever said about this "escape attempt," if one actually had taken place.

Very likely, there might have been an escape attempt; Fort Mifflin had experienced many successful escapes before. After Howe's confinement there, the newspapers figured that Howe would have been part of it. Rumor and innuendo continued to plague the tragic young man. And, the impact on the public—both private citizens and persons in positions of power—might have made Randall's job of obtaining mercy much more difficult.

A week after the announcement of the court-martial decision, Randall wrote to Judge Advocate General James Holt, respectfully calling his attention to the case. Randall indicated that the circumstances surrounding the courts-martial were such that the board should have come to a more favorable decision. The main point, in the attorney's mind, was that Frink sat as president of the court and had, in fact, prepared the charges against Howe. Such preknowledge of the case, Randall felt, prejudiced any decision on Frink's part. And, his ruling to admit all testimony, whether it was legally or illegally obtained, prostituted the credibility of the court. There were other examples just as grievous, he wrote Holt, which destroyed Howe's chances of a fair trial. Unfortunately for his client, Randall stated that the most important point was, in his own mind at least, the admission of documents omitting Howe's middle initial, thereby "proving the offence against another person of a different name." The attorney added, "I feel quite confident, when this case is reviewed by an officer as well as jurist of your known reputation in our profession that justice will be done." [3]

It was probable, however, that Holt had no notion of what Randall was requesting. It was not until April 18, 1864, five weeks or more after the trial, that papers were forwarded by General Couch to Holt's office.

According to the rules governing courts-martial, the judge advocate, as the recorder of a general court-martial, was directed to transmit the proceedings and decision of the court as quickly as possible to the secretary of war, where the papers would then be examined by the judge advocate general. [4] Though the rules are quite specific, they were never carried out promptly. Perhaps Randall's letter accelerated Couch's processing of the paperwork.

Regardless, time was running out for William H. Howe. His execution was scheduled for June 24 at Fort Mifflin. Having received nothing concrete from his letter to Holt, Randall tried again. This time, he sent Holt a portion of his defense statement, since he was uncertain that it had been sent along with the court's proceedings. If Holt had not already reviewed the case, Howe's attorney pleaded with him to give it his "carefull & earnest consideration." [5]

Still Randall received no reaction from Washington.

Frightened by the lack of news, and with a firm belief in his client's innocence and the inequities of the justice that had been meted out to Howe, Randall, on April 30, wrote directly requesting a commutation of Howe's sentence. "I am sure," he told Lincoln, "could your Excellency take the time to examine into his case you would find his conduct free from either guile or malice. His character as a Soldier he can safely leave to the judgement of all the officers of his Regiment." He concluded his plea with a request that Lincoln commute Howe's sentence to imprisonment—"even tho' it be as long as the term of his life." [6]

Randall's letter did not, however, go directly to the White House; nor did William Howe's previous letters to the president. As early as August 23, 1863, Howe had tried to tell his story to someone with a compassionate ear—Abraham Lincoln.

In a letter mailed from the provost marshal's barracks in Philadelphia, Howe told the president that he had enlisted in the 116th Regiment as a private. He stated that his enlistment began on August 8, 1862, and that he left the regiment on Christmas Eve, arriving home January 21. Howe explained that:

LIBERTY AND UNION FOREVER

Philadelphia Provost marshals
Hedquarters - August 23. 1863

Mr:
President: Sir, I will
inform you afewlines this is
that I William H Howe frume
Frederick Township Montgomery County
Pa, have Enlisted in the 116th P.V. Reg
as private i Enlisted on the Eights of
August 1862 and left the Regtment
one day Before Crismas and Recived
home the 21 of January the reason
that i left the Regtment was this
i was not well the hole time
that i have Been in Servis and
i Could not get in no Hospital
i hut to do my duty like the rest that
was well and so i thought i
would live the Regtment and go
home till i was well againe and
when i was at home about three

*Letter from William Howe to President Lincoln, August 23, 1863:* National Archives

K. 1039 Aug 63

Not tell who he was and then i
Shot at him and then i went
upstares againe opened a window and
Looked out but Everything was all
Quiet and then i jumpt out and
Hollart. Murder Murder and runt
to my next nabour and toled him and
to a Coulle more and whent there
and Back againe
then i hait Shat the Enrulen Officer
from New Hanover township he was
going to Cetch me and then they
Cant me and tucked me to philadephia
and put me in a Sell about eight
feet Leeng and about four feet witer i
am all most Smatering in there i
am in now five weeks it is no air
aer coming in atall and Dark to if
he would come there like a man
he could Cetch me but not like
a murder: and this i can prove
By a dessen of Witnesses. Wm H Hoove

the reason i left the regtment was this i was not well the hole time that i have been in servis and i could not get in no Hospital. i hat to do my duty like the rest that was well and so i thought i would live the regtment and go home till i was well againe and when i was at home about three months i was nere over it then i was going to go out againe and then my Nabers found it out and they came to my house and told me that you had let Printed in the news Papers that every Deserter that would Not be in his Regtment till the first day of Apill would get Shot are hung they mate me afraid because I was to late then and further they told me that i should Stay at home they would fite for me before they would lieve me go and so i did Not no what to do i was afrait to go out and i was afrait to Stay at home and then i thought i would stay two three weeks yet then i would go and in that time they commenced to enrole the Peoples for the Draft and So one Sunday Nite three men came at my house to catch me one was the Enrolen Officer from Newhanover Townshp and the others was two Citicence from the Same Township and i Lived in Frederick Township and on Sunday nite at Eleven O Clock Somebody Came nocking at the Dore and my wife heret it and She went down to See what was the matter then She ask what was the matter and then Somebody out Side Set She Should open the doore and She ask what for then She got anser rite away then he Set if She would not open the dore he would push her in and then he tried to push her in and my wife came running upstares and told me and i looked out upstares then i seen Two men out Side and So Soon i looked out they Shot at me two times and then i went Back againe and get my gun and then i Hert them at the doore againe and i Seen one out Side to but i could Not tell who he was and then i Shot at hime and then i went upstares againe opened a window and Looked out but Everything was all quiet and then i jumpt out and Hollert Murder Murder and went to my next naberer and told him and to a coulle more and whent there then i came back again hat Shot the Enrolen Officer from New Hanover township he was going to cetch me and then they caut me and tucked me to philadelphia and put me in a Sell about eight feet Long and about four feet wite I am allmost Smotering in here I am in now Six weeks it is no aer coming in atall and Dark to if he would come here like a man he could catch me but not like a murder and this i can prove by a dossen of Witnesses. '

The letters all went to the office of the judge advocate general. The transmittal note on Randall's correspondence, dated May 4, indicated that the final determination rested with the president. Accompanying this material was the judge advocate general's report on the proceedings of the court-martial.

Holt's report outlined Randall's objections, and his plea for clemency. He then explained to the president how he saw the case: Desertion was certain, the judge advocate general determined, because the original muster roll proved that he was mustered into the army on August 8, 1861. Hobart's testimony, the report continued, confirmed the dates and, further, that Howe had in fact deserted. Howe's witnesses, Carrigan and Ewing, Holt added, could not attest to the same facts. "The Court, weighing this Conflicting testimony," the judge advocate general wrote, "probably came to the Conclusion that Hobart was the more reliable witness, and that his positive testimony over-balanced that of Carrigan and Ewing, which was rather negative. The finding of guilty is clearly well sustained, if the identity of the prisoner was made out, and the conclusion of the Court upon this question cannot be disturbed upon any of the principles applicable to trials of issues of fact."

Holt indicated to Lincoln that the "evidence respecting the alleged murder was still more Conflicting, though that adduced by the prosecution, when taken in connection with the Confessions of the prisoner, appears to Establish his guilt beyond a reasonable doubt."

The testimonies of both Eisenberry and Wagner were considered by the judge advocate general to be more reliable than that of Richard Bolton, whose testimony could not be corroborated. The Court, he indicated, probably rejected his statements "as unworthy of credit."

Holt felt, and he expressed it to Lincoln, that the deserter Howe could conceivably know that these men wanted to arrest him and that it was possible—if not probable—that he would shoot Bertolet. He nonetheless admitted that these men had made "a bungling attempt to capture him."

Regardless, Holt conceded, Howe was defended "with much skill by a lawyer, the same who now appeals to the President for mercy in behalf of his client." He added that nothing was presented at the trial which demonstrated Howe's character or his conduct as a soldier.

In his conclusion, the judge advocate general told Lincoln that, in his estimation, the court did not overstep its authority. In short, Holt's opinion was that William H. Howe should die. If Lincoln thought differently, that was the president's own concern.[8]

While his fate rested in Washington, Howe was removed from Fort Mifflin. On May 6, 1864, through an arrangement between civil and military authorities, he was transported to Eastern Penitentiary on Fairmount Avenue in Philadelphia.[9]

Suddenly local newspapers injected an exciting but erroneous dimension to the prisoner's story. On May 28, *The Press* reported that William Howe had escaped from Fort Mifflin. Confined in a bomb-proof, the paper stated, Howe had escaped in a mysterious manner. The fugitive was described as "a desper-

*Eastern Penitentiary. Guard towers and main entrance on Fairmount Avenue, Philadelphia.* Photograph by author

ado, an illiterate, brutalized fellow, who avoided arrest and defied the officers of the law for several months." Howe's escapade was indeed mysterious, as at the time he was still confined in Eastern Penitentiary. Three days later *The Press* acknowledged red-faced that Howe had not escaped, and that the fugitive from Fort Mifflin was named Taylor.

Throughout the flurry of excitement, there was still no reaction from the president. Randall did not wait—he could not wait—any longer. Panicky, he travelled to Washington four days before the scheduled execution and hand-delivered yet another plea for clemency. In an affidavit, Randall recounted the inequities of the trial, including the fact that Colonel Frink "had had [Howe] in custody and had acted *as his jailor for several months.*" In addition, the court "*without allowing the Prisoner* (as was his undoubted right) *to examine the challenged member on his oath* as to his qualifications to sit on the trial, allowing Col. Frink to make an *ex parte statement, not under oath*, in his own behalf." Realizing this, Randall "concluded it was of little use or avail to challenge *two other members of the Court, who had prejudged the case also, by having tried the Prisoner Howe some two months before for the same offence*, which trial however was set aside for informality. *This last mentioned fact does not appear on the Record, for the reason stated*, but it is nevertheless *true*, as can be fully verified of an examination of the two orders from Genl. Couch' Hd Qr's detailing the various officers to constitute the two Courts.

"Independently of the above facts, the whole proceedings on the trial were so irregular and illegal as to leave no doubt, but the *Prisoner was deprived of that full, fair impartial investigation of his case, that law & justice allows him.*

"This Statement of objections is not made with any desire of your Excellency's granting the Prisoner a *full pardon*, but only with the hope that, in conjunction with the Prayer of the officers of the Prisoner's Regiment and his Spiritual advisor—your Excellency may deem this case fit for the exercise of *your clemency in commuting the sentence from death to imprisonment.*" Randall urged Lincoln to act with speed because "the sentence is fixed for *next* Friday, June 24/64."[10]

In addition to his own plea, Randall attached two letters. In the first, the present and former officers of Howe's unit asked Lincoln "if the exercise of your charity towards the Prisoner and his unhappy family will not be contrary to the good of the service *we would pray you to commute the Prisoners Sentence from death to imprisonment.*" It was signed by Col. St. Clair A. Mulholland, Capt. Francis E. Crawford, Adj. Lewis J. Sacriste, Maj. John Teed, Lt. Thomas McKnight, and former officers Lawrence Kelly, Philip A. Boyle, Dennis Heenan, and Thomas S. Ewing.[11] Transmitting the officers' document, Holt noted that he could make "no recommendation."

The second letter was written June 19, by the Rev. G. F. Krotel, pastor of St. Mark's Lutheran Church in Philadelphia. Krotel had visited Howe in Eastern Penitentiary and analyzed the man. The pastor spoke with the prisoner in German "with which he is more familiar than he is with English." Seeking an objective view, the minister listened to Howe's account of "the sad affair." It was, he remembered, delivered "in a very simple, candid and straightforward way, and made a favorable impression upon my mind." Krotel believed the young man when he told him that "he had not the slightest idea of deserting, but simply wanted to go home to get that medical attendance and rest which he so much needed. He was," Krotel continued,

To His Excellency
           President Lincoln.
    ,We would most Respectfully re=
=quest of your Excellency to take into consider=
=ation the case of William H. Howe, Private
Co "A" 116th Regt. Penna Volunteers now under sen
-tence to be hung on the 27th of June 1864, and
if the exercise of your charity towards the Prisoner
and his unhappy family will not be contrary to the
good of the service we would pray you to com-
=mute the Prisoners sentence from death to im=
=prisonment.

                St. Clair A. Mulholland
                   Colonel 116th Penna, Vols
        Francis E. Crawford Capt. 116' Pa
               Lewis J Sacriste Adjutant 116 Pa
        John Teed Major 116 ton Penna. Vols.
        Thomas McKnight Lieut 116 P V.
        Lawrence Kelly, late Capt. Co G 116 P V

    Dennis Heenan
                Late Colonel 116th Regt. Pa
    Thos S Lenig  late Capt 116 Regt P V

*Letter from Howe's unit to President Lincoln.* National Archives

*Rev. G. F. Krotel, c. 1854.* Archives, Lutheran Theological Seminary,
Philadelphia

"under the Doctor's hands for several weeks after he reached his home, and he made no attempt to conceal his presence at home from any of his neighbors or friends. He alleges that when he discharged his gun into the midst of the persons who were endeavoring forcibly to enter his house, at night, he did not know that they had come to arrest him as a deserter, and he did not aim at any particular person."

Krotel was distressed that Howe's spirits were high based on the efforts of his friends to secure clemency from Lincoln. The Lutheran minister felt that the prisoner appeared to "cling to the hope that something would be done to save him from execution." Krotel told Howe that there was little or no hope, and "that it was my simple duty to urge him to prepare to meet his God. He professes to trust in the Saviour, and that he is prepared to die, if die he must, but cannot help declaring that it seems very hard to die for a crime he did not mean to commit. He appears to be a plain, simpleminded Pennsylvania German; and the impression made upon the chaplain [of the prison, the Rev. John Ruth], who has considerable experience in reference to the deportment and character of prisoners, as well as upon myself, has been and is still, that his story is a true one. I subsequently conversed with Rev. H. Wendt, his pastor, whose account of the affair differed from Howe's, but, . . . a further investigation of the circumstances, in the neighborhood in which the sad affair took place, has led him to the conclusion, that Howe has told the truth."

Krotel did not demand absolute clemency but "there appears to me to be so much in this particular case to call for the exercise of mercy, that I sincerely rejoice at your proposed application to our honored and merciful President. The poor man has a wife and children, who tremble at the thought of his approaching doom. It is a terrible thing to die the death of a malefactor, and I am sure that if the President can satisfy the stern demands of justice by some other punishment, he will spare the life of a poor simpleminded, humbled man who volunteered as a soldier of the Union, and conducted himself bravely and well for a long time, and who has learned the bitter lessons of long imprisonment."[12]

Randall's plea—and his advantageous use of supporting documents must have attracted some attention because the order was rendered to stay the execution, pending the decision of the president.

On June 21, 1864, Holt's office presented to President Lincoln a detailed documentation of the questions raised by Howe's defense. The most important question, Randall had indicated, was Frink's position as president of the court-martial board. Holt felt that Frink's statement that "he had no knowledge of the facts of the case," was sufficient. Without the colonel's explanation, his signature on the charges would disqualify him from sitting in judgment. He would be expected to harbor some bias. Frink, Holt affirmed, appeared to have been a nominal prosecutor; the court was correct. Holt did, however, think that Frink's statements, though true, were not made under oath, and, as such, were "irregular and should not be countenanced."

Howe should have insisted Frink be questioned under oath. But, since neither Randall nor Howe objected, this right was waived. In other words, the irregularity was permitted, simply because the question had not been asked. It is possible that Randall had not raised the question of the oath simply because he felt it futile in face of the closed-session determination by the court-martial board to seat Frink.

Regarding the certification of Howe's desertion, Holt insisted that the court's decision was not based entirely on Captain Hobart's testimony. The judge advocate general agreed with the defense that Captain Jack's testimony was improperly admitted, since Jack had no firsthand knowledge. His statements should have been proved, Holt thought, by others. "But," Holt opined, "admissions of the prisoner were not extorted by promises or threats, and were therefore competent."

Even removing Jack's testimony from consideration, Holt continued, left enough evidence in the record to justify the finding of the court. Howe, he wrote, "appears to have confessed the homicide to Taylor . . . Johnson . . . and Captain Freedley."

Holt did not feel that the other points required any notice on his part.

Randall, in his affidavit, had raised the question of the prior court-martial. He deposed that two members of the panel, besides Frink, had sat in judgment of Howe when their decision was subsequently set aside for irregularity. "But as this fact does not appear in the record," Holt added, "and was not mentioned at the trial, this office refrains from any comment upon the point."

From the judge advocate general's final comments, it appears that the letters from Krotel and from the officers of the 116th were not forwarded with the recommendations, but were summarized. The minister, Holt wrote, listened to Howe's confessions and admission of guilt; the officers, on the other hand, asked for clemency but did not set forth any new facts on the case.

Another communication, however, was forwarded through Holt's office, which might have weighed heavily against William Howe. On June 27, Henry R. Bertolet wrote to the president. The transmittal note alleged that it was from Bertolet's parents demanding that the sentence be carried out. Bertolet was, in fact, Abraham's brother—and he had so indicated in his letter.

"Respected Sir," Bertolet began, "I communicate these few lines in behalf of the family of my dec[eased] Bro[ther] Abraham R. Bertolet who was murdered by William H. Howe about one year since the time for his execution having passed. His sentence having been commuted to an indefinite period we fear some bad influence has been used in representing his case before you. If any petitions or any Thing of the kind have come before you purporting as coming from his wife or friends that he should not be executed, we have only to say that it is false & a forgery. We have waited patiently & long for Justice to be meted out to him & when upon the eve of realizing those expectations we are unhappily informed that execution has been stayed. The enemy's of our glorious Union are already rejoicing. Hoping & expecting that their friend Howe who has not only murdered my Bro[ther] but also deserted the flag of his country will be again released & amongst his friends. However we Trust & pray that those hopes of theirs may be blasted. There have quite a number of union men been murdered through the state that it seems but proper that an example should be made of this man Howe. For if all are pardoned it only lizences Traitors to murder our citizens. I would earnestly solicit an early reply to this letter."[13]

It is not known whether Henry Bertolet ever received a reply. But, on July 8, 1864, Abraham Lincoln took his pen in hand and wrote two words on the transmittal documents, "Sentence approved," and then signed his name.

Lincoln had a reputation for leaning towards mercy. He did not particularly like the death sentence. John Hays was constantly amused at Lincoln's ploys to circumvent the death penalty. "He was only merciless," Hays wrote, "in cases where meanness or cruelty were shown." There was a pattern to Lincoln's merciful dole. In strictly military crimes, like sleeping on guard duty, insubordination, or desertion, the president usually accepted the recommendation of the man's commanding general or the judge advocate general, especially when they recommended clemency. When the death sentence was presented, he often ordered a reduced sentence. The only area where his decision was stern was in cases of crimes against civilians—rape, robbery, arson and the like. These he treated severely.

There was one case, similar to Howe's, in which Lincoln showed great clemency. A private from a New York artillery regiment deserted, enlisted as a substitute, and then deserted again. He was finally captured and imprisoned at Elmira. While there he made an unsuccessful attempt to escape, poisoning some of the guards and killing one.

When Lincoln got the papers on this case, he ordered the execution take place. The soldier's lawyer, in the meantime, pleaded with the president that the man was a mental defective. Lincoln contacted a Utica physician and asked him to examine the soldier. The doctor's report indicated that the man was not insane, and that he had control over his faculties when he killed the guard. After receiving the doctor's statement, Lincoln commuted the man's sentence to ten years' imprisonment at hard labor.[14]

Why then did Lincoln not respond to Howe's plea? Was it because a man

*Letter from Henry R. Bertolet to President Lincoln, June 27, 1864.* National Archives

*Transmittal documents signed by Lincoln, approving Howe's death sentence.* National Archives had been murdered? Could it be that Lincoln never received all the material Randall had dutifully conveyed to Washington? Or, was the entire idea of executing William H. Howe created for the purpose of stopping the evil of desertion, Copperheadism, draft evasion and resistance in Pennsylvania?

Three weeks after Lincoln signed Howe's fate, Major General Couch issued General Order No. 41 announcing that William H. Howe would "be hung by the neck until dead" between 11:00 A.M. and 4:00 P.M. on Friday, August 26, 1864, at Fort Mifflin, Pennsylvania. The fort's commandant was charged with complying with the order.[15]

This directive did not satisfy the adjutant general's office. On August 20, E. D. Townsend, assistant adjutant general, requested Couch to give reason why the sentence had not been carried out sooner.

"Howe was directed . . . to be executed June 24th following previous to which time he was respited by authority from the War Department," Couch responded.

"Upon receiving the order of the President of July 21st, ultimo, approving and confirming the sentence, directing that he be hung by the neck until dead—I deemed it humane to give him some little time to prepare for death, as it were natural to infer that when respited he expected to escape execution, and consequently had to do over what had been undone.

"The above are my reasons for not carrying out the President's order sooner."[16]

There could be no more delays. All that now remained was for William H. Howe to die.

## A MILITARY EXECUTION

*William H. Howe, of Co. A, 116th Pennsylvania Volunteers, is to be executed tomorrow morning, at Fort Mifflin. At the time of the enrolment, having deserted from the army, and being at his home in Perkiomen township, Montgomery county, Howe, who is described as a perfect desperado, vowed that he would resist the draft, and the manner he did it was thus: He armed himself, and, taking advantage of a favorable opportunity, he waylaid and shot the enrolling officer of his district, who was quietly pursuing his duty. Information of this being conveyed to this city, Deputy Marshals Jenkins, Sharkey, and Schuyler started out in pursuit of the murderer. Having the start of his pursuers, he escaped to the mountains, armed with revolvers and bowie knife, being in fact little short of a walking armory. He roamed at large in the forests and wilds of Western Pennsylvania, committing numerous depredations upon their inhabitants who became in dread of his approach for nearly a year. Finally, however, about three or four months ago, he was entrapped and made prisoner. Trial and conviction by court martial soon followed, and if the Presidential mercy does not intervene, this double criminal will soon suffer the fate which his acts have courted.*

*The Press*
August 25, 1864

# 11

# The Execution

IT WAS NO longer dark at half-past six when Lt. Sylvester Bonafon of the 99th Pennsylvania arrived at Eastern Penitentiary. With an ambulance and three-man guard, Bonafon had been entrusted with the "delicate duty" of escorting William H. Howe from the prison and delivering him to Fort Mifflin.

Within minutes of the lieutenant's arrival, Howe was ready to leave, dressed in dark pants, a light linen coat, white shirt, and laced shoes—a departure from the usual prison attire. There was nothing left for him to do but go. He had met with Hannah for the final time on Thursday afternoon, and that meeting was quite emotional.

The ride was "the most painful and quiet he ever took," Bonafon later confided to a reporter. Neither of them spoke while they traveled from the prison through West Philadelphia and the Darby road. The trip took more than an hour, and they arrived at the fort about eight o'clock.[1]

As they entered the main gate, the river to their backs, Howe saw the gallows for the first time. Though it was supposed to have been erected the day before, workmen from the Moyamensing Prison were still nailing boards to complete it when the ambulance and its passengers arrived. It was, the workmen were sure to inform anyone who asked, the same one which "launched into eternity" Arthur Spring, the Skuplinski brothers, Maddocks and Armstrong—well-known criminals of the time. For the first time since he had picked up the prisoner, Bonafon noticed "a twinge of nervousness" surfacing on the young, condemned man.[2]

They took him from the ambulance and walked him across the parade to the small guardhouse near the main gate. From its windows the prisoner could see the gallows. For several hours he sat not more than ten feet from the scaffold and pondered his fate.

While William Howe sat, alone with his thoughts, a steamboat, filled with spectators and thrill-seekers, was making its way to the fort. Aboard the *Don Juan*, a Confederate craft that had been captured on Sabine Bay in April 1863, was a ninety-man detachment of the 186th Pennsylvania Regiment, commanded by one of Howe's accusers, Captain Jack; the Rev. Mr. Krotel; representatives of the press; and a motley collection of military and civilian personnel. Edmund Randall was with them and so was Colonel Frink. The *Don Juan* steamed down the Delaware from the Vine Street wharf shortly before nine o'clock. It arrived at the fort an hour later, after stopping at Washington Street to pick up another squad of soldiers.

Before the spectators were allowed to leave the steamer, the soldiers were ordered ashore. Their officers drew them up on the dock and marched them over a bridge spanning the weed-choked moat into the main portion of the fortification. Inside the fort, they stacked their arms. The soldiers then broke ranks and wandered about the installation until they were summoned for the execution.

Though it was possible for William Howe to see these men milling about the guardhouse and to overhear their ribald comments and snide remarks about the scaffold, he seemed to pay little attention. But he could be seen . . . pacing up and down in his cell.

Mr. Krotel, who had prayed long and hard with Howe in prison, finally received permission to leave the *Don Juan* and accompanied a military aide to Howe's cell. The minister remained with the young man, praying and talking, later confiding that the prisoner had resigned himself to die.[3]

At half-past eleven, the conference between the two came to an end. Escorted by a small guard, Howe walked across the parade ground. Though passing the gallows and the hearse, which would later carry his body back to Philadelphia, he remained calm, displaying no emotion. The *Public Ledger* reported that the day before, Howe had told Randall he "would rather die than live, as he had come to the conclusion that the country was going to destruction; that civil war would rage for years, and he would be better off away from strife."[4]

Fifteen minutes after Howe left his dismal cell, the drums were beat and the troops picked up their weapons and fell into line. Two companies of the

Provost Guard and a detachment of soldiers from the fort's own garrison marched to the foot of the gallows. There they formed two sides of a hollow square. The guardhouse, in which Howe had been confined, and the small, brick arsenal formed the other two sides.

This procedure was in strict conformance with military regulations. According to the courts-martial manual, death by hanging was conducted less ceremoniously than execution by a firing squad.[5] When the troops were properly formed, William H. Howe was led to the center. His hands were shackled, as if to keep him from escaping.

At the foot of the scaffold, his handcuffs were removed by a guard. Then, with Krotel at his side, Howe walked up the steps of the gallows to the platform. The scene was a most solemn one. The soldiers stood around the scaffold silent and at rigid attention. Captain Pritner's company was formed at the entrance to the parade, facing the gallows; Captain Jack's unit was drawn up facing both the entrance and the gallows. Between the two lines of soldiers, a number of officers entered and stationed themselves on that side of the hollow square opposite the guardhouse. Prominent among them was Col. Daniel Powers Whiting, commandant of the post and the "venerable, gray-haired, noble-looking veteran of the regular service and 'Florida War' fame." With Whiting were Captain Pritner, Captain Jack, the doctors who would later examine the body, and several others.[6]

The workmen, who remained to watch the spectacle, climbed to the ramparts and stared. Within ten feet of the scaffold itself, a party of deserters and bounty-jumpers, who were confined in one of the fort's casemates, was afforded a full view of the proceedings. The *Ledger* reporter added in his account, "it is hoped that it will not be lost upon them." As he stood on the platform of the gallows, all eyes were fixed on William H. Howe. After apparently being prompted by his chaplain, he drew a small piece of white paper from his pocket and began to read in a low voice, tinged with the echoes of his German ancestry:

> Fellow-soldiers and officers: I am now about to go before my God, to answer for the crime of having taken the life of a fellow-creature. I bow with submission to my sentence, and fully forgive those who passed it and all who were witnesses against me. They did their duty as well as they could, and I take this opportunity to thank you from my heart, the members of the court-martial who tried me, and especially Captain Clarke, the judge advocate, and Mr. Edmund Randall, my lawyer, for their kindness to me. But as I have to leave my dear children but my record and good name as a soldier, I feel it a duty I owe to them to state now that I never sought the life of the man I killed, and never wanted it; and I feel God will pardon me for taking

it as I did. I know my fellow-soldiers and officers in the army never blamed me for leaving, as I was an invalid, and had no hospital to go to in my regiment. And now I am about to leave this life and I commend my wife and little ones to the charity of the world, and as a last request I ask pardon of those I injured, and hope they will forgive me and pray for my soul.[7]

Mr. Krotel then asked William Howe to kneel. Joining him on the wooden platform, the minister delivered a prayer, which was "beautiful and affecting" for the salvation of the young man, his wife, and children. During the prayer, and for that matter the entire proceedings, Howe remained composed, even when references were made to his wife and children. The assembled spectators listened to Mr. Krotel's prayer in deep silence. Their heads were bare as if in respect, and "as the deeply uttered 'Amen' dropped from the lips of the minister, Howe, who had remained immovable during the utterance of the prayer, opened his lips evidently adding his own 'Amen' to the one just pronounced."

Mr. Krotel whispered a few final words to Howe and then descended the scaffold steps. A noncommissioned officer, reportedly a cousin of Bertolet, fastened the manacles to Howe's wrists. The noose was adjusted around his neck and a white cap placed over his head. William H. Howe was left alone, his face turned in the direction of Perkiomenville.

At the signal from the provost marshal, the executioner, on temporary duty from the Moyamensing prison, removed the supports, unfastened the hook, and at precisely seven minutes past noon, grabbed the rope and jerked it toward him. The trap doors opened and Howe "was launched into eternity." His body descended about four to five feet and he died without a struggle. Eye-witnesses could only discern "two or three convulsive movements . . . a few nervous twitchings of the legs and arms ensued and all was quiet."

At half-past twelve, Dr. William Blackwood, the fort's surgeon and a resident of the city, announced that William H. Howe was dead—of a dislocated neck. Howe's body was cut down and given into the hands of Mr. Black, the government's undertaker. Black would embalm it that afternoon and send it to Hannah Howe. But Howe's death was not the end of the controversy.

"The execution," the *Sunday Dispatch* reported two days after the event, "was attended with certain features which were not noticed in the daily papers." The *Dispatch* was, however, the only Philadelphia newspaper to take exception to events that allegedly took place at the execution. Neither the *Public Ledger* nor the *Inquirer* commented on the procedures or editorialized on any indecorum. The *Daily Evening Bulletin*, on the other hand, did indicate in its account that "everything concerned with the execution was conducted in the most unexceptionable manner." *The Press* did not comment one way or another, but on August 27 concluded its report by saying . . . "but society at that time, in that part of Pennsylvania, was tainted with Copperheadism, and it may be well supposed that the draft-resisting, dark-lanterned conspirators had the effect to instill into the mind of Howe some of the poison for which their victim was hung instead of themselves."

The *Dispatch* was more vocal. Its editorials denounced the proceedings as a travesty. "Those entrusted with the unpleasant duty of carrying out the orders from head-quarters endeavored to do their duty," the newspaper wrote, "in such a manner that which the effect upon the bounty-jumpers and deserters would be a decided one, the prisoner should be treated with all the kindness due to his unfortunate position." Some of those in charge, the paper felt, did not harbor any of those noble sentiments.

The *Dispatch* itemized the charges: Howe was made to witness the completion of the gallows even though there had been sufficient time to finish construction earlier. Further, he was left alone for four hours in full view of the platform. His minister, Mr. Krotel, was not permitted to console him until two hours before the execution. "Thus the few remaining hours of the prisoner, which should have been devoted to solemn things," the *Dispatch* cried, "must have been disturbed by the sight of the preparations for his death. He could see all that passed, and could hear the thoughtless remarks of those who came to examine the structure. After passing through such a terrible ordeal, it was surprising to see him display so much fortitude when brought out and placed upon the platform." It was unnecessary, the paper stated, to subject him to this horror. This fact was admitted by Colonel Whiting, "who stated that it was an oversight, and was not noticed until too late to make any change. Here the error ended so far as Howe was concerned."

The *Dispatch* contended that the entire execution was staged to produce the maximum effect on the bounty-jumpers and deserters who were imprisoned at Fort Mifflin. The effect, the newspaper reasoned, was lost because of the disgraceful manner in which the event was conducted.

Adding to the charges, the *Dispatch* noted that the man who pulled the rope was neither concealed, as was usual, nor disguised in the traditional manner. "He stood boldly forward to the centre of the group of soldiers, and when he had pulled the rope seemed to regard the result with an eye to the artistic effect." But that was not all. "When the body remained suspended about half an hour, preparations were made to take it down." The civilian in charge of the gallows was not affected by the presence of death. "On the contrary, his attention was about equally divided between the dullness of his knife and the mouth of bread he was munching at the time! There was but one sentiment," the *Dispatch* concluded, "—that of disgust—in the whole assemblage." The officers of the fort were sorry when they saw the final result and swore it would never happen again at Fort Mifflin.[8]

The officers' oath was correct. There were no more executions at Fort Mifflin after that of William Howe. In fact, there were no more military executions carried out in Philadelphia or its surrounding counties.

The prisoners confined in the fort on August 26, who were forced to witness the death of Private Howe, did not seem greatly influenced by the incident. The only effect reported was that four prisoners—Arnold Audenhutter, Samuel Smith, William H. Alexander, and William Fisher—escaped at 2:00 A.M. on Sunday, August 28, from the post hospital attached to the fort. Fisher, a later account indicated, was shot by the guard and died the same day as a result of his wounds. The others escaped and were never caught.[9]

The citizens of Philadelphia did not take much notice of William Howe's execution. No letters were sent to the editors of the newspapers agreeing or disagreeing with the execution or the posture of the paper. One interesting commentary did, however, appear on the front page of the *Daily Evening Bulletin* the day after the execution. It read:

> HANGING.—There was a great demand, both on Thursday and yesterday, for tickets to witness the hanging of William H. Howe, at Fort Mifflin, who suffered the penalty of death by hanging, upon his conviction for murder by a court-martial.
>
> Hanging is a terrible and disgraceful death, and the friends of any unfortunate victim of such, weep with shame and mortification at the occurrence of such a calamity to any kinsman, whilst those who are obliged to have any Paper Hanging done upon the most expeditious, substantial and reasonable terms, rejoice and are glad that they have entrusted this work to Mr. Thomas Murray, a practical and thorough-going workman, whose store is at the N.W. corner of Eleventh and Shippen streets . . .[10]

What continued was a long advertisement for Mr. Murray and his firm. Perhaps William H. Howe's death was not in vain. Perhaps Mr. Murray profited by it.

WAR DEPARTMENT
ADJUTANT-GENERAL'S OFFICE
Washington, May 29, 1865.

The Secretary of War directs that you send a list of names
of the prisoners who would be discharged under the following order to this office immediately, giving number of order
promulgating sentence, and that the prisoners be not discharged until you receive further instructions from here:

GENERAL ORDERS,       WAR DEPARTMENT
No. 98                ADJUTANT-GENERAL'S OFFICE
                      Washington, May 27, 1865

Ordered. That in all cases of sentences by military tribunals
of imprisonment during the war the sentence be remitted and
that the prisoners be discharged. The Adjutant-General will
issue the necessary instructions to carry this order into effect.
By order of the President of the United States:

                              E. D. TOWNSEND,
                              Assistant Adjutant-General.

Acknowledge receipt.

                              E. D. TOWNSEND,
                              Assistant Adjutant-General. [1]

# 12

# The Aftermath

**W**ILLIAM H. HOWE was dead. After his body had been embalmed, it was transported back home and turned over to his widow.

Excitement in the Montgomery County area, which had been high during the court-martial and the appeals, reached almost a fever pitch. The sympathy of the majority of the inhabitants rested with Hannah Schoener Howe, and against the enrolling officers. Many supporters of William Howe came to Keelor's Church in Obelisk, Pennsylvania, to attend the funeral. The Rev. Henry Wendt, pastor of the congregation, conducted the services.

Even in death, William Howe could not rest in peace. Hannah had arranged for his body to be buried in the church grounds. The church council, which did not want to publicly support the antidraft sentiments of the community, voted not to allow burial of his body in that sacred ground. And, their decision was final.

With a sad heart, Hannah Howe, her children, and a few friends buried her husband near a low stone fence within a few yards of her home. Later, much later, a small stone was placed on the site to mark Howe's grave. Time and the effects of nature cracked the stone, much as Howe himself had been broken. The stone was replaced with another. Neither this marker nor its predecessor carried any legend.

Howe's execution and burial had taken place swiftly because the federal

169

government planned it that way. But even with the speed, General Couch received a mild reprimand from his superiors for not acting more quickly. Perhaps Assistant Adjutant General Townsend's demand for speed was predicated on something more than military expediency. Why did the federal officials want William Howe executed as rapidly as possible? There were other condemned men confined in prisons and cells throughout the North. Why was this case so important?

The first answer would be that the federal government had knowledge that irregularities in the trial existed. Any disclosure of these discrepancies might have embarrassed the government and could have been used by opponents to the Lincoln administration in the coming election. Furthermore, it would have cast doubt on the information presented at other men's courts-martial. In addition, it would have indicated that the government, while espousing firm adherence to law and order was, in reality, prostituting justice for its own political ends.

William H. Howe's court-martial was a travesty. Besides being denied his basic rights as an American citizen, he had been convicted on forged or fabricated muster rolls. William Hobart, the key witness for the prosecution, had lied under oath. Both the documentation sent to the court-martial board from Washington and Hobart's testimony established August 8, 1861, as the date of Howe's enlistment in Company A. The original muster roll, on the other hand, stated quite clearly that Howe had joined the unit on August 8, 1862, and in fact Colonel Heenan did not begin recruiting efforts for his three-year regiment until June of 1862. But the adjutant-general's affidavit carried a date one full year earlier.

Perhaps, when the evidence was introduced, the error was so minor that it completely escaped everyone's attention. While Randall argued the difference between William Howe and William H. Howe, he missed this discrepancy in dates—the first clue to the prosecution's determined drive for his client's execution. If Randall had discovered this, he might have been able to prove Hobart's perjury, a fact that was passed over at the court-martial.

Hobart's lies under oath might have been made because he was an ambitious, if not courageous, individual. During his enlistment in the Union army, he was never in a combat situation. He had engineered his way to the staff of the provost marshal at headquarters. He did not want to be involved in the war, just reap benefits his military position could bring. He might have seen his testimony as just another step he had to take in order to solidify his position, reputation, and advancement in the army. Perhaps he knew the truth, but thought his own personal success was more important than the life of William Howe.

Hobart's knowledge of Howe's alleged desertion was never substantiated. It was very convenient for him that the unnamed orderly sergeant who had relayed the information to him was, at the time of the court-martial, in Richmond's Libby Prison. Hobart's attitude seemed to be that the court must simply take his word as an officer and gentleman. Besides, he tried to please the court with his disclosures of Howe's confession, his escape route, and other confidences. The prisoner's statement of guilt to Hobart, any admission by Howe of "leaving the army" could, and probably was, accepted by the court as an admission of desertion.

Lt. Col. Henry A. Frink, another ambitious person, had served in Howe's previous court-martial, as did three (not two, as Randall contended) other officers: Capts. James McCann, John C. Dobleman, and Charles Fair. No matter what evidence Randall unearthed in his research to save Howe's life, it seems highly unlikely that their minds could have been swayed from their earlier decision. They might even have resented that their first verdict was thrown out. It is even possible that orders were given to them beforehand that the government would appreciate a guilty verdict. Such a suggestion is plausible since when the board adjourned on February 15, 1864, to discuss the defense's "Special Plea in Bar," its decision was rendered the next morning without further discussion or deliberation.

In addition, the strength of the army, and the nation, was seriously affected by the deserter problem and the organized attempts to obstruct the draft. From a purely personal standpoint, the officers sitting on Howe's court-martial could not have been unbiased in their feelings toward the prisoner or his alleged crimes.

The court-martial board, by the transcript of the proceedings, indicated a favorable attitude toward all prosecution witnesses, but a negative one toward those of the defense. Judge Advocate General Holt's evaluation of the case stated that the witnesses Randall brought forth were "negative." Negative to what? Negative to the case the government had planned for William H. Howe?

But there were others, Mulholland and the rest, who came to Howe's defense. It seems highly improbable that, with their military futures at stake, they would intercede on Howe's behalf if they thought he was in any way guilty of the crimes with which he was charged.

Even more surprising was Lincoln's refusal to consider the request of these officers with more compassion. Lincoln might have been swayed by their military records. Mulholland, at the time he signed the letter to the president, had been awarded a Medal of Honor for his bravery at Chancellorsville. He was not a desk-bound, ambition-blinded man like William Hobart. Lewis Sacriste was an officer of similar merit. He also was a recipient of the Medal of Honor, for heroism at Bristoe Station, November 14, 1863. Mulholland, Sacriste, and the others were men of proven military skill and had been rewarded with brevet rank. Mulholland was brevetted major general, and Sacriste, major. They would not sacrifice their names or reputations to the petition of a coward and a murderer.

But the Lincoln administration weighed the evidence at hand and relied on the words of William Hobart. In reality, the government did not have to go to the extreme of falsifying records to prove Howe deserted. On two separate occasions, the ex-soldier had written to Lincoln, telling the president what actually had happened—how he left the army, expecting to return, and how Bertolet was accidentally killed on that fateful June night.

All the prosecution had to do to destroy Edmund Randall's case was to present Howe's own letters. The young attorney could not have prevented the admission of such telling evidence. Thereafter, his objections based on William Howe versus William H. Howe would have been moot.

The prosecution might not have had the letters in their possession. And, if they had the documents, they might have been reluctant to enter them as evidence since they contained mitigating circumstances—his sickness, refusal of medical attention—which might have reduced the first charge to absence without leave.

If the first charge were reduced, the death of Bertolet might not be considered murder, but manslaughter or even justifiable homicide. William Howe admitted to leaving the army, not deserting, with every intention of returning. He also acknowledged firing his gun into a crowd of men who came to his house in the dead of night. But he did not admit to taking deliberate aim to shoot and kill Abraham Bertolet.

That the two letters were not admitted, while they were in both his military service record file and the records of the adjutant general's office, is a strong indication that the information was withheld. The suppression of valuable evidence and the admission of the spurious affidavit are representative of Howe's "fair and impartial" treatment at the hands of the court-martial board.

The prosecution could not prove, beyond a shadow of a doubt, that Howe had actually deserted. Records were ill-kept and not readily available. For this reason, the fabricated papers were produced. Failing to establish desertion, the charge of murder would have been questionable and trial by court-martial for a civil offense would have aroused the dissident factions in the North.

A major clue to the true significance of Howe's death lies in the reaction of the government to Couch's delay of his sentence, and to other actions taken by Couch. At this time, the situation in Couch's jurisdictional area was quite grave. In Columbia County, Pennsylvania, the voting population leaned heavily toward the "Peace Democrats." Though generally complying with the draft, the residents of the area were outspoken in their opposition to it. The *Columbia Democrat* fired up its readers and condemned the Lincoln administration for drafting white men to pursue the government position of "War and Niggers."[2] The "Fishing Creek Confederacy," as it was called, was about to erupt into open warfare against the government. Couch had tried to deal with the problem of deserters by making an offer of pardon, hoping to resolve the situation without bloodshed. In addition, he delayed Howe's execution as a "humane" gesture.

Federal officials disagreed with this solution; they did not want to reason with any dissident faction. They wanted to force them into submission—the only way to deal with the deserter problem and draft resistance was with strength. Anything that showed weakness or mercy was to be avoided at all costs. The offer of pardon was rescinded, and Couch was directed to focus all his attention and efforts on the hanging of one man.

William H. Howe was at the wrong place at the wrong time. The government saw his case as an excellent opportunity to strike fear into the hearts and souls of the draft resisters, deserters, and certain factions of the Democratic party. The charges against him were such that he would make an ideal example. He could be tried, sentenced, and executed in short order. This would encourage anyone who resisted the government to think twice.

On August 26, 1864, the political prisoners at Fort Mifflin were forced to watch Howe die on the gallows. It was intended that the sight of his death would cleanse their minds of dissension. It was a heavy-handed demonstration —one that did ultimately kill the political dissension of the "Fishing Creek Confederacy" . . . but did not stop the evil of desertion.

William H. Howe had served his country.

# Notes

Chapter 2
Recruitment

1. Samuel P. Bates, *History of Pennsylvania Volunteers 1861-65*, p. 1228.
2. *The Press*, July 29, 1862.
3. *Public Ledger and Daily Transcript*, June 7, 1862.
4. *Philadelphia Inquirer*, July 24, 1862.
5. *Sunday Dispatch*, July 13, 1862.
6. *Public Ledger*, August 2, 1862.
7. St. Clair A. Mulholland, *The Story of the 116th Regiment Pennsylvania Volunteers in the War of the Rebellion*, p. 2.
8. *Philadelphia Inquirer*, August 16, 1862.
9. National Archives, Record Group 153, "Records of the Judge Advocate General's Office," Courts-martial records of William H. Howe; William H. Howe to Abraham Lincoln, August 23, 1863.
10. Ibid., Rev. G. F. Krotel to Edmund Randall, Esq., June 19, 1864.
11. *The Press*, July 17, 1862.
12. Rev. J. J. Kline, comp., *A History of The Lutheran Church in New Hanover, Montgomery County, Pennsylvania*, p. 631.

13. "The United States Census of 1850, Montgomery County," *Bulletin of the Historical Society of Montgomery County, Pennsylvania*, XIV (1965) 4:378.
14. Kline, *The Lutheran Church*, p. 604.
15. Interview with genealogist Edgar Grubb.
16. *Montgomery Ledger*, undated clipping.
17. Ella Lonn, *Foreigners in the Union Army and Navy*, pp. 7–8.
18. Mulholland, *The Story*, pp. 386–88.
19. *Philadelphia Inquirer*, August 16, 1862.
20. *Public Ledger*, August 20, 1862; *Philadelphia Inquirer*, August 19, 1862.
21. *Philadelphia Inquirer*, August 22, 1862; *The Press*, August 22, 1862.
22. *Daily Evening Bulletin*, August 22, 1862.
23. *The Press*, August 23, 1862.
24. David Power Conyngham, *The Irish Brigade and Its Campaigns*, p. 101.
25. *The Press*, September 2, 1862.
26. *Sunday Dispatch*, September 7, 1862; *The Press*, September 3, 1862; *Daily Bulletin*, September 3, 1862.
27. Mulholland, *The Story*, p. 385.
28. Frank H. Taylor, *Philadelphia in the Civil War 1861–1865*, pp. 210–12.

Chapter 3
The Journey South

1. Henry Steele Commager, ed., *The Blue and the Gray*, p. 272.
2. National Archives, Record Group 94, "Records of the Adjutant General's Office, 1780s-1917," Muster Rolls of Volunteer Organizations, Civil War, 116th Pennsylvania Infantry, Company A, June-August, 1862, and November-December, 1862.
3. Bruce Catton, "Union Discipline and Leadership in the Civil War," *Marine Corps Gazette* 40 (1965) 1:18–25.
4. National Archives, Record Group 94.
5. *Antietam to Appomattox with the One Hundred and Eighteenth Pennsylvania Volunteers, "Corn Exchange Regiment,"* p. 19.
6. St. Clair A. Mulholland, *The Story of the 116th Regiment Pennsylvania Volunteers in the War of the Rebellion*, p. 30.
7. William Hanchett, *Irish: Charles G. Halpine in Civil War America*, p. 69.
8. Ibid., p. 17.
9. David Power Conyngham, *The Irish Brigade and Its Campaigns*, p. 319.
10. Mulholland, *The Story*, p. 32.
11. Bell I. Wiley, *The Life of Billy Yank, The Common Soldier of the Union*, p. 133.

12. Ibid., pp. 126–27.
13. Samuel P. Bates, *History of Pennsylvania Volunteers 1861–65*, p. 1228.
14. Mulholland, *The Story*, p. 38.
15. Ibid., p. 39.
16. National Archives, Record Group 94.
17. Ibid.
18. Ibid.
19. Mulholland, *The Story*, p. 39.
20. National Archives, Record Group 94.
21. Bates, *Pennsylvania Volunteers*, p. 1229.
22. Ibid.
23. *The Press*, November 12, 1862.
24. *Philadelphia Inquirer*, November 20, 1862.

Chapter 4
Bivouac of the Dead

1. Vorin E. Whan, Jr., *Fiasco at Fredericksburg*, p. 27.
2. *The Press*, November 22, 1862.
3. *Philadelphia Inquirer*, November 22, 1862.
4. St. Clair A. Mulholland, *The Story of the 116th Regiment Pennsylvania Volunteers in the War of the Rebellion*, p. 47.
5. Frederick L. Hitchcock, *War from the Inside, The Story of the 132nd Regiment Pennsylvania Volunteer Infantry in the War for Suppression of the Rebellion 1862–1863*, p. 147.
6. *Philadelphia Inquirer*, December 3, 1862.
7. Warren Lee Goss, *Recollections of a Private, A Story of the Army of the Potomac*, p. 9.
8. *Philadelphia Inquirer*, December 5, 1862.
9. Lt. Thomas H. Evans, "The Cries of the Wounded Were Piercing and Horrible," *Civil War Times Illustrated* 7 (1968) 4:28–33.
10. *The Press*, December 10, 1862.
11. David Power Conyngham, *The Irish Brigade and Its Campaigns*, p. 325.
12. *Philadelphia Inquirer*, December 10, 1862.
13. *The Press*, December 12, 1862.
14. Bell I. Wiley, *The Life of Billy Yank, The Common Soldier of the Union*, p. 70.
15. James F. Rusling, *Men and Things I Saw in Civil War Days*, pp. 45–46.
16. U.S. War Department, *The War of the Rebellion: A Compilation of the Official Records of the Union and Confederate Armies* (hereinafter cited as OR), I, v. 21, p. 221.

17. Ibid., pp. 221–22.
18. Ibid., p. 240.
19. Ibid.
20. Ibid.
21. Henry Steele Commager, *The Blue and the Gray*, p. 500.
22. Whan, *Fiasco at Fredericksburg*, p. 57.
23. *Philadelphia Inquirer*, December 13, 1862.
24. Conyngham, *The Irish Brigade*, p. 152.
25. *OR* I, v. 21, p. 241.
26. Thomas Francis Galwey, *The Valiant Hours*, ed. Col. W. S. Nye, p. 57.
27. *The Press*, December 17, 1862.
28. *OR* I, v. 21, p. 241.
29. Whan, *Fiasco at Fredericksburg*, p. 87.
30. *OR* I, v. 21, p. 241.
31. Mulholland, *The Story*, p. 53.
32. St. Clair A. Mulholland, "Heroism of the American Volunteer," *Public Ledger*, April 2, 1902.
33. James A. Shipton, "Campaign and Battle of Fredericksburg 1862," Army War College, Session 1911–12.
34. Mulholland, *The Story*, p. 62.
35. *OR* I, v. 21, p. 241.
36. Mulholland, *The Story*, p. 63.
37. *Philadelphia Inquirer*, December 15, 1862; *The Press*, December 15, 1862.
38. Mulholland, *The Story*, p. 64.
39. *OR* I, v. 21, p. 241.
40. Samuel P. Bates, *History of Pennsylvania Volunteers 1861–65*, p. 1229.
41. Ibid., p. 1230.
42. Mulholland, *The Story*, pp. 65–66.
43. Avery Craven, *An Historian and the Civil War*, p. 28.
44. Goss, *Recollections of a Private*, p. 127.
45. Conyngham, *The Irish Brigade*, p. 154.
46. Galwey, *The Valiant Hours*, p. 42.
47. Don Congdon, ed., *Combat: The Civil War*, p. 310.
48. Ned Bradford, ed., *Battles and Leaders of the Civil War*, p. 295.
49. *OR*, I, v. 21, pp. 242–43.
50. Mulholland, "Heroism," *Public Ledger*, April 2, 1902.
51. *OR* I, v. 21, pp. 242–43.
52. *Montgomery Ledger*, undated clipping.
53. *OR* I, v. 21, pp. 243–44.
54. Evans, "The Cries of the Wounded."
55. Conyngham, *The Irish Brigade*, p. 156.

56. Mulholland, *The Story*, p. 74.
57. *The Annals of the War Written by Leading Participants North and South*, p. 261.
58. Joseph H. McRae, "Campaign of Fredericksburg to Include the Attack on Marye's Hill," Army War College, Session 1910-11, p. 33.
59. *The Press*, December 15, 1862.
60. Clarence Edward Macartney, *Highways and Byways of the Civil War*, pp. 107-8.
61. Bradford, *Battles and Leaders*, p. 299.
62. B. A. Botkin, ed., *A Civil War Treasury of Tales, Legends and Folklore*, pp. 202-3.

Chapter 5
A Time to Go Home

1. St. Clair A. Mulholland, *The Story of the 116th Regiment Pennsylvania Volunteers in the War of the Rebellion*, p. 68.
2. Willard Glazier, *Battles for the Union*, p. 219.
3. Warren Lee Goss, *Recollections of a Private, A Story of the Army of the Potomac*, pp. 132-33.
4. Ella Lonn, *Foreigners in the Union Army and Navy*, pp. 392-93.
5. Mulholland, *The Story*, pp. 75-76.
6. David Power Conyngham, *The Irish Brigade and Its Campaigns*, pp. 355-56.
7. *Montgomery Ledger*, undated clipping.
8. *Public Ledger*, December 17, 1862.
9. *Philadelphia Inquirer*, December 17, 1862.
10. National Archives, Record Group 153, "Records of the Judge Advocate General's Office," Courts-martial of William H. Howe.
11. Henry Steele Commager, *The Blue and the Gray*, p. 779.
12. Lt. Thomas H. Evans, "The Cries of the Wounded Were Piercing and Horrible," *Civil War Times Illustrated* 7 (1968) 4:28-38.
13. Ned Bradford, ed., *Battles and Leaders of the Civil War*, p. 319.
14. *Frank Leslie's Illustrated*, March 21, 1863, p. 401.
15. Gideon Welles, *Diary of Gideon Welles: Secretary of the Navy Under Lincoln and Johnson*, 1:191-92.
16. Rev. A. M. Stewart, *Camp, March and Battle-field; or, Three Years and a Half with the Army of the Potomac*, p. 283.
17. Charles Carleton Coffin, *Four Years of Fighting: A Volume of Personal Observations with the Army and Navy, From the Battle of Bull Run to the Fall of Richmond*, p. 174.
18. James F. Rusling, *Men and Things I Saw in Civil War Days*, p. 291.

19. Wood Gray, *The Hidden Civil War. The Story of the Copperheads*, p. 133.
20. Richard Harwell, ed., *Hardtack and Coffee, The Unwritten Story of Army Life by John D. Billings*, p. 98.
21. Thomas Francis Galwey, *The Valiant Hours*, ed. Col. W. S. Nye, p. 72.
22. Harwell, *Hardtack and Coffee*, p. 183.
23. Aida Craig Truxall, ed., *"Respects to All," Letters of Two Pennsylvania Boys in the War of the Rebellion*, pp. 35–36.
24. George Templeton Strong, *Diary of the Civil War 1860–1865*, ed. Allan Nevins, p. 255.
25. Dr. Gordon W. Jones, "Sanitation in the Civil War," *Civil War Times Illustrated* 5 (1966) 7:12–18.
26. Bell I. Wiley, *The Life of Billy Yank, The Common Soldier of the Union*, p. 137.
27. Stewart, *Camp, March and Battle-field*, p. 283.
28. William W. Teall, "Ringside Seat at Fredericksburg," ed. Wilbur S. Nye, *Civil War Times Illustrated* 4 (1965) 2:17–34.
29. Rusling, *Men and Things*, p. 292.
30. Frederick L. Hitchcock, *War from the Inside, The Story of the 132nd Regiment Pennsylvania Volunteer Infantry in the War for the Suppression of the Rebellion 1862–1863*, p. 159.
31. David S. Sparks, ed., *Inside Lincoln's Army, The Diary of Marsena Rudolph Patrick, Provost Marshal General, Army of the Potomac*, p. 196.
32. Evans, "The Cries of the Wounded."
33. *Philadelphia Inquirer*, December 29, 1862.

Chapter 6
The Night Callers

1. *OR* I, v. 25, Part 2, p. 149.
2. *Montgomery Ledger*, undated clipping.
3. *OR* I, v. 25, Part 2, p. 86.
4. Ella Lonn, *Desertion During the Civil War*, p. 151.
5. Ibid., p. 161.
6. *OR* I, v. 25, Part 2, p. 73.
7. Records of St. Luke's, Keelor's Church, p. 17.
8. *Final Report*, Provost Marshal General, March 17, 1866, p. 218.
9. *OR* II, v. 2, p. 54.
10. Ibid., p. 1.
11. Ibid., pp. 15–16.
12. Ibid., pp. 501, 938–39.

13. National Archives, Record Group 110, "Records of the Provost Marshal General's Office," Records of Office Subdivisions, 1862–66; Disbursing Branch, General Records, Letters Received, 1863–68, 89-F-1863.
14. Eugene C. Murdock, *One Million Men, The Civil War Draft in the North*, pp. 28, 30.
15. Ibid., pp. 27–28.
16. Ibid., pp. 101–9.
17. Daniel H. Bertolet, comp., *A Genealogical History of the Bertolet Family*, no. 427.
18. The foregoing account is taken from: National Archives, Record Group 153, "Records of the Judge Advocate General's Office." Courts-martial of William H. Howe; testimonies of Bolton, Eisenberry, and Wagner.
19. *Montgomery Ledger*, June 23, 1863.
20. Bertolet, *A Genealogical History*, p. 76.

Chapter 7
Escape to Doom

1. *Compendium of General Orders, Adjutant General's Office* (Washington: March 24, 1863), General Order No. 73.
2. *Montgomery Ledger*, June 30, 1863.
3. Ella Lonn, *Desertion During the Civil War*, p. 205.
4. Eugene C. Murdock, *One Million Men, The Civil War Draft in the North*, pp. 23–24.
5. *Public Ledger*, August 1, 1863.
6. Ibid., July 21, 1863.
7. *The Press*, July 1, 1863.
8. *Philadelphia Inquirer*, May 6, 1863.
9. Ibid., May 9, 1863.
10. Ibid., May 11, 1863.
11. Ibid., June 2, 1863.
12. Ibid., June 3, 4, 1863.
13. Ibid, June 15, 1863.
14. Murdock, *One Million Men*, pp. 45–48.
15. Gideon Welles, *Diary of Gideon Welles: Secretary of the Navy Under Lincoln and Johnson*, 1:232.
16. Lonn, *Desertion*, p. 221.
17. *Philadelphia Inquirer*, June 27, 1863.
18. *Montgomery Ledger*, July 21, 1863.

19. National Archives, Record Group 153, "Records of the Judge Advocate General's Office," Courts-martial of William H. Howe.
20. *OR* II, v. 2, pp. 41–42, 134.
21. Ibid., p. 156.
22. *Montgomery Ledger*, July 21, 1863.
23. Ibid., undated clipping.
24. National Archives, Record Group 153.
25. *Montgomery Ledger*, July 21, 1863.
26. *Public Ledger*, July 15, 1863.
27. National Archives, Record Group 153.
28. Ibid.
29. *OR* II, v. 6, pp. 689–90.

Chapter 8
The Court-martial

1. National Archives, Record Group 153, "Records of the Judge Advocate General's Office," listed as "Case of Private William Howe" and "Case No. 163."
2. *Articles of War*, no. 79.
3. Alexander Macomb, *The Practice of Courts-martial*, pp. 20–21.

NOTE: All other information is derived directly from the official transcripts of the courts-martial of William H. Howe, found in: National Archives, Record Group 153, "Case No. 163."

Chapter 9
Justice Revisited

1. National Archives, Record Group 153, "Records of the Judge Advocate General's Office," listed as "Case of Private William Howe" and "Case No. 163."
2. *Public Ledger*, February 17, 1864; *The Press*, February 17, 1864.
3. Alexander Macomb, *The Practice of Courts-martial*, pp. 20–21.
4. Ibid., p. 51.
5. Ibid., p. 53.

NOTE: All other information is derived directly from the official transcripts of the courts-martial of William H. Howe, found in: National Archives, Record Group 153, "Case No. 163."

Chapter 10
Out of the Depths

1. National Archives, Record Group 153, "Records of the Judge Advocate General's Office," listed as "Case of Private Williarr Howe" and "Case No. 163."
2. General DuChanal, "How Soldiers Were Tried," *Civil War Times Illustrated* 7 (1969) 10:10–15.
3. National Archives, Record Group 153, "Records of the Judge Advocate General's Office," Courts-martial of William H. Howe; Randall to Holt, March 15, 1864.
4. DuChanal, "How Soldiers," pp. 10–15.
5. National Archives, Record Group 153, Randall to Holt, April 20, 1864.
6. Ibid., Randall to Lincoln, April 30, 1864.
7. National Archives, Record Group 94, "Records of the Adjutant General's Office, 1780s–1917," Compiled Military Service Records, 116th Pennsylvania Volunteers; Howe to Lincoln, August 23, 1863.
8. National Archives, Record Group 153, Holt to Lincoln, May 4, 1864.
9. "Warden's Daily Journal," Eastern State Penitentiary, Pennsylvania Historical and Museum Commission, Record Group 15, no. 2 (1856–77) entry for May 6, 1864.
10. National Archives, Record Group 153, Affidavit, June 20, 1864.
11. Ibid., Officers to Lincoln, undated.
12. Ibid., Krotel to Randall, June 19, 1864.
13. Ibid., Henry Bertolet to Lincoln, June 27, 1864.
14. Bell I. Wiley, *The Life of Billy Yank, The Common Soldier of the Union*, pp. 217–18.
15. National Archives, Record Group 153, General Order No. 41.
16. Ibid., Couch to Townsend, August 23, 1864.

Chapter 11
The Execution

1. *Daily Evening Bulletin*, August 26, 1864.
2. Ibid.
3. *Public Ledger*, August 27, 1864.
4. Ibid.
5. Alexander Macomb, *The Practice of Courts-martial*, p. 76.
6. *The Press*, August 27, 1864.
7. *Public Ledger*, August 27, 1864; *The Press*, August 27, 1864; *Daily Evening Bulletin*, August 26, 1864; *Philadelphia Inquirer*, August 27, 1864.

8. *Sunday Dispatch*, August 28, 1864.
9. *Public Ledger*, August 30, 1864; *Philadelphia Inquirer*, August 29, 1864; *Daily Evening Bulletin*, August 29, 1864.
10. *Daily Evening Bulletin*, August 27, 1864.

Chapter 12
The Aftermath

1. *OR* II, v. 8, p. 500.
2. William W. Hummel, "The Military Occupation of Columbia County: A Re-examination," *Pennsylvania Magazine of History & Biography*, 80 (1956) 3:320–338.

# Bibliography

Alcott, Louisa May. *Hospital Sketches*. New York: Sagamore Press, 1957.

Angle, Paul M., ed. *Three Years in the Army of the Cumberland, The Letters and Diary of Major James A. Connolly*. Bloomington: Indiana University Press, 1969.

*The Annals of the War Written by Leading Participants North and South*. Philadelphia: Times Publishing Co., 1879.

*Annual Report of the Adjutant General of the Commonwealth of Pennsylvania for the year 1862*. Harrisburg, Pa.: Singely & Myers.

*Antietam to Appomattox with the One Hundred and Eighteenth Pennsylvania Volunteers, "Corn Exchange Regiment."* Philadelphia: F. McManus, Jr., 1903.

Barton, Michael Lee. *The Character of Civil War Soldiers: A Comparative Analysis of the Language of Moral Evaluation in Diaries*. Doctoral Dissertation, University of Pennsylvania, 1974.

Bates, Samuel P. *History of Pennsylvania Volunteers, 1861-5*. Harrisburg: B. Singely, 1870.

*Bauern Freund*. (German language newspaper) Pennsburg, Pennsylvania.

Bearss, Edwin C., ed. "The Civil War Diary of Lt. John Q. A. Campbell, Company B, 5th Iowa Infantry." *Annals of Iowa*, (1949) 39 (3rd Series):519:41.

Beck, Harry R., ed. "Some Leaves from a Civil War Diary." *Western Pennsylvania Historical Magazine*, (1959) 42:363–82.
Bell, John T. *Civil War Stories*. San Francisco: Whitaker and Ray Co., 1903.
Bertolet, Daniel H., comp. *A Genealogical History of the Bertolet Family*. Bertolet Family Association, 1914.
Biggs, Charles Lewis, ed. *The Civil War Diary of Capt. Uriah Nelson Parmelee*. Guilford, Connecticut: privately published, 1940.
Birkhimer, Lt. William E. "Response to 'The Power of Military Courts to Punish for Contempt.'" *Journal of the Institution of the United States*, (1892) XIII:758–60.
Blackburn, George M., ed. *With the Wandering Regiment: The Diary of Capt. Ralph Ely of the Eighth Michigan Infantry*. Mt. Pleasant: Central Michigan University Press, 1965.
Botkin, B. A., ed. *A Civil War Treasury of Tales, Legends and Folklore*. New York: Random House, 1960.
Bradford, Ned, ed. *Battles and Leaders of the Civil War*. New York: Appleton-Century-Crofts, 1956.
Brigham, Loriman S., ed. "The Civil War Journal of William B. Fletcher." *Indiana Magazine of History*, (1961) 57:41–76.
Byrd, Cecil K., ed. "Journal of Israel Cogshall, 1862–63." *Indiana Magazine of History*, (1946) 42:69–87.
Byrne, Frank L., ed. *The View from Headquarters, Civil War Letters of Harvey Reid*. Madison: State Historical Society of Wisconsin, 1965.
Carman, Harry J., ed. "Diary of Amos Glover." *Ohio Historical Quarterly*, (1935) 44:258–72.
Catton, Bruce. *The Army of the Potomac: Glory Road*. Garden City, New York: Doubleday & Co., 1952.
——. *The Civil War*. New York: American Heritage Press, 1970.
——. "Hayfoot, Strawfoot." *American Heritage*, (1957) v. 8, no. 3:30–37.
——. "Union Discipline and Leadership in the Civil War." *Marine Corps Gazette*, (1965) v. 40, no. 1:18–25.
"Civil War Diary of Jabez Thomas Cox." *Indiana Magazine of History*, (1932) 28:40–54.
"The Civil War Diary of John Howard Kitts." *Transactions of the Kansas Historical Society*, (1918) 14:318–32.
Coffin, Charles Carleton. *Four Years of Fighting: A Volume of Personal Observations with the Army and Navy, From the Battle of Bull Run to the Fall of Richmond*. Boston: Ticknor and Fields, 1866.
Commager, Henry Steele, ed. *The Blue and the Gray*. New York: Bobbs-Merrill Co., 1950.

*Compendium of General Orders, Adjutant General's Office.* Washington: March 24, 1863.

*A Compendium of the History of Upper Frederick Township.* The Bicentennial Committee of Upper Frederick Township, Pennsylvania, 1975.

Congdon, Don, ed. *Combat: The Civil War.* New York: Delacorte Press, 1967.

Conyngham, David Power. *The Irish Brigade and Its Campaigns.* Boston: Patrick Donahoe, 1869.

Craven, Avery. *An Historian and the Civil War.* Chicago: University of Chicago Press, 1964.

Curry, Richard O. "The Union As It Was: A Critique of Recent Interpretations of the 'Copperheads.' " *Civil War History,* (1967) v. 13, no. 1:25–39.

*The Daily Evening Bulletin.* (newspaper) Philadelphia, Pennsylvania.

Dana, Charles A. *Recollections of the Civil War.* New York: Collier Books, 1963.

*Der Neutralist.* (German language newspaper) Skippackville, Pennsylvania.

"Diary, October 8, 1862, to August 3, 1864." (William H. Ibbetson) *Publications of the Illinois State Historical Library.* (1930) 37:236–73.

"Diary of Capt. John N. Bell of Company E, 25th Iowa Infantry." *Iowa Journal of History,* (1961) 59:181–221.

"A Diary of Prison Life in Southern Prisons." (Amos Ames) *Annals of Iowa,* 3rd series 40:1–19.

Donovan, Frank. *The Medal.* New York: Dodd, Mead & Co., 1962.

"The Draft Riots of 1863." Military Order, Loyal Legion of the United States, Ohio Commandery, 1916.

DuChanal, General. "How Soldiers Were Tried." *Civil War Times Illustrated,* (1969) v. 7, no. 10:10–15.

Dwight, Lt. Henry O. "Each Man His Own Engineer – A First Person Account." *Civil War Times Illustrated,* (1965) v. 4, no. 6:4–7, 30, 31.

Dye, John Smith. *History of the Plots and Crimes of the Great Conspiracy to Overthrow Liberty in America.* Freeport, New York: Books for Libraries Press, 1969.

Dyer, Frederic H. *A Compendium of the War of the Rebellion.* New York: Thomas Yoseloff, 1959.

Evans, Lt. Thomas H. "The Cries of the Wounded Were Piercing and Horrible." *Civil War Times Illustrated,* (1968) v. 7, no. 4:28–38.

Evans, Lt. W. P. "Response to 'The Power of Military Courts to Punish for Contempt.' " *Journal of the Military Service Institution of the United States,* (1892) XIII:1186–87.

Fatout, Paul, ed. *Letters of a Civil War Surgeon.* Purdue University Studies, 1961.

Fite, Emerson David. *Social and Industrial Conditions in the North During the Civil War.* New York: Macmillan Co., 1910.

Fox, William L., ed. "Corporal Harvey W. Wiley's Civil War Diary." *Indiana Magazine of History*, (1955) 51:139-62.

*Frank Leslie's Illustrated Newspaper.* New York.

Frederick, J. V., ed. "An Illinois Soldier, in North Mississippi: Diary of John Wilson, February 15 to December 30, 1862." *Journal of Mississippi History*, (1939) 1:182-94.

Galwey, Thomas Francis. *The Valiant Hours.* Edited by Col. W. S. Nye. Harrisburg, Pennsylvania: Stackpole Co., 1961.

Glazier, Willard. *Battles for the Union.* Hartford, Connecticut: Gilman & Co., 1878.

Godcharles, Frederick A. *Pennsylvania: Political, Governmental, Military and Civil.* New York: American Historical Society, 1933.

Goss, Warren Lee. *Recollections of a Private, A Story of the Army of the Potomac.* New York: Thomas Y. Crowell & Co., 1890.

Gould, Benjamin Apthorp. *Investigations in the Military and Anthropological Statistics of American Soldiers.* (Published for the U.S. Sanitary Commission by Hurd and Houghton) Cambridge: Riverside Press, 1869.

Gray, Wood. *The Hidden Civil War, The Story of the Copperheads.* New York: Viking Press, 1942.

Greenleaf, Maj. Charles R. "Personal Identity in the Recognition of Deserters." *Journal of the Military Service Institution of the United States*, (1889) X:561-75.

Greenleaf, Margery, ed. *Letters to Eliza from a Union Soldier, 1862-1865.* Chicago: Follett Publishing Co., 1970.

Hale, Edward E., ed. *Stories of War Told by Soldiers.* Boston: Roberts Brothers, 1879.

Hanchett, William. *Irish: Charles G. Halpine in Civil War America.* Syracuse: Syracuse University Press, 1970.

Harstad, Peter T. "Draft Dodgers and Bounty Jumpers." *Civil War Times Illustrated*, (1967) v. 6, no. 2:28-36.

Harwell, Richard, ed. *Hardtack and Coffee, The Unwritten Story of Army Life by John D. Billings.* Chicago: Lakeside Press, R. R. Donnelley & Sons Co., 1960.

Harwell, Richard D., ed. *The War They Fought.* New York: Longmans, Green & Co., 1960.

Hatch, E. E. "Campaign and Battle of Fredericksburg." Typescript. U.S. Army War College, 1915.

Hicken, Victor. *The American Fighting Man*. New York: Macmillan Co., 1969.

Hill, A. F. *Our Boys, The Personal Experiences of a Soldier in the Army of the Potomac*. Philadelphia: John E. Potter, 1864.

Hitchcock, Frederick L. *War from the Inside, The Story of the 132nd Regiment Pennsylvania Volunteer Infantry in the War for Suppression of the Rebellion 1862-1863*. Philadelphia: J. B. Lippincott Co., 1904.

Hood, J. B. *Advance and Retreat, Personal Experiences in the United States and Confederate States Armies*. New Orleans: Hood Orphan Memorial Fund, 1880.

Howe, Mark De Wolfe, ed. *Touched with Fire, Civil War Letters and Diary of Oliver Wendell Holmes, Jr., 1861-1864*. Cambridge: Harvard University Press, 1946.

Hummel, William W. "The Military Occupation of Columbia County: A Reexamination." *Pennsylvania Magazine of History & Biography*, 1956, 80 (3):320-338.

Jones, Evan Rowland. *Four Years in the Army of the Potomac: A Soldier's Recollections*. London: Tyne Publishing Co., Ltd., undated.

Jones, Dr. Gordon W. "Sanitation in the Civil War." *Civil War Times Illustrated*, (1966) v. 5, no. 7:12-18.

"Journal of Melville Cox Robertson." *Indiana Magazine of History*, (1932) 28:116-37.

Keesy, Rev. William Allen. *War . . . As Viewed from the Ranks*. Norwalk, Ohio: Experiment and News Co., 1898.

Klein, Frederic S. "On Trial." *Civil War Times Illustrated*, (1969) v. 7, no. 9:40-46.

Klement, Frank L., ed. "Edwin B. Bigelow, A Michigan Sergeant in the Civil War." *Michigan History*, (1954) 38:193-252.

Kline, Rev. J. J., comp. *A History of The Lutheran Church in New Hanover, Montgomery County, Penna.* New Hanover: published by the congregation, 1910.

*Phil Koempel's Diary*. Privately published, undated.

*List of U.S. Soldiers Executed by United States Military Authorities during the Late War*. Washington: Adjutant General's Office, August 1, 1885.

Lonn, Ella. *Desertion During the Civil War*. New York: Century, 1928.

———. *Foreigners in the Union Army and Navy*. Baton Rouge: Louisiana State University, 1951.

Lossing, Benson J. *A History of the Civil War 1861-65 and the Causes That Led Up to the Great Conflict*. New York: War Memorial Association, 1912.

Lucey, Rev. William L., ed. "The Diary of Joseph B. O'Hagen of the Excelsior

Brigade." *Civil War History*, (1969) 6:402-09.

Lyle, Rev. W. W. *Lights and Shadows of Army Life*. Cincinnati: R. W. Carroll & Co., 1865.

Macartney, Clarence Edward. *Highways and Byways of the Civil War*. Philadelphia: Dorrance & Co., 1926.

Macomb, Alexander. *The Practice of Courts-martial*. New York: Harper & Brothers, 1841.

Martin, John Hill. *Bench and Bar in Philadelphia*. Philadelphia: Rees Welsh & Co., 1883.

Maslowski, Pete. "A Study of Morale in Civil War Soldiers." *Military Affairs*, (1970), v. 34, no. 4:122-26.

McAnaney, Lt. William D. "Desertion in the United States Army." *Journal of the Military Service Institution of the United States*, (1889) X:450-65.

McRae, Joseph H. "Campaign of Fredericksburg to Include the Attack on Marye's Hill." Typescript. U.S. Army War College, session 1910-11.

Meredith, Roy. *Mr. Lincoln's Contemporaries, An Album of Portraits by Mathew B. Brady*. New York: Charles Scribner's Sons, 1951.

Mitchell, Joseph B. *The Badge of Gallantry*. New York: Macmillan Co., 1968.

*Montgomery Ledger*. (newspaper) Pottstown, Pennsylvania.

Mooney, Chase C., ed. "A Union Chaplain's Diary." *Proceedings of the New Jersey Historical Society*, (1957) 75:1-17.

Moore, Wilton P. "The Provost Marshal Goes to War." *Civil War History*, (1959) v. 5, no. 1:63-71.

——. "Union Army Provost Marshals in the Eastern Theatre." *Military Affairs*, (1962) v. 26, no. 3:120-62.

Morgan, H. Wayne, ed. "A Civil War Diary of William McKinley." *Ohio Historical Quarterly*, (1960) 69:272-90.

Morton, Joseph W., Jr., ed. *Sparks from the Camp Fire or Tales of the Old Veterans*. Philadelphia: Keystone Publishing Co., 1895.

Mulholland, St. Claire A. "Heroism of the American Volunteer." *Philadelphia Public Ledger*, April 2, 1902.

——. *The Story of the 116th Regiment Pennsylvania Volunteers in the War of the Rebellion*. Philadelphia: F. McManus, Jr., 1903.

Murdock, Eugene C. *One Million Men, The Civil War Draft in the North*. Madison: State Historical Society of Wisconsin, 1971.

——. *Patriotism Limited, 1862-1865, The Civil War Draft and the Bounty System*. Ohio: Kent State University Press, 1967.

National Archives. *Record Group 15, Records of the Veteran's Administration*. Pension Files, WC-#113447.

———. *RG 94, Records of the Adjutant General's Office*, 1780s–1917. Muster Rolls of Volunteer Organizations, Civil War, 116th Pennsylvania Infantry.

———. *RG 94, Records of the Adjutant General's Office*, 1780s–1917. Compiled Military Service Records, 116th Pennsylvania Volunteers.

———. *RG 110, Records of the Provost Marshal General's Bureau*. Records of Office Sub-divisions, 1862–66, Disbursing Branch. General Records, Letters Received, 1863–68, 89-F-1863.

———. *RG 110, Records of the Provost Marshal General's Bureau*. Records of Office Sub-divisions, Branch for Disbursing the Collecting, Drilling and Organizing Volunteer Fund. General Records, Letters Received, 1862–84, 25-F-1868.

———. *RG 110, Records of the Provost Marshal General's Bureau*. Records of the Office Sub-divisions, 1862–66, Disbursing Branch. General Records, Reports.

———. *RG 153, Records of the Judge Advocate General's Office*. Courts-martial of William H. Howe.

Niccum, Norman, ed. "Diary of Lt. Frank Hughes." *Indiana Magazine of History*, (1949) 45:275–84.

Norton, Oliver Willcox. *Army Letters, 1861–1865*. Chicago: O. L. Deming, 1903.

"On the March with Sibley in 1863, the Diary of Pvt. Henry J. Hagadorn." *North Dakota Historical Quarterly*, (1903) 5:103–29.

*Pamphlets Issued by the Loyal Publication Society*. New York: Loyal Publication Society, 1865.

*Philadelphia Inquirer*. (newspaper) Philadelphia, Pennsylvania.

Power, R. McKinlay. "The Power of Military Courts to Punish for Contempt." *Journal of the Military Service Institution of the United States*, (1892) XIII: 331–37.

*The Press*. (newspaper) Philadelphia, Pennsylvania.

Price, William H. *The Civil War Handbook*. Fairfax, Virginia: Prince Lithographic Co., 1961.

*Public Ledger and Daily Transcript*. (newspaper) Philadelphia, Pennsylvania.

Quinn, William. *The History of a Soldier*. Washington: Gibson Bros., undated.

Redway, Major G. W. *Fredericksburg: A Study in War*. New York: Macmillan Co., 1906.

Robertson, James I. "Military Executions." *Civil War Times Illustrated*, (1966) v. 5, no. 2:34–39.

Rusling, James F. *Men and Things I Saw in Civil War Days*. New York: Eaton & Mains, 1899.

Sellers, James L., ed. "The Richard H. Mockett Diary." *Mississippi Valley Historical Review*, (1939) 26:233-40.

Shipton, James A. "Campaign and Battle of Fredericksburg." Typescript. U.S. Army War College, session 1911-12.

Small, Harold Amos, ed. *The Road to Richmond, The Civil War Memoirs of Maj. Abner R. Small of the 16th Maine Volunteers; with his Diary as a Prisoner of War.* Berkeley: University of California Press, 1957.

Smith, David M., ed. "The Civil War Diary of Col. John Henry Smith." *Iowa Journal of History*, (1949) 47:140-70.

Sparks, David S., ed. *Inside Lincoln's Army, The Diary of Marsena Rudolph Patrick, Provost Marshal General, Army of the Potomac.* New York: Thomas Yoseloff, 1964.

Stackpole, Edward J. "Battle of Fredericksburg." *Civil War Times Illustrated*, (1965) v. 4, no. 8:4-47.

Staudenraus, P. J., ed. *Mr. Lincoln's Washington, Selections from the Writings of Noah Brooks, Civil War Correspondent.* New York: Thomas Yoseloff, 1967.

Stern, Bernard J., ed. *Young Ward's Diary.* New York: G. P. Putnam's Sons, 1935.

Stewart, Rev. A. M. *Camp, March and Battle-field; or, Three Years and a Half with the Army of the Potomac.* Philadelphia: Jas. B. Rodgers, 1865.

Stillwell, Leander. *The Story of a Common Soldier of Army Life in the Civil War 1861-1865.* Franklin Hudson Publishing Co., 1920.

Stine, J. H. *History of the Army of the Potomac.* Washington: Gibson Bros., 1893.

Stinson, Byron. "Scurvy in the Civil War." *Civil War Times Illustrated*, (1966) v. 5, no. 5:20-25.

Strong, George Templeton. *Diary of the Civil War 1860-1865.* Edited by Allan Nevins. New York: Macmillan Co., 1962.

*Sunday Dispatch.* (newspaper) Philadelphia, Pennsylvania.

Taylor, Benjamin F. *Pictures of Life in Camp and Field.* Chicago: S. C. Griggs & Co., 1875.

Taylor, Frank H. *Philadelphia in the Civil War 1861-1865.* Philadelphia: City of Philadelphia, 1913.

Teall, William W. "Ringside Seat at Fredericksburg." Edited by Wilbur S. Nye. *Civil War Times Illustrated*, (1965) v. 4, no. 2:17-34.

Thompson, D. G. Brinton., ed. "From Chancellorsville to Gettysburg, A Doctor's Diary." *Pennsylvania Magazine of History & Biography*, (1965) 89:292-315.

Throne, Mildred, ed. "The Civil War Diary of John Mackley." *Iowa Journal of History*, (1950) 48:141–68.

Thurner, Arthur W., ed. "A Young Soldier in the Army of the Potomac: Diary of Howard Helman." *Pennsylvania Magazine of History & Biography*, (1963) v. 87, no. 2:135–55.

Tilley, Nannie M., ed. *Federals on the Frontier, the Diary of Benjamin F. McIntyre.* Austin: University of Texas Press, 1960.

Townsend, George Alfred. *Rustics in Rebellion: A Yankee Reporter on the Road to Richmond, 1861–65.* Chapel Hill: University of North Carolina Press, 1950.

Truxall, Aida Craig. *"Respects to All," Letters of Two Pennsylvania Boys in the War of the Rebellion.* Pittsburg: University of Pittsburg Press, 1962.

U.S. War Department. *The War of the Rebellion: A Compilation of the Official Records of the Union and Confederate Armies.* Prepared by LTC Robert N. Scott. Washington, D.C.: Government Printing Office, 1880–1901.

"The United States Census of 1850, Montgomery County." *Bulletin of the Historical Society of Montgomery County, Pennsylvania*, (1965) v. XIV, no. 4.

Wainwright, Nicholas B. "The Loyal Opposition in Civil War Philadelphia." *Pennsylvania Magazine of History & Biography*, (1964) v. 88, no. 3:294–315.

Walton, Clyde C., ed. *Private Smith's Journal.* Chicago: R. R. Donnelley, 1963.

Webb, Willard, ed. *Crucial Moments of the Civil War.* New York: Bonanza Books, 1961.

Weigley, Russell F. *History of the United States Army.* New York: Macmillan Co., 1967.

Welles, Gideon. *Diary of Gideon Welles: Secretary of the Navy Under Lincoln and Johnson.* Boston: Houghton Mifflin, 1911.

Whan, Vorin E., Jr. *Fiasco at Fredericksburg.* State College, Pennsylvania: Pennsylvania State University Press, 1961.

Wiley, Bell I. "The Common Soldier of the Civil War." *Civil War Times Illustrated*, (1973) v. 12, no. 4:1–64.

———. *The Life of Billy Yank, The Common Soldier of the Union.* Garden City, New York: Doubleday & Co., 1971.

Williams, Charles G., ed. "Down the Rivers: Civil War Diary of Thomas Benton White." *Register of the Kentucky Historical Society*, (1969) 67:134–74.

Williams, T. Harry, ed. "The Reluctant Warrior, the Diary of Norman K. Nichols." *Civil War History*, 3:17-39.

Wolseley, Field Marshal Viscount. *The American Civil War, An English View.* Edited by James A. Rawley. Charlottesville: University Press of Virginia, 1964.

Wright, Edward Needles. *Conscientious Objectors in the Civil War.* Philadelphia: University of Pennsylvania Press, 1931.

# Index

**Robert I. Alotta,** writer, historian, journalist, and teacher, is a native Philadelphian. He has written *Street Names of Philadelphia* (Temple University Press, 1975), the award-winning Bicentennial radio series, "Past Prolog," and is a regular historical columnist for the Philadelphia *Evening Bulletin,* the *Germantown Courier,* and other local newspapers. As president and founder of The Shackamaxon Society, he spearheaded the drive to restore historic Old Fort Mifflin and has written extensively on the fort's role in American military history.

Alotta is currently writing and narrating a radio show and working on the final chapters of another non-fiction book. He lives in center city Philadelphia in the former home of a Civil War general and Medal of Honor winner.

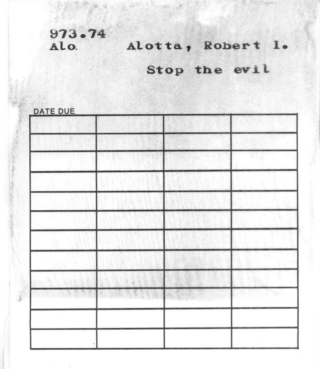